D0730808

Exploring Worship

by Virginia Talmadge

Exploring Worship

Virginia Talmadge

THE SALVATION ARMY SUPPLIES
1424 NORTHEAST EXPRESSWAY, N.E.
ATLANTA, GEORGIA 30329

ABOUT THE AUTHOR

Virginia E. Talmadge, complementing her husband, Colonel Charles Talmadge, in his various appointments, particularly in the field of training, has a national reputation as an authority on worship resources and as an instructor in Christian education, creative writing and drama.

Author of the book, *Dear God...Little Prayers to a Big God*, and for many years a columnist for the *War Cry*, Mrs. Colonel Talmadge was for eighteen years editor of the Junior Sunday School Quarterlies for The Salvation Army in the U. S. A.

Born in Pittsburgh, Pa., this gracious lady has filled training appointments, divisional and territorial duties with distinction.

While in New York, she majored in elementary education at Hunter College and established the Child Care Center for the Eastern School for Officers' Training. This responsibility she later continued for children of cadets in the South.

Adopting the southland as their home, the Talmadges reside in Atlanta, Georgia, from which location the Talmadges reach out in ministry across the North American continent.

● ●

Verses marked TLB are taken from THE LIVING BIBLE © 1971 owned by assignment by Illinois Marine Bank N.A. (as trustee). Used by permission of Tyndale House Publishers, Inc., Wheaton, IL 60189. All rights reserved.

Quotations noted NIV are from the *Holy Bible, New International Version*, copyright © 1973, 1978, 1984 International Bible Society. Used by permission of Zondervan Bible Publishers.

Available through Book Stores or Salvation Army Supplies

Published by The Salvation Army

Supplies and Purchasing Department

1424 Northeast Expressway

Atlanta, Georgia U.S.A. 30329

To

All Who Enjoy Worship

and

Seek to Enrich the Worship Experience

DEDICATION

In love, I dedicate this resource manual to my husband Charles, and daughter Charlene. In all our Salvation Army service Charles has given me opportunity for the expression of creativity as we have accepted and kept divine appointments. The fulfillment of our ministry has been a partnership of calling. Charlene with her artistic skills and insight has added design and color to my writings, visuals, and worship presentations.

ACKNOWLEDGEMENTS

I wish to express special appreciation and thanks to The Salvation Army for the publication of this book.

I am grateful to Lt.-Colonel Houston Ellis for encouragement and cooperation in the publication.

To Mr. Ralph Miller, I express my gratitude for his fragile sensitivity as the editor of the book and Salvation Army Southern Territory Publications.

I am deeply indebted to Dianne Lyons, of the Graphic Arts Department of the Supplies and Purchasing Department of The Salvation Army, who has faithfully contributed her time and skills to the publication.

I owe a great deal to the astute eye and sagacious judgment of Linda Keller in the typesetting of the manuscript.

Contents

FOREWORD

PREFACE

Part I

WHAT IS WORSHIP ?

The Nature of Worship 5

The Function of Worship 7

The Structure of Worship 10

The Expression of Worship 17

The Practice of Worship 20

Personal Worship 20

Family Worship 20

Family Worship Workshop 24

Part II

CHORAL SPEAKING

Understanding Choral Speaking 36

Definition and Interpretation 39

The Speaking Ensemble 42

Techniques of Interpretation 49

Organization for Performance 57

Part III

WORSHIP RESOURCES

The Call To Worship 72

Choral Speech-Interpretative Selections 93

The Litany 181

Responsive Readings 207

Youth Group Devotions 265

Part IV

THE WORSHIP CENTER

Worship Centers-General 277

Worship Centers-Holy Week 313

FOOTNOTES 339

SUBJECT INDEX 340

TITLE INDEX 343

SCRIPTURE INDEX 349

FOREWORD

Mrs. Colonel Charles (Virginia) Talmadge (R) has long been a master of creating the right mood and in providing meaningful and momentous worship services.

This book fills a long felt need for Salvation Army produced worship resources. We enthusiastically endorse its concepts believing their utilization will enrich the worship experience for all.

We are indebted to Mrs. Talmadge for this book and for her unusual talent so long employed, leading the way to creative and compelling worship.

James Osborne
COMMISSIONER

Atlanta, Georgia
October, 1988

PREFACE

Everyone needs to not only learn *how* to worship but also we must understand the *what* of worship. Neither the *how* of worship nor the *what* of worship is automatic. Both are accomplishments.

The *how* of worship is the establishment of a line of communication with God, while the *what* of worship is the channel used to move into worship.

Entering and enjoying worship takes on exciting dimensions when we open our hearts to worship stimuli. In such an experience there is a re-breathing of the Spirit of God into the spirit of man.

There are many concepts and ideas about worship so that we can easily become confused when we try to satisfy the urge for worship. The ancient cry of the man of God, "O, that I knew where I might find Him?" (Job 23:3) becomes our cry as we endeavor to approach God.

Because worship is a conscious effort to know God and to find His will concerning our lives, any thought, act, or feeling, or any stimuli that inspires a closer relationship with our God will open the door of worship.

It is relatively easy to admonish, to suggest, to advise about the importance of worship, but it requires study and experience to become a competent guide in the worship experience.

Although there is no set, pre-determined model, frame, or form for the worship service or experience, we do know that in every worship experience some realities happen:

> A sense of God's presence
> A sense of one's need
> A realization of our dependence upon God
> A commitment to Christ's way of living
> A dedication to the principle of truth revealed in worship.

The enrichment of the worship experience involves related source material as well as creating a worshipful attitude through musical preludes, postludes, or worship centers. The resources in this book are not planned programs or services, but rather devotional resources to be adapted to programs that are being planned.

The media or techniques suggested have grown out of a desire to share with others material I have used to enrich worship services. I believe that, in addition to hymns, scripture, prayer, musical contributions, and the sermon, there should be plans for congregation participation. This can be accomplished through unison prayers, the call to worship, litanies, responsive readings, choral speech or worship centers.

Every effort has been made to determine authorship of resource material that is not my own and credit has been given.

It is my desire and design that in both our personal worship and our corporate worship, we may maintain the flow of worship through the use of various media or stimuli. May they be thoughts that breathe and words that burn with aspiration as you explore worship.

May you walk through these gates of worship and enjoy God!

September, 1988   Virginia Talmadge
Atlanta, Georgia

Part I

What is Worship?

WHAT IS WORSHIP?

THE NATURE OF WORSHIP

Have you ever felt dissatisfied with an experience of worship, or have you ever felt that you really didn't worship when in a worship service?

Do you think that our worship services are not speaking to man's needs in this twentieth century, space age?

Has our traditional concept of worship given worship a sense of irrelevance?

Have we unwittingly made worship common and ordinary?
Have you ever left a worship service with no conscious awareness of being in the presence of God?

Could it be that we have been standing on the perimeter of worship, and wondering what it is all about?

Public worship then, is far from being as simple a matter as we might think it to be. This would explain some of the following comments:

"That worship service didn't do much for me." "I get so weary of just going through the familiar motions of a Sunday service."

"We do the same thing Sunday after Sunday." "Our Sunday morning service is so predictable a song, a prayer, the songsters, the band, and the sermon."

Just going through the motions will never be worship, no matter how effective the program items may be. The quality of worship is less than fulfilling or meaningful if we feel as though we are not worshiping personally. Understanding the nature of worship will bring renewal in worship with no dull, sterile sameness. An understanding of the nature of worship relates to the essentials, the character, and the essence of worship. If the

definition of worship

the desire for worship

the delight in worship

became the focus of our worship, then life and spontaneity would be the climate of our worship. As we identify these three areas of worship we will be better able to create an atmosphere which will be conducive to an inner response and a worship experience.

DEFINING WORSHIP

Worship is a noble word. The term comes into our modern speech from the Anglo-Saxon word "weorthscipe". Later it developed into "worthship", and finally as we know it today "worship". Loosely we say, he worships money, success, home, car, or a hobby. A deeper meaning is the honorary title, "His worship the Mayor", which dignifies the first citizen of our city. Worth-ship stirs a sense of value, of goodness, of virtue, of rightness, of worth.

In our worship we acknowledge God is worthy of our love, our devotion, our allegiance, and our praise. The supreme worth, the excellent worthiness of God is echoed in scripture.

"Give unto the Lord, the glory due His name." Psa. 96:8

"Thou art worthy, O Lord, to receive glory and honor and power." Rev. 4:11

SOMETHING HAPPENS WHEN WE WORSHIP

Worship may be inherent in all of us, but it is not a natural accomplishment. We must learn "how" to worship God so that something will happen to our spirit, so that we will know we have come into the presence of God. It must be more than singing, praising, reading the Word of God, or praying. Not even God can command our worship response. Perhaps, we could phrase it like this:

Worship is not what someone does FOR us - the worship program

Worship is not something done TO us - the worship sermon

Worship is something we DO - (I worship) - worship experienced.

In other words, there are any number of things that may lead us to worship; what we OBSERVE, or what we HEAR, or the atmosphere CREATED. However, something happens in worship only when we are INVOLVED.

THE FOCUS OF WORSHIP

The distinguishing mark of worship as taught by Jesus and seen in the early church was an awareness of the presence of God. This awareness makes a line of communication which is the avenue of worship. The person who learns to worship in "spirit and in truth" experiences a change both in character and conduct. Although the cross is central in worship, the triune God is involved in every worship experience.

THE LINE OF COMMUNICATION

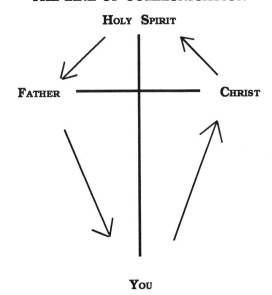

HOLY SPIRIT

FATHER

CHRIST

YOU

THE FUNCTION OF WORSHIP

PRESENTATION-WHAT DO I FEEL?

Worship will reach down into the inner depths of our being where words cannot go if we understand its function as "being", "becoming" and "doing". We must prepare to meet God, commune with Him, and be sent forth by Him.

> *"He that cometh to God must believe that He is, and that He is a rewarder of them that diligently seek Him."* (Heb. 11:6)

> *"Let us draw near with a true heart in full assurance of faith."* (Heb. 10:22)

Our worship must always involve our whole being. It never just embraces our spirit. It demands all of us. Our intellect, our emotions, our will, our interests, our time, our energies, our whole being must be aligned to God's will. Because we are not all spirit we must be spirit controlled.

We cannot worship God and still cheat, lie, steal, or hate. We cannot worship God and have anger, resentment, rebellion, pride, disobedience, or independence in our heart. If we envision worship as something happening outside of us, or around us, no interaction with God will take place. Worship is "being" and you feel it going on inside you. You experience God speaking, you feel His presence, His love, His joy, His power. You sense the indescribable majesty and splendor of God. You enter into a spirit of intimacy and affection. You relate to the mercy, concern, protection, and strength of God. You feel excited, and expectant. You enjoy worship!

COMMUNICATION-WHAT HAPPENS TO ME?

> *"And the Lord spake to Moses face to face, as a man speaketh to a friend."* (Ex. 33:11)

> *"And Moses was not aware that His face was radiant because he had spoken with the Lord".* (Ex. 34:29 NIV)

Moses could not see the face of God, but he came away from talking with God with his face aglow. Everyone knew where Moses had been.

Worship as communion, or communication, means something will happen to me. I am not only involved, but I am "becoming". I become alive to Christ, and I become shaped by an awareness of His presence.

As we respond to "being" in contact with God, we begin to become like Him. Our behavior, our conduct, our manner of living, our demeanor, our comportment, our whole person "becomes" open to the triune God. "Becoming" will happen when we focus on what God is doing. It is not what someone is doing for us, or to us. It is a discovery that God is acting while we are worshiping.

Yes, something is happening to me, and it is more than a conscious awareness of God:

It is renewing and refreshing my spirit

It is rekindling my faith

It is energizing my love

It is nourishing my spiritual life

It is sharing His power

It is making me adequate

It is new insights, new confidence, new courage, new growth

It is increased understanding

It is greater devotion

It is a whole new dimension with a fresh approach to all of living. And this will happen too: the Word of God will take on new meaning and there will be a new sense of guidance and direction in our lives. The total effect is that worship becomes dynamic in our daily living.

APPLICATION - WHAT MUST I DO?

Our worship embodies much more than our feelings, even though *"In His presence is fullness of joy"*. (Psa. 16:11) Worship embraces more than changes that are brought about in the character and conduct of the worshiper as he prays, *"Create in me a clean heart, O God, and renew a right spirit within me."* (Psa. 51:10) Worship includes responsibility and commitment. *"Not everyone that says, Lord, Lord... but those who are obedient to my Father in Heaven"*. (Matt. 7:21 WEY) Therefore, the worshiper must celebrate his worship experience by application. He must become a channel permitting God the Holy Spirit to flow out through him in blessing and ministry. Worship necessitates action by the worshiper.

In presentation we say, "What do I feel?" and we "verbalize" in worship. In communication we say, "What happens to me?" and we "internalize" in worship. In application we say, "What must I do?" and we "actualize" in worship. I have always thought of Psalm 100 as a Psalm of worship although it is designated as a Psalm of praise. To me it has all the elements of worship. To put it in focus with our thinking on worship, let us change the order of the verses. Note that each verse begins with a verb, with two additional verbs in verse four. To summarize that worship is an experience, or is experienced, whether it be individual or corporate, let us illustrate with Psalm 100.

Verse 4 *"Enter into His gates"*

Get quiet before the Lord. Tune in to His love, mercy, goodness and faithfulness. Get in harmony with His will, His thoughts, His plan. Meditate and prepare to meet with God. Even your posture may contribute to this preparation of entering. Kneeling, just sitting quietly, resting your hands in your lap, or bowing your head, closing your eyes, or standing in His presence and maybe speaking aloud. Enter and be comfortable.

Verse 2 *"Come before His presence with singing"*

A singing heart is a delightful thing to bring into worship. We can become so caught up with our needs, so anxious about our problems, so discouraged, or distressed that we bring a depressed mood to worship. God is our help in every need, and we come believing that God is instantly, constantly available and rushes to our aid in every circumstance of life. We come bringing our faith in the overwhelming power of God. We bring our lithe, open, yielded, singing self, and in the valleys, the plains, or the mountain tops, with a singing heart we keep stride with God.

Verse 3 *"Know ye that the Lord, He is God."*

We acknowledge God - His majesty, His greatness, His authority, and power. We adore and revere Him. He is God, the good omnipotent. As we meditate we feel a great sense of peace. "Be still and know that I am God," (Psa. 46:10) speaks to us of God's surrounding, enfolding love. As we verbalize our knowledge of who God is, we are gripped with the understanding of what He can do for us. We know too, that He has the right to tell us what He wants us to do, and that always He gives us grace to be responsible to do it.

Verse 1 *"Make a joyful noise unto the Lord."*

The heart of God is made happy when He is our joy. Joy is strong, grand, and noble. *"The joy of the Lord is our strength."* (Neh. 8:10) We carry the seed of joy within our hearts and minds, and joy can find expression in worship, then in our living. Joy will make the bitter sweet and heavy burdens seem light.

Verse 2 *"Serve the Lord with gladness"*

If we serve unwillingly our service is bondage, but if we serve with gladness our service is ministry. It is witness and it is support. Serving the Lord with gladness because His power is at work within us comes from worshiping with gladness. We worship with gladness! We serve with gladness!

Verse 4 *"Be thankful unto Him"*

This is the result of entering into His presence. He makes me thankful! Our hearts overflow with thanksgiving for we realize we give so little and He gives so much. We are so undeserving. and we get so much. In our worshiping, thanksgiving gets right into our souls.

Verse 4 *"Bless His Name"*

In worship we behold God in all His glory, and when we see His splendor, all that is inside us cries out, *"Bless the Lord, O my soul"* (Psa. 103:1) O Lord, you are very great, you are big enough for everything. We bless and magnify your holy Name, is the expression of our hearts.

The understanding of the function and essence of worship as related to the worshiper brings meaning and satisfaction to the experience. Being, becoming and doing is vital to presentation, communication and application of all worship. As we listen and worship,God speaks to us, enfolds us in His presence, and guides us into exciting service.

THE STRUCTURE OF WORSHIP

The structure or order of our worship should make a great statement of what we believe. Worshipers have the imprint of a great love, a great faith, and spiritual power by the shape of our worship service.

DISCOVER THE SHAPE OF WORSHIP - FOCUS

The focus of worship should be God at work, speaking to us, and moving us to devotion through a conscious awareness of God. It is feeling God acting -- loving us, caring for us, renewing our relationship with Him, and giving form to all of our life.

A commentary on our worship today might be that it has become a form instead of a force. It is a Sunday exercise often rather dull, cold, formal and unrelated. If our worship is flat, and characterized by sameness, or passive indifference, it has little affect on what the worshiper is, or what is going on in his life the rest of the week.

If it is true that the shape of worship is somewhat out of balance today, let us think about the factors that have contributed to this passive structure.

Is our worship service dominated by the Corps Officer?

Is the congregation, our soldiers and fellow worshipers, nothing more than an audience?

Are they passive spectators who listen and watch?

Is the worship service, sermon-centered, rather than worship experience centered?

Are we treating hymns, prayers, scripture, and music as preliminaries -- just a mere path to the sermon?

Do we feel that the order of the service is written in cement; it must not be altered or changed?

Is our worship service controlled by the timing factor?

Does any single element of the worship program dominate timing?

Does the order of the worship service guide the worshipers into an individual response?

Is there a sense of freedom -- a space for spiritual breath in the worship service?

Is there variety in the worship service program?

Does the order of worship communicate the truth to be taught in the sermon?

The answers to these questions emphasize that order and form in worship will communicate. It also reminds us that poor form and order rob the worshiper of a meaningful experience.

A purposeful sequence of worship opens the door to freedom in our worship and directs our thinking toward a satisfying worship experience. Therefore a quickly put together, haphazardly planned program does not go anywhere. In fact, such an unstructured service can be distracting, disturbing, and engender emptiness, tension, confusion, and preoccupation with self. Consequently, if we throw together hymns, scripture reading, prayer, and some music, as a "fill in" leading to the sermon, in all probability there will be little or no worship experienced. We will entertain, divert, and just indulge our audience.

In conclusion, we note that there are various styles or shapes to the worship service, some formal and some informal, but with a sequence that permits a great deal of flexibility and spontaneity. It is never worship without order, rather it is a sequential ordered presentation that allows God to 'speak and act, and the worshiper to hear and respond in faith and love.

Such a worship experience will not be mechanical, dictated or a required ritual, a duty, or an obligation. It will be a privilege and a joy for all will "worship in spirit and in truth". (John 4:24)

UNCOVER-NEW APPROACHES

If God has designed the worship experience as an avenue for releasing His love and blessing, for communicating with Him, and for His children to appropriate and embrace His power, it should have very exciting dimensions. Certainly it should be an ever-ascending, ever-growing experience. Worship should always produce more worship. For this to happen we need to "UNCOVER" some new approaches.

While worship is an ever-growing experience, it must be noted we do not grow into worship. We grow in worship. Growing into worship can be a routine, comfortable, accommodating position to assume. Growing in worship is a responsible, demanding, determined and involving response. As we grow, our response will grow. Only new insights and a fresh approach to the corporate worship experience can make this a reality.

To uncover fresh, new approaches will require constant change in methods of presentation, content, in timing, in structure, in sequence, and style.

In a word it will require an adaptability that will keep us in touch, relevant, and innovative. It will mean examining our present worship service, and being adventurous in changing our program. It will require abandoning "pet" (almost sacred) ideas, and practices, and becoming open to creative thinking. The challenge is change, modification, and variation.

There will be freedom of expression, initiative, imagination, and the nonstifling of new ideas. There will always be a flow of new approaches because worship was never intended to be a stagnant pool. In Nehemiah 8 there is a sequence of verses that describe a flow of participation by worshipers:

> "Ezra the scribe stood upon a pulpit of wood. . .
> and opened the book. . . .
> and blessed the people. . . . .
> and all the people answered, 'Amen, Amen'
> with lifting up their hands. . .
> and they bowed their heads and worshiped God."

THE CALL TO WORSHIP

While our practice of personal worship and devotion, prepares us to a degree to enter into corporate worship, the structure of the service can and should be an avenue for communion with God. For instance, so frequently the "Call to Worship" is a verse of scripture printed on the order of service and read by the Corps Officer. It could be a united reading or it might be a responsive reading or a litany. A silent reading of scripture, song, or poetry with piano or organ accompaniment could move us into worship. Or for a change just open the service with a time of silence introduced by a short verse: - *"Thy face will I seek. I will wait on the Lord"*. (Psa. 27:8, 14)

Many hymns are essentially a call to worship and an effective solo of a hymn could signal meditation. Above all the call to worship should not be just an item in the service. It should be purposely and relevantly planned. In the resource section of this book there are suggestions for the call to worship. Could I insert here, that before the call to worship, preparation for worship initially begins with our attitude as we enter the place of worship. The expression of Psalm 24:4 speaks of this:

> *"One thing I ask of the Lord, one thing I seek: that I may be constant in the house of the Lord, to gaze upon His beauty and to seek Him in His temple."* (NEB)

THE PRAYER

Some Corps Officers believe that the Sunday morning prayer should be a pastoral prayer. This does have merit, but a new approach might be to have a soldier give an invocation or blessing after the opening song. It could be a prayer of adoration and praise, of rejoicing and thanksgiving. The pastoral prayer could be later. The pastoral prayer was non-existent in the early church. Prayer belonged to the people. We can give it back to our people. Ask for a prayer of intercession. Suggest areas of prayer for the needs of the congregation or the world. This could be a change, and the pastoral prayer for the Sunday would be accomplished. A local officer could occasionally give the pastoral prayer, for primarily we of the faith are all called to function as priests.

> *"Ye as lively stones, are built up a holy priesthood. Ye are a chosen generation, a royal priesthood."* (I Peter 2:5)

There is a priesthood of believers which affirms the responsibility of caring, concern, and intercession by the total worshiping congregation. This was also the concept of the worship service as perceived and practiced by General William Booth.

THE BENEDICTION

The conclusion of the morning worship service is equally significant. After we have worshiped, the benediction or the blessing should send us forth to be ambassadors with the word of reconciliation.

> *"God. . . hath committed to us the word of reconciliation. . . we are ambassadors for Christ."* (2 Cor. 5:19,20)

The closing song should focus on this by combining the central truth that has been taught with the action desired. As the congregation participates in the singing the response is determined and assured. The benediction, then, concisely resolves the end of worship and the beginning of service. This can be accomplished in a variety of ways as well as making effective the familiar pattern.

The songsters could sing an appropriate benediction with a concluding "Amen".

The congregation could sing one of the several benedictions in the Army Song Book.

The band or a quartet could accompany a spoken benediction from the Song Book.

A soloist could sing an appropriate benediction. Recently I was at a service where the soloist sang the last phrase of the Lord's prayer, "For Thine is the kingdom, the power and the glory, forever, Amen." Occasionally a benediction of unity could be used as everyone takes hands across the aisles and sings a benediction.

We could revive the Army doxology, "Praise God, I'm Saved".

SCRIPTURE READING (Have Congregation Stand)

The Word of God should always be treated with the greatest reverence and respect. In the reading of the scripture we should always be aware that God the Holy Spirit is actively present. Therefore, we should give attention to "how" it is read. Nehemiah 8:8 accents the importance of the reading of scripture:

> *"They read the law of God distinctly, and gave sense, and caused them to understand the reading."*

The apostle Paul makes this practice very clear in his writing to Timothy:

> *"Devote your attention to the public reading of the scriptures, to preaching and to teaching."* (I Tim. 4:13 NEB)

Whenever the scripture is read and heard in faith, the response is the sense of God's presence, and a fresh and new meaning from the Word.

HOW DO WE READ?

The Word of God is not a preliminary. It is not just something we do at the beginning of the service. It is God speaking and he who reads it needs to read it well. We cannot be too insistent or demanding in the manner in which the Bible is read in public. It should not be read carelessly, stumbled over, or hurriedly presented. The Word of God is powerful! It is dynamite if read distinctly and with meaning. We don't ask people to sing who can't sing well. Let us not ask people to read the Word who can't read well. Perhaps a Scripture Reading Seminar in our Corps would greatly improve our Scripture Reading skills, and breathe life into the public reading of the Word. If not a Seminar, we could train one or two, or more, who are interested and have potential for Bible Reading, thus developing their skills.

LITANY- RESPONSIVE READING

Generally Scripture Reading is an assigned text by one person. However, the use of a Litany or a Responsive Reading will add variety and also elicit participation by the congregation. In the resource section you will find theme and topically indexed responsive readings and litanies. Scripture reading should not be only by the officer or the officer's wife. We should involve the congregation as active participants.

13

Scripture reading need not be a one-way delivery system.

The Antiphonal reading will also lend variety, and has a visual element too. It could be a question and answer, or a reply, acknowledgement, or echo type. One reader could be at the rear and another at the front. The aisles also are adaptable for reading. The center of the congregation and the platform could be used to imply the Word of God among us. No matter how it is done the reading of the Word is of vital importance, and the congregation participation seals the Word in the heart and life.

DRAMA

Dr. James Young, of Wheaton College, views worship "as not only a celebration of the Christ life, but also a dramatic presentation or reenactment of it." It is the conflict between good and evil in our everyday lives, and how we confront it and resolve it by the power of God within us. It is a great drama culminating in triumph, praise and thanksgiving. To use a variety of the art forms would certainly enhance our worship. It is not a suggestion to secularize, debase, or make common the worship experience.

I read recently of a pastor who wanted to have a dramatic bent to the Easter Sunrise Service. In celebration of the Resurrection and in a mood of rejoicing, he released dozens of colorful, helium-filled balloons. It did not have the effect he anticipated. It did not create a sense of joy and gladness, but rather an awkward and uneasy sense of a gimmick. We must carefully and prayerfully consider the art form, the dramatic expression to be used, assured it will be worshipful in nature and an inducement to worship. For special occasions, visuals, characterizations, readings, Biblical dialogue, or Biblical symbols could be introduced.

CHORAL READINGS

The Choral Reading (which is not a Responsive Reading) when effectively presented by a well rehearsed group and a leader with a dramatic sense, truly communicates. In the resource index you will find a number of Choral Readings as well as instructions for presentations. Some are for first-time (beginner) groups and others more exciting and dramatic for well trained groups. All will add a new dimension to worship. Speech dialogue and interaction, which includes monologues, mini-scenes, and interpretative choreography can be symbolic methods of "adding to" the worship experience.

WORSHIP CENTERS

A valuable tool in the worship experience is the worship center. This medium is a vehicle of focus, both for the worship atmosphere and the individual worship experience. There is no limit for the creative mind that sees worship in pictures, objects, symbols, nature, color, space, candles and all of art. Certainly art forms are not necessary to worship, but they are not a hindrance either. It is an aesthetic contribution to the worship that interprets and communicates truth. The principle is that all creation joins in worship. Helpful guidance and designs with interpretations for worship Centers are to be found in the resource section.

THE CHRISTIAN CALENDAR

Because worship is linked to the daily life of the worshiper, it is natural that it should also celebrate the sacred events of the church year. To these we also add secular celebrations and Salvation Army observances. The planning of a lectionary including these will keep us in touch with truths that shape our lives, and the building blocks of spiritual formation.

In the Christian Calendar Lectionary we should consider the following in our worship program:

Advent	Lent	Pentecost
Christmas	Palm Sunday	Bible Sunday
Epiphany	Good Friday	Watch Night
	Easter	New Year's Eve

Some of the secular celebrations that we should plan for might be:

Mother's Day	Children's Day	Father's Day
Commencement	Graduation	Thanksgiving

Salvation Army Observances include:

All Senior and Youth Program Observances

Founder's Day

Music Sunday, Home League Sunday, League Of Mercy Sunday, etc.

In such a lectionary every service is followed by a comma, not a period.

ORDER AND FREEDOM

Professor Boyd of Asbury Seminary makes this statement, "Preaching is not the whole ball of wax ever!" Preaching should always be careful to be the servant of worship. It is true there is a rising tide of participation in worship, but there are still many places where the Officers do everything -- lead, read the scripture, pray and preach. Our people must not be just spectators; they must be participants. We could perhaps phrase it, "Worship by the people, for the people". It is the sense of a lively, active faith, a spontaneity of response by something the worshiper is doing.

Let me give you an example:

> Mrs. Colonel Gordon Swyers sang a solo in a service at the Atlanta Temple Corps, "Nothing but the blood can save me". At the conclusion of her solo she invited the congregation to sing the chorus. As we sang together you sensed an aliveness and involvement. But the power and presence of the Holy Spirit was intense when we individually and directly became involved. It happened when we finished singing the chorus. Mrs. Swyers said, "If you believe this, say "Amen". The passive role was broken. We were involved.

Acclamations of praise, hallelujah, amen, and thank you Lord, were once a free and spontaneous part of Salvation Army services. Why not restore these responses to our worship?

Congregation participation demands forethought by the leader, but it pays big dividends in worship. Simple ideas like the following could be used:

Short responses of praise and thanksgiving can create a sense of unity and involvement. For instance, after the Scripture reading the person doing the reading might quote *"Thy word is a lamp to our feet"* and the congregation could respond, *"And a light unto our path."* (Psa. 119:105) In the same manner you could use Psalm 119:97.

READER: "O, how I love thy law"

CONGREGATION: "It is my meditation day and night"

Before the sermon the congregation could repeat Psalm 19:14 or something similar:

> *"Let the words of my mouth and the meditation of my heart be acceptable in thy sight, O Lord, my strength and my Redeemer."*

If we can adapt and use creative thought and ideas for a new approach to our worship services, there will be an increased "aliveness" in our worship. Let us open the door of doing something as a congregation and never permit our worship to be just something we watch others do.

RECOVER OUR SALVATION ARMY HERITAGE

In 1963, General Wilfred Kitching wrote an article on "Worship in The Salvation Army" for the International Review of Missions in which he states, "The Salvation Army wants reality and not ritualism in our worship. Our constant aim is to avoid becoming merely an audience that does not participate. We want a congregation where all in spirit and truth are one in worship. Our emphasis has always been on personal participation."

General Kitching purposed six characteristics of Salvation Army worship, which are an echo of the worship services conducted by General William Booth. He further states that he believes they should be retained by present day Salvationists. They are the following:

> A freedom of spirit
> Simple meeting places
> Hearty singing
> Instrumental music
> Liberty in prayer
> An altar invitation
> Link worship and work

Methods and practices are not timeless. Principles and truths remain the same. If we can retain the above principles, and become adventurous and imaginative, our worship will recover our heritage.

In 1907-1908, William Booth asks in "The Founder's Message to Soldiers" "Is there not a certain amount of brain lying unemployed within your borders?" and then he suggests "might not some fresh plans be invented?"

"TRADITION! TRADITION!" you say. NO! Innovation, initiative, creativity, adaptability, ingenuity, flexibility, all harnessed to these timeless principles.

THE EXPRESSION OF WORSHIP

The expression of worship, because of differing personalities, may vary in style, wording, or manner. However, there are basic principles that must be understood and accepted. There are five general concepts that are essential tenets of the act of worship:

Adoration /Praise

    Confession

        Thanksgiving

           Praise

              Supplication

In our worship services our whole person -- mind, will, heart, emotions, and yes, our senses -- is drawn into the act of worship. That is, if we give or are led to give, expression to all five.

WE ADORE

We adore, we glorify, we magnify, and we recognize the majesty, the greatness, the power of the eternal God. In our worship there must be adoration as we revere and pay homage. In the Orders and Regulations for Officers we read, "The one unchanging command ever to be remembered is, "Give to Jesus glory!"

Again and again in the scripture we are reminded of this principle in worship,

> *O magnify the Lord with me, and let us exalt His name together"*. (Psa. 34:3)

> *"Let such as love thy salvation say continually, 'The Lord be magnified.' "* (Psa. 40:16)

What could be a more appropriate culmination to the act of worship than the benediction:

> *"Now unto the King eternal, immortal, invisible, the only wise God, be honor and glory for ever and ever."* (I Tim. 1:17)

Colonel Milton Agnew in "More Than Conquerors" writes:

> "When God has been deprived of His glory, men are also deprived of theirs."

When "we adore" Him, we go up to the mount of the Lord where the vision is too big for our heart to hold so "Christ is magnified in our life." (Phil. 1:20)

We adore Him, and discover that, 'Nothing is ever lost that glorifies the Saviour's name." General Clarence Wiseman - *The Desert Road to Glory*

WE CONFESS

Woven into our worship there must always be the sensitivity that God is aware of the inner condition of those who worship. If there has been disobedience to the mind and will of God, if there is sin in the heart, then there must be confession and rebirth of the spirit. Confession is also our road to renewing and maintaining our relatedness to God. Confession establishes again a broken line of communication. Sometimes it may just be a line that needs repairing, and it happens as "We confess" in worship. Perhaps, we should plan for some open-ended moments where any need for confession could take place. These could be directed by a responsive reading, a solo, a song, a prayer, or a quiet pause. It need not be a time kept for the mercy seat invitation. These moments may be very private, passing moments, during the worship service. In the quiet of the mind and spirit with an attitude of listening, God speaks and reveals.

Lt-Colonel William Burrows has said, "Confession to God is a primary need of the human heart."

The Bible says:

> "He that covereth his sins shall not prosper, but whoso confesses and forsakes them shall have mercy." (Prov. 28:13)

> "If we confess our sins, He is faithful and just to forgive us our sins and to cleanse us from all unrighteousness." (I Jn. 1:9)

WE PRAISE AND GIVE THANKS

Praise and thanksgiving may be twins, but they are individual entities in our worship. Praise is related to a spontaneous joy. It is concentrated in the love, the goodness, the faithfulness, the mercy, the peace and care of God. It is the "Alleluia" and "Amen" of the heart. It is the feeling, the emotion, the response to what God is. It is expressed in the Psalms:

> "With all my heart I say, 'Praise the Lord! you are my God, and you are very great.'" (Psa. 104:1)   -Donald Demaray (Alive to God)

Thanksgiving emphasizes something that is specific and particular, such as friends, food, home, loved ones, healing victory in temptation, and the meeting of every need of our life. It is gratitude for country, school, church, nature, art, and every good and perfect gift.

Praise and thanksgiving should skip happily through all our worship. Mrs. General Catherine Booth has expressed it best when she wrote:

> "Bless the Lord, we ought to get up and sing a song of praise before we go any further."

Thomas a'Kempis in "Of the Imitation of Christ" writes:

> "Thank you, Heavenly Father, for being so good as to remember all my needs, because I need all the help I can get."

WE PETITION

All worship is framed in petition or supplication. In supplication

We ask

We request

We appeal

We entreat

but we do more!

We listen

We wait

We trust

We rejoice

Truly the picture of prayer expression, with adoration, confession, praise and thanksgiving, blends together in the sturdy frame of petition. Every worship service we plan should have breathing spaces - the opportunity for worship expression. We must not rush from one item to another, but rather permit each item to flow into each other. In the flowing, prayer will naturally spring from the worshiping hearts.

THE PRACTICE OF WORSHIP

PERSONAL WORSHIP

A renewal of corporate worship has a pronounced effect upon personal worship. Certainly it stimulates a desire for consistent, faithful, creative personal devotions and study of the Word. Our desire for worship and delight in worship is enhanced and heightened. Corporate worship and personal worship are interwoven into a design of personal growth in our walk with God. The great truth is expressed by Eugenia Price "the more we know Him, the more we long to know Him". In other words, the cry from the heart of the apostle Paul is the cry of our heart, *"that I may know Him,* (Phil. 3:10) and in knowing Him there is no ending. We are always unsatisfied, but not dissatisfied; just longing, desiring, yearning and aspiring for more of God. *"My soul yearns for thee, O God. I will seek thee earnestly."* (Psa. 63:1 NSB)

Let us find time each day to "dwell in the secret place," to experience a closeness, by the presence of the Holy Spirit. The loving Father, who created you and your longing for Him, through the Holy Spirit, wants to give you more of Himself, and more, and more, and, yes, MORE!

FAMILY WORSHIP

If we truly believe that the home is the strongest influence in a person's life, then family worship should be an imperative. In the home children's values are set. They learn to be responsible, to learn skills, attitudes, ideals, and discipline.

We often admit the importance of these moral values, but we hesitate to initiate family worship. Family life is so fragmented today that family worship is a necessity to family Christian growth. The Christian nurture of the family is not the sole responsibility of the church or the Salvation Army Corps. In Deuteronomy 6:7 we are commanded, *"to teach the scripture diligently to our children, to talk about it when we sit at home, or walk along the road, or when we lie down or when we get up."* (NIV)

Louis H. Evans has said, "the family who kneels to God can stand up to anything. Family prayers are the best remedy for family cares." One of the prime and vital concerns of the Salvation Army Corps should be preserving and stabilizing the home life. The family altar is the source of that strength. If we have vital Christian faith in the home we will have it in the Corps.

There are five major responsibilities of parents to their children:

> To love
>
> To provide
>
> To control
>
> To train
>
> To teach

In this relationship of parent-team to children, the family worship structures, guides, and reinforces all these responsibilities. The plus is - with the power of God the Holy Spirit - when there is a family altar. Our home is a Christian home only if God's Word is exalted and prayer is heard. A vital, interesting, zestful family worship is as welcome as the aroma of homemade bread or apple pie.

There are two devotional experiences associated with family life; grace before meals, and the family worship.

A prayer of thanks is a pleasant interlude as well as a recognition of God's goodness. It should start the meal with all members of the family present. Mealtime, primarily the evening meal, should be very special. Nothing can fragment a family like having meals in front of the TV or not foreseeing time conflicts in meal planning.

So many families today do not have sit-down meals. It is so needful, so essential, so necessary to strengthen family life. My observation of grace before meals has resulted in these guide lines:

Keep it short

Make it thoughtful, not always the same.

Let it add a worshipful note to meals.

All participate, not just the children.

Family members take turns saying grace.
    Perhaps grace in unison; sometimes, a verse of hymn, scripture or doxology.

Hold hands around the table.

Be creative -- all will be eager to be there for grace.

WHAT ARE THE INGREDIENTS OF FAMILY WORSHIP?

The essential ingredients of family worship should be considered in the focus, knowledge, and atmosphere of each family.

Preparation

    Prayer - Praise

      Scripture

        Music

          Reverence

            Communication

            Communion

              Something for everyone

HOW DO YOU START?

When you as parents have decided you want to have family worship, the next best thing to do is to discuss it with the children. The import of the discussion will be dependent upon the age of the children. You might call it a family council. All members should be present when the idea is introduced. Each family member should tell what he would like included, what he hopes it will mean to him, and how he would like family worship to be conducted. Speak frankly about some of the difficulties and hindrances to having family worship. Be accepting of all ideas, and involve the suggestions in the plans you decide upon.

WHEN DO YOU HAVE IT?

It should be at the most convenient time for the family to be together. The particular time should give consideration to the varying schedules of the family. Everyone should be flexible, and the time should fit the family. The family should not be made to fit a time schedule. Of course, there will be occasions when a member cannot be there, but the family worship should proceed as usual.

Interruptions should be planned for. Decide as a family what you will do if the phone rings. Leave the phone off the hook during prayer time or to answer and say, "We're having family prayers now, could you call back later?" This could be a silent witness. If a guest arrives, ask them to join with you. Think of the possible interruptions and formulate your plan before they happen.

Family worship should be an appointment with God that is kept regularly. Morning, evening, or mealtime, it is a priority on the family schedule. It may be twice a week, or every other day, or every day. Don't wait until you have a large segment of time. Take the time you have and use it.

WHERE DO YOU HAVE IT?

The place you have it is not as important as the fact that you choose a place apropos to your family's personality. You should not do just whatever is convenient for the day. The place can be open-ended to consider the preferences of everyone. On a monthly or quarterly basis the place could change. For instance, you could meet around the table at the evening meal. Some families like to gather around the piano and sing. This, then, would make a suitable place for family worship. Sometimes a mother may like to get all the children ready for bed, then let them crawl on a big bed with her and daddy for a Bible story and worship. Some families love to relax in the family room around a fireplace and a comfortable sofa, perhaps with a guitar and have family worship. Whatever your family enjoys will help to make the place special. It will always be a vivid place in their memory as they recall the many times they talked with God, listened in prayer, and sensed God's presence. A Korean veteran with his back injured and his feet frozen lay for hours in a ditch, where he had been left for dead. During the time he was conscious, he spent the time praying for himself, his buddies, and the folks at home. After his rescue he wrote a letter home, and told this story. While I was praying, I looked at my watch and began to figure out what time it was back home. I had to do these things to keep me awake. Then I discovered it was just the time you were having family prayers around the table. I could almost hear you, Dad, saying, "Bless Jim, wherever he is now, give him strength for his need." What a lift it gave me. It was like a shot in the arm. I continued to pray, and in the morning I was rescued. Thank God for our family prayers.

HOW LONG SHOULD IT BE?

Keep it brief! Good timing would be about 15 minutes, and again this would depend on the ages of the children. Worship should not be tiring, or a lengthy experience that is tolerated or endured. With that we defeat our primary purpose. A short period will stimulate interest, and create a desire to know, love, and serve God.

WHAT DO WE DO?

Do what your family enjoys. Make it a blessed, happy time. Make it a time all will look forward to with gladness. Always be looking for better ways to do it. Make it informal, but always a setting of reverence. It should include scripture, prayer, music, conversation, discussion and study helps. Do whatever will make it special.

SCRIPTURE

Be sure the Bible is visible. If you are using a devotional book, a Bible story book, or study helps, read from the Bible itself. The King James Version has beauty and majesty that should not be denied the family. Many expressions are found in literature and it will enhance such reading for the family when they recognize the origin. Of course the many versions of the Bible should be used for translation and interpretive purposes. Bible resource material sometimes has charts, maps, key thoughts, memorization suggestions, etc., that will enrich scripture. If parents hold the Bible important and use it, children will deem it important and use it. Family worship can make scripture alive, for the Bible is a book to be read, loved, and lived. (See the Family Worship Workshop)

PRAYER

Prayer should be short and specific. A prayer focus for the week, sentence prayers by everyone, or conversational prayer where one member prays briefly, and each person adds to the prayer, or silent prayer on the same subject. You may want to give some thought to your position for prayer. You could kneel, or you could stand, or form a circle and hold hands, or sit and bow your head. One time we made a football huddle. It was a great feeling! The Family Worship Workshop details prayer ideas for varying ages.

MUSIC

Singing and music can set the tone and mood for worship. It always enriches and enforces truth. It may be a hymn or a chorus; it could be a record or a tape; it might be a solo from a family member who plays an instrument, or a vocal solo from one of the children as everyone hums in the background; if there are two or three younger children they could have rhythm sticks or bells or a tambourine to accompany the singing. The delight of the music, plus the incentive for developing musical skills, honors God in our worship. Let us "sing praise unto our God, and be glad in the Lord." (Psa. 104:33,34)

DIALOGUE AND DISCUSSION

Conversation about ideas, concepts, and insights involving the whole family result in a closeness of family relationships. A personal point of view, an illustration or a related experience, or even a confession or the acknowledgment of a problem brings new understanding and deepens the spiritual life of everyone. Sharing takes time, but sharing is so productive. Everyone is learning not only the techniques of effective discussion, but also the privilege of talking over everything with the Lord.

STUDY HELPS

There are many excellent devotional guides, useful literature, character studies, book studies, pictures, poetry, and other material which can be used in family worship. Acquaint yourself with them, look them over and decide what will be best for your family. Money may be a factor here, but sacrifice something not so important and get the best for your family worship time.

WHO SHOULD LEAD?

There is the idea, especially in structured families, that the father is the head of the house and should just naturally lead the family devotions. Assuming the man of the house doesn't want to lead, we immediately have an obstacle to face.

However, as women have made their way into the work-place, this role has changed and both parents are accepting mutual responsibilities. Therefore, both moms and dads can work together in establishing and leading family worship. The important thing is not who leads, but that every Christian home has family devotions. In fact, it need not be mom or dad, it could be a teen-age son or daughter, a child in the work force, or any of the children old enough to give expression of worship.

A relative visiting in the home would be a delightful change, like Grandma or Grandpa. You could invite the corps officer for dinner, and ask him or her to lead. Active involvement and planned participation will keep all the family interested. No one will be bored or restless and the leadership is not a problem.

Every leader should prepare for his time of leadership, be it a day or a week. Waiting on the Lord in prayer, considering the family, being mindful and attentive to the needs of friends and relatives, observing spiritual growth in the family, and being aware of world situations and the needs outside the family are the concerns of each leader. To bring it all under a scriptural umbrella will adequately fulfill the role of the leader. Every leader will change the pattern from time to time so that family worship never gets in a rut. The leader will keep the atmosphere fresh with new ways of doing things. There is no limit to originality.

FAMILY WORSHIP WORKSHOP

In sharing our faith with the family through worship, we want it to be a helpful time of information, instruction, inspiration, and spiritual fellowship. This workshop is a presentation of resources, down-to-earth creative ideas to make family worship meaningful.

INFANT

A child is impressed long before he can express. As we cuddle, hold, and kiss our baby, we can pray. Say a sentence prayer following the times you say "I love you", like "I thank God for you" or "You know Jesus loves you, too", or "I pray God will keep you good". A child can feel a prayerful, reverent spirit.

At feeding time when he recognizes the bottle, as you hold him, say a prayer, "Thank you, God, for this good milk for my baby". Later teach him grace before meals by folding his little hands together as you thank God aloud. Soon you can say, "Pray" and he will say it. This is a time for 'one word' so you can not only teach mommy and daddy but Jesus and God. "I love mommy, daddy, sister, Jesus." In worship hold your baby when you pray and let him feel the reverence.

PRE-SCHOOLER

Sing action songs.

Use finger plays that you create or those prepared in books. Two good books are *Fascinating Finger Fun*, by Eleanor Doan and *Christian Finger Plays and Games*, by Edna Bevan, both published by Zondervan.

Have the child draw or color a picture and bring it to worship time. Bring an object from nature - a twig, leaf, flower - and have a show and tell time.

Use records - listen and pray.

Relevant pictures and objects to talk about or pray about. A 'what-not' tree is a small branch in a styrofoam base on which they can hang cut-outs such as leaves of thanksgiving.

It is also good for memorization. Cut out apples from construction paper and have one word from a verse of scripture printed on each apple. "Be ye kind one to another." Be sure to put the reference on an apple.

Have an ABC chart with alphabet listed and verse for each letter. Learn a verse each week. Put a seal or star on a chart when verse is memorized. A "feely bag" is good when you want to thank God for your senses. Have something sharp, soft, hard, rough etc. in the bag. The child reaches in the bag and, without seeing the object, guesses what it is. Then you thank God for it, and for the sense of touch.

Have the children pray a sentence prayer for something special. Storytime with a picture book, or pictures should be brief and simple. Let the children tell one of the stories that has been read to them. Utilize holidays like Valentine's Day. Have a verse hidden in the pocket of a large heart. Let the children take out the verses. An adult or older child could read them and everyone repeat the verse.

JUNIOR

Have question and answer period after the story time.

Make a prayer mural for the family room using a suggested phrase like "Children praying around the world" or "God made all things beautiful" Everyone could participate. Be sure to have all the materials ready.

Make a prayer envelope. Use a legal size envelope with words printed or a picture on the outside. Inside cut out pictures of people or things for which you should pray. Use the envelopes by taking out something each day and pray accordingly.

Memorization can be a family project by using selected portions of scripture such as Psalm 23 or Psalm 1, the beatitudes or other meaningful passages. Learn a verse a week, or two verses according to the ages of the children. Have a verbal fill-in by someone starting the verse saying a few words, then stopping and the next person adding a few more words, etc., until the verse or verses have been completed. When you are not schedule conscious you could play a Bible Story, Juniors especially enjoy being a character they like.

Juniors also like being original. Let them write the Bible story in their own words.

For juniors, who are beginning to read well, let them read the story or the memory verse to be learned.

Visuals have great appeal to juniors and can assist in recall. Use them and create them. At Christmas time scripture verses can be attached to decorations on a small tree and either added as they are read or taken off and read by juniors. It could also be a centerpiece or "Our Bible Christmas Tree".

If you have a bulletin board in the kitchen, have a junior draw a Bible picture or some Bible symbol to be displayed during any of the holidays. Bible pictures, attitude pictures, conduct pictures, relationship pictures are real incentives to meaningful worship.

Pray about specific attitudes that juniors may display, such as being bossy, unkind, unwilling to share, not helpful, unforgiving, etc.

Children are not made prayerful by force or rule, but by climate and attitude. Teach your junior to listen for God to speak.

Make a family worship scrap book.

TEENS AND ADULTS

Be sure to have dialogue and discussion on relevant issues coming out of the scripture.

Prayer focusing - suggest a prayer focus for each day or for the week.

Use maps and charts to explain Bible places, times, and symbols. Do some problem solving with strong emphasis on obedience to God's rules in Christian living.

Have a talk-a-thon on God's guidance, forgiveness, judgment, temptation, moral values, etc.

Research and report on Christian witnessing, dating relationships, etc.

Worship outdoors, or take a prayer walk.

Review a book.

Write a prayer or praise litany and use it at worship time.

Bring something from a newspaper or magazine that could be a prayer focus.

Have someone read a poem or an article that has been helpful, a blessing, or an inspiration to them.

Read a letter from a friend or relative that needs prayer support or a letter that cites an answer to a prayer.

Decide to reach out in your prayer life in unusual ways:

> Breathe a prayer for the first person who says "Good morning" to you.

> Silently pray for a person you pass on the street.

> Quietly pray for the person who passes the sugar, salt or pepper to you if it be at home, or even the school cafeteria.

> In your heart pray for someone who says, "Thank you".

Whisper a prayer for the person who gives you change when you make a purchase.

There are so many ways to reach out. Decide what you will do for one week, and make each day different. It will surprise you what it does for you, as well as for the person for whom you pray.

Plan special centerpieces that may contribute to worship like a "Cornucopia of Thanks" for Thanksgiving. On small cards write names of people whom you especially appreciate, or scripture references of praise or thanksgiving. At worship time take one of the cards and use it in worship. You might even want to write a thank-you note to one of the persons named.

Try a prayer basket using last year's Christmas cards. Put several cards in the prayer basket, and take out one, enjoy reading it again, talk about the sender, and pray for him. Everyone could take a card and pray briefly for the person sending the card.

Choose red letter days on the calendar, -- Independence Day, Mother's Day -- and write a prayer to be read.

Occasionally, break up in pairs and go together and have prayer and worship. We had a prayer "huddle" one time (just like the football huddle). Everyone prayed briefly in the huddle and then we said the Mizpah benediction together.

Make a prayer notebook with a column for Prayer Requests and one for Prayers Answered. A column beside each of these for the date would be interesting too, so that you know the time lapse between the request and the answer. Always remember God answers our prayers in at least three ways: no, wait, yes.

A good exercise in family worship is to follow a chain reference with a word such as love, or to study a Bible character.

There is no substitute in the Christian home for a planned, consistent, scheduled time of devotion, prayer, and communication with God.

Suggested Devotional Aids

Pre-school

The Bible in Pictures for Little Eyes, by Kenneth N. Taylor, Moody Press, Chicago.

Today I Feel Like a Warm Fuzzy, by William L. Coleman, Bethany House Publishers, Minneapolis, MN.; also *Today I Feel Loved.*

Bible Stories for Family Devotions, by Jo Ann Merrell, Bethany House Publishers, Minneapolis, MN.

The Goodnight Book, by William Coleman, Bethany House Publishers, Minneapolis, MN.; also *Counting Stars.*

Primary and Junior

The Child's Story Bible, by Catherine Vos, Wm. B. Eerdmans, Grand Rapids, MI.; also *Egermeir's Bible Story Book,* by Elsie Egermeir.

Little Visits with God, by Allan Hart Jahsmann, Concordia Publishing House, St. Louis, MO.

Tell Me About God, by Mary Alice Jones, Rand McNally and Co., New York, NY.

Listen to the Animals, by William L. Coleman, Bethany House, Minneapolis, MN.

Forty Five Simple Object Talks, by Barbara Ebert, Standard Publishing Co. Cincinnati, OH.

Teens

Does Anyone Care How I Feel, by Mildred Tengbom, Bethany House, Minneapolis, MN.

A Daily Look at Jesus, by Mary Lillian Miles, Moody Press, Chicago, IL.

Lord, I Have a Question, by Betty Westrom Skold, Augsburg Publishing House, Minneapolis, MN.

Day by Day, by Amy Bolding, Baker Book House, Grand Rapids, MI.

Falling Off Cloud Nine, by Lorraine Peterson, Bethany House, Minneapolis, MN.

Just Between God and Me, by Sandra Drescher, Zondervan Publishing House, Grand Rapids, MI.

Adults

Your Family Worship Guidebook, by Reuben Herring, Broadman Press, Nashville, TN.

Devotions for your Family, by Marjorie Bloom, Word Books, Waco, TX.

Salt in My Kitchen, Jeanette Lockerbie, Moody Press, Chicago, IL.

Celebrate the Feasts, by Martha Zimmerman, Bethany House, Minneapolis, MN.

Joy and Strength, by Mary W. Tileston, World Wide Publications, Minneapolis, MN.

Five Minutes a Day, by Robert Speer, Westminster Press, Philadelphia, PA.

THE FAMILY

FAITH IN THE FAMILY

Let us hold fast the profession of our faith, without wavering. For without faith it is impossible to please Him, for he that cometh to God must believe that He is and that He is a rewarder of them that diligently seek Him.

For we walk by faith and not by sight.

We thank God that your faith groweth exceedingly. . . For this is the victory that overcometh the world.

THE ALTAR IN THE FAMILY

And Abram moved toward Bethel and pitched his tent, and there he built an altar and called upon the name of the Lord. And these words which I command thee this day shall be in thy heart, and thou shalt teach them diligently to thy children, and thou shalt talk of them when thou sittest in thy house, and when thou walkest by thy way, and when thou liest down, and when thou risest up, and thou shall write it upon the gates of thy house. And God said, "Go rear an altar unto the Lord." For man shall not live by bread alone, but by every word that proceedeth out of the mouth of God.

MELODY IN THE FAMILY

0 come let us sing unto the Lord. Sing unto the Lord a new song for He hath done marvelous things.

Let the word of Christ dwell in you richly, singing with grace in your hearts unto the Lord, speaking to yourselves in psalms and hymns and spiritual songs; singing and making melody-in-your heart to the Lord.

INSTRUCTION IN THE FAMILY

All scripture is given by inspiration of God, and is profitable for doctrine, for reproof, for correction in righteousness that the man of God might be perfect, thoroughly furnished unto every good work. Thy word have I hid in my heart that I might not sin against thee. I will instruct thee and teach thee in the way thou shouldst go. This book of the law shall not depart out of thy mouth, but thou shalt meditate therein day and night; then shalt thou make thy way prosperous and then shalt thou have good success.

LAW AND LOVE IN THE FAMILY

The law of the Lord is perfect. 0 how I love thy law. Open my eyes that I may behold wondrous things out of thy law. The Lord give thee wisdom and understanding that thou mayest keep the law of the Lord thy God. Discipline your children while they are young. If you don't you are helping them destroy themselves. Withhold not correction from thy child. If you don't punish your child, you don't love him. If you do love him, you will correct him.

YOU IN THE FAMILY

I pray your love may abound yet more and more in knowledge and judgment;

That you may approve things that are excellent.

Speaking the truth in love, may you grow up into Him in all things.

May you walk within your house with a perfect heart.

Scripture Selections: Heb. 10:23, Heb. 11:6, 2 Cor. 5:7, 2 Thess. 1:3, 1 Jn. 5:4, Gen 12:8, Duet. 6:6,7, 2 Sam. 24:18, Matt. 4:4, Psa. 95:1, Psa. 98:1, Col. 3:16, Eph. 5:9, 2 Tim. 3:16, Psa. 32:8, Joshua 1:8, Psa. 19:7, Psa. 119:97,18, Prov. 23:13, Prov. 13:24, Phil. 1:9,10, Psa. 101:2.

Part II

Choral Speaking

INTRODUCTION

Choral Speaking is an art form of expression, but because it has been so frequently thought of as a "responsive reading", much of its meaning, impact, and significant effect in worship is unknown and unexplored.

TUNNEL VISION

As an instrument of expression in worship, it has untold possibilities that are just waiting to be explored by worship leaders, teachers in Sunday School or Corps Cadets, Home League, Bands and Songsters, Drama Clubs, and almost any area of Salvation Army programming.

Never Lock In

To One System

Not only is Choral Speech a valued performance tool for worship leaders, but it also brings deep personal satisfaction to everyone who becomes involved in the Choral Speaking ensemble. For you see, Choral Speaking, if it is to be worthy as an avenue of expression, must first be interpreted, understood, individualized, and experienced in a creative and projecting image. Therefore, we need to recognize the nature, the scope, the dynamic, the personal and instructive values as well as the extensive usefulness in worship programming.

Of Worship...

CREATE!

RE-CREATE!

Choral Speaking can be exciting and dramatic, inspirational and enriching, intellectual and spiritual, imaginative and communicative. Worship is a rare and wondrous privilege. May God bless to your understanding and use the suggestions, the principles, the procedures, and the selections that I trust will add freshness, vitality, and originality to the reading. I would want to encourage and stimulate you to unusual accomplishments in Choral Speaking.

This is a brief, but I hope a practical text with illustrated theory, practice materials, and suggested reading selections so that it may be a valuable and useful tool.

Virginia Talmadge

UNDERSTANDING CHORAL SPEAKING

CHORAL SPEAKING AS AN ART

Choral speech or choral reading has been used throughout the ages in religious services and, to a degree, in the field of drama, especially by the Greeks. The revival of choral reading in the Twentieth Century has spread from religion and the theater to the radio, television, and education. It includes all forms of communication from current events to the announcement of a football game.

Thus today, its form includes more than the rituals of worship, but also lyrics, poetry, narration, refrains, hymns, and particularly Scripture. These are all being used singly or in combination for arrangements in effective choral speaking renditions.

Of course, the value of a revival in an art form such as a verse speaking choir is not in the emulation of the past achievements, but in its new, creative contemporary expression which evolves from the early forms and expressions. A true revival of this art form is virile, vital, and relevant. It creates a current Twentieth Century mood, but always preserves the unity of interpretation in the selection.

NEW

CREATIVE

CONTEMPORARY

EXPRESSION

VALUES

COMMUNICATE

AN IDEA. . .

A CONCEPT

One of man's greatest gifts is his ability to communicate; and, like all art, choral speaking seeks to convey or communicate an idea and a concept, to arouse a feeling or a response.

Charles Laughton has underscored this truth when he said, "the whole thing is bound up in wanting to communicate something you like to others and have them like it, too." [1]

Meaningful and moving choral speech will lead people into a genuine and satisfying worship experience and inspire in the worshiper feelings of wonder, love, and praise. The use of choral speech can also enable the leader to draw attention to specific ideas and insights through appreciative hearing as well as creating the spiritual climate for the leader's goal in the service. A genuine spiritual fellowship is created by the cohesive inner forces at work in a Speaking Ensemble. This is the result of the devotion to a common task by the Choral Speaking Ensemble.

Choral speech also has an intrinsic "individual" value quite apart from the spiritual implications; the enrichment of daily living, the improvement of speech and oral reading, meeting a basic need to belong, developing self-confidence through participation, and encouragement of team spirit through achieving group unity. These are but a few of the inherent values; for essentially, the member of a verse speaking choir is a growing, improving, flowering, and enhanced person because of his or her exposure to the selections for reading.

It will invariably create a love for the Word of God, for hymns and Army songs, for Salvation Army doctrine and ceremony, and Christian poetry and literature. Very often, there is also the opportunity for writing and arranging which is a value of individual significance. Not to be overlooked is the contribution that choral speaking makes to "learning by heart". Today, there seems to be such a lack of emphasis on memorization. In choral speaking, it can happen almost without effort through study of the selection, rehearsal, expression, and interpretation.

The oral interpreter may have a variety of attitudes regarding the selection he is to read aloud, but we must always bear in mind, as Charlotte Lee has said, ''The reader's aim is to present the material so that it conveys the effect which the author intended. The writer is the creative artist; the interpreter, the re-creative artist." [2] Let us not judge its value by the performance quality alone, but let the grand value be in what it does for each person taking part.

INTRINSIC

INDIVIDUAL

VALUES

READER

IS

A

CHANNEL

PURPOSE

There is "music of speech" as well as that of song; and as the musician interprets the written symbols and the musical notes of the composer, so the reader of choral speech interprets and recreates the meaning of words. The musician often thinks of himself as the instrument through which the interpretation flows; so the reader in choral speech is a channel through which freely flows his insights and concepts.

Always in creative choral speaking, the author is interpreted with understanding, meaning, and feeling. Frequently in reading, we see words, words, words when we need to see thoughts, ideas, observations, principles, and

37

concepts. It is when we concentrate on the idea that words become interesting, convincing, effective, personal, suggestive, and the avenue of communication.

Bishop James Pike, in the New York Times, underscored this concept when he said, ". . .knowledge of God comes through people--people who can communicate. Communication is of the very essence of God. As made in God's image, man's greatest gift is his ability to communicate." [3]

Let us, therefore, describe the purpose of choral speech in the following four statements:

1. Improving our understanding and appreciation of the Scriptures.

2. Promoting our skill in the interpretation of God's Word.

3. Enriching the Bible meaning with creativeness, aliveness, vitality, freshness, and clarity of expression.

4. Stimulating individual thinking and developing flexibility and discipline in sharing ideas and meanings.

Because of the creative process involved in choral speech, it has purposes not always obvious in a cursory evaluation of the subject. There is the individual purpose of developing artistic expression, a sense of the rhythm and power of words. The delightfulness as well as the energy of the united tones; the beauty, and sometimes the surprise, that comes from understanding the contents of the selection will certainly enhance the quality of life that one inherits from the interpretation of fine literature or the Word of God. The total purpose, then, must be to convey an idea, a mood, or a concept.

To these intrinsic purposes we must also be aware of the added dimensions of choral speech as a media of instruction in speech, articulation, tone, imagination, creativity, and dramatic expression. While the highlight of a Choral Speaking Ensemble will be sharing through public performance, the values of clear thinking, deep feeling, and honestly expressing thought, emotion, and contrasting moods far outweigh the performance experience.

How blessed it would be if some day in the future, because of participation in a Choral Speaking Ensemble, it could be said, as Charles Brown wrote in his text, "He opened the Book (Bible) as a skilled interpreter of its deeper meaning. He made clear its rich content by the very manner of his reading. He uncovered to the souls of men the divine message which lay beneath the surface of the written word by his own intelligent, sympathetic modulation. He showed its bearing upon present need and duty. He related its agelong helpfulness to the moods and opportunity of the hour." [4]

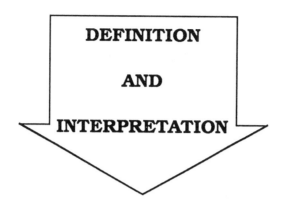

DEFINITION AND INTERPRETATION

Choral speech is a type of group interpretative reading. For Salvation Army purposes, the Choral Speaking Ensemble, through tempo, rhythm, tone, texture, repetition, and imagery, enriches the Word of God as the Band Selection enriches the simple hymn tune.

A Scripture Speaking Ensemble strives for direct communication, clarity, and strength in their oral interpretation of the great truths of the Bible. Sometimes, because of familiarity with a passage of Scripture, we neglect preparation in reading, and the result is bad reading. Curry, in his writings on the interpretation of the Bible, warns us against this and says, "However familiar a man may be with the Scripture, he will not allow himself to neglect the thorough preparation of the lesson he is to read. He may have studied it thoroughly years before, but he knows that this is not enough. There must be a present readiness, a freshness of thought and feeling."[5] It can be a simple, straightforward reading of a passage, a quiet inspirational study, or a dramatic, exciting, turbulent portrayal of the great Bible classics.

In every Choral Reading interpretation, there are three considerations--the selection, the interpretators or readers, and the audience. Thus, that which is shared is influenced by all three.

Lawrence Mouat supports this in *Reading Literature Aloud* when he writes, "It is necessary for the oral reader to assist the listener in comprehending and appreciating what he hears."

There are various forms of choral reading or suggested methods for arranging choral speech. The selection itself, the purpose or use intended, the group composition, and the nature of the interpretation will be factors to consider in determining the method which would be most effective.

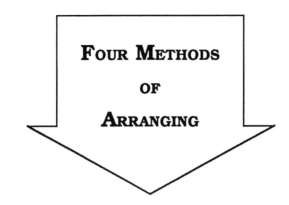

FOUR METHODS

OF

ARRANGING

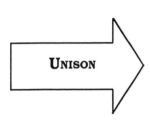

UNISON

Unison Reading is essentially considered to give the effect of several voices speaking as one. Thus, you create the idea, the pattern, the mood of unity with each person of the group speaking in his own voice. By varying and well defined emphasis, stress, pauses, rhythm, tempo, and sharp contrast, you bring all the voices together as one. These modulations must be agreed upon by the director and the chorus. They must also be sensed by the individuals and spoken effec tively as one. It will never be monotonous, but rather unified and effective by the variety of inflections. Poetry, hymns, Army songs, rituals, Army doctrine, covenants, pledges, Proverbs, some Psalms, and Paul's letters could be effectively used in Unison Reading.

Refrain work may, on the surface, seem to be a simple style to achieve in choral speech; but if the flowing, tripping, unaffected, rhythmical balance is to be accomplished, there must be exact guidance given to the speaking ensemble.

While a refrain may seem very close to a "jingle" type, the sense of unity in the total narration must be understood and preserved. To maintain this, the group could be divided into heavy or light voices, low or high voices with one speaking the story or verse lines while the other group intones the refrain. It is also acceptable to use a solo speaker whose voice can give life and color to the verses and yet smoothly swing into the rhythm of the refrain.

REFRAIN

The definition, then, of *refrain* arrangements would be a two-part work in which either a group or a solo speaker delivers the narrative and the rest of the choral group join in a refrain.

Sometimes the reading ensemble may be divided into three parts--*high, medium,* or *low*--with the selection being divided as seems fitting for the parts.

Consideration should be given in the study of the selection to rhythm and pace, strong and weak stress, rhyme and repetition, and the changing moods of the selection. It is extremely important in refrain arrangements to have the accuracy and distinctiveness of speech, and the chorus lines change with the moods of the selection. This means that all will be in harmony with the interpretations.

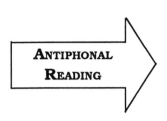

In selections that have questions and answers, or appeal and response, a very effective arrangement for interpretation is the antiphonal reading. This really is a two-part arrangement in which two contrasting voice groups read alternate lines.

Two-part work calls for *light* and *dark* voices with a group contrasting or a solo voice contrasted with the whole group.

Light voices usually ask the questions, and the *dark* or heavy voices give the answer or response. *Light* voices usually speak tender, delicate passages; and *dark* voices the heavy, strong, active, moving passages.

This type of arrangement is very well suited to any selection where parallels are used, the repetition of an idea in different words, or where the writer will balance one idea with another. While rhythm and stress are equally important to the interpretation of antiphonal passages, the principle emphasis must be given to pitch. this is not always easily or immediately achieved; but if given the right value by the leader and not forced, both contrasting voices will gain freedom of range.

Antiphonal work will require much practice, training, and study for interpretation and meaning of the selection if it is to be an effective method. It is truly worth the effort because of the beauty and precision of form, with the plus of variety in the expression of a passage.

This technique gives opportunity for individuality according to the ingenuity of the director or the members of the choir as the contrasting groups speak alternately, separately, or together.

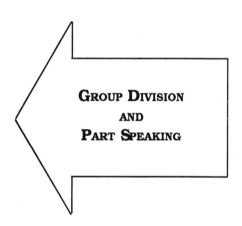

GROUP DIVISION AND PART SPEAKING

Group division and part speaking presents opportunities for more variety than does any other kind of choral speech. A smooth flowing movement is achieved by the sections and full chorus as well as by a combination of voices in solo, duet, trio, and quartet parts. Warmth, dash, color, and bravado, together with delicate or robust tones, can create interesting contrasts of interpretations.

The varying values of expression, speech, and tone are built up or diminished, yet knit together, so as to give unity to the selection. It is truly many voices speaking as one.

The group divisions are arranged in parts according to the normal key of voices -- high, medium, or low. This could make three divisions, or you could separate the group into two divisions with an equal number of voice keys; high, medium, and low being in each division. In the final analysis, the total number in the speaking chorus would determine the group division. The treatment of part speaking such as the moods, images, and special effects are accomplished by the adding and subtracting of voices, thus enriching the interpretation of the selection.

Bible narratives from both the Old and the New Testaments, poetry, selections from the prophets, particularly Isaiah, and some of the Psalms are adaptable to this development of material.

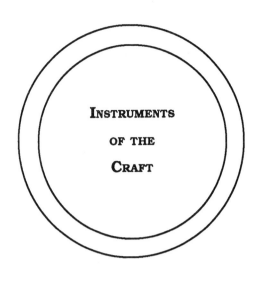

INSTRUMENTS

OF THE

CRAFT

THE SPEAKING ENSEMBLE

So frequently, we imagine because we can talk and read that a speaking ensemble is an easy, simple performance. THIS IS FALLACY. In a singing group, the organ or piano accompaniment may cover up for a poorly trained group. A poorly trained speaking ensemble has nothing to save it. There can be no mistakes in a speaking ensemble. A breath on the wrong beat, a slur, poor enunciation, or the wrong stress will detract from the entire performance.

Therefore, diligent attention must be given to blending the voices together so the timing and rhythm shall be in perfect accord, and the speaking ensemble will freely and naturally express the thought and feeling in the selection.

The first consideration in choral reading is adequate tone quality. This is followed closely by tempo and rhythm. "Keeping in step" is a necessity; and for effectiveness, there must be a variation of both tempo and rhythm. While there will be fast lines and slow lines, the sense of rhythm must never be interrupted.

This gives opportunity for flexibility and also aids in breaking up faulty speech habits of pronunciation, enunciation, and emphasis. The improvement of speech will inevitably contribute to the desired blending of voices.

To interpret effectively, the group must also recognize other techniques such as change of pitch, inflections, pauses, emphasis, and stress. To get these desired effects, the material is arranged so that lines will be effectively spoken according to the style of arrangement selected. The result of such a study of the selection will be solo readings, part readings, unison readings, division readings, adding and subtracting voices, occasionally using refrains, echoes, and antiphonal passages.

Each member of the speaking ensemble speaks in his normal range, moving up and down the scale as the response to the idea or interpretation demands. Tone color is most important to the speaking ensemble; however, we must not work for tone quality and sacrifice the "idea" or interpretation of the reading while endeavoring to preserve voice harmony.

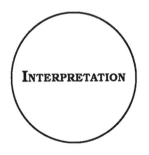

INTERPRETATION

The speaking ensemble will certainly want to give considerable thought to the meaning and the mood of the selection to be performed. This would immediately indicate a study of the passage, the style of the writing, perhaps something about its composition such as the date of writing, the author, or its place in literature. A relaxed, leisurely reading of the material would stimulate an appreciation for the selection. For the members of the verse chorus, this would also open the door for a mental, emotional, and spiritual reaction to what he reads. How the reader feels about the passage, the joy he experiences, and the light of understanding it communicated to him, is the beginning of his oral interpretation expression. The reader must develop an appreciation of the material before he can rightly interpret it.

To interpret or communicate the message of any selection, the reader must then study and reflect on its deeper meaning. He must become personally involved with the content of the selection and give himself to the task of communicating what the author intended. The speaking ensemble should not alter, modify or overly garnish the text, but they will give self-expression to the idea so that the speaking ensemble becomes a vehicle of interpretation or communication. The speaking ensemble has something to share when they have studied the selection until they feel they "want to" and they "must" share it. This eagerness to share makes them communicate not only words -- the letters -- of the selection, but go beyond to the "spirit" and "life" of the material.

Richard Whately has given expression to this relationship of the reader and the material, in Elements of Rhetoric when he writes, "He who not only understands fully what he is reading but is earnestly occupying his mind with the matter of it, will be likely to read as if he understood it and, thus, to make others understand it; . . .and he who not only feels it but is absorbed with that feeling will be likely to read as if he felt it and to communicate the impression to his hearers." [7]

Suggestions

The following suggestions would be helpful in preparing for interpretation:

1. Read the selection individually and unhurriedly.

2. One or several members read it.

3. The director will read it.

4. Discuss it; reading lines or paragraphs.

5. Clarify images or unusual wordings.

6. Ask questions regarding the total meaning of the selection.

7. Relate the selection to the experiences of the group.

8. Take time for individual, quiet thinking.

9. Give expression in the session to the individual thinking.

10. Let the group thinking be crystallized from the individual thinking.

11. Imagine, dramatize, sense, create the mood; -- gay, sad, mysterious, serious, light, etc.

12. Discover the tempo and rhythm. Does it move quickly, walk, gallop, or saunter?

13. Never force an interpretation, but lead the group to insight and understanding through planned discussion in keeping with the group thinking.

The Speaking Ensemble must always remember it is a channel through which interpretation of literature flows. Our channel should be cut deep, it should be free of any obstruction with strong banks to direct, guide, and preserve the message God would speak through the voice of the ensemble.

43

The Speaking Ensemble in The Salvation Army should always be dominated by the desire to interpret the great truths of God so that the listener will comprehend the message as it meets his personal needs.

SKILLS

Choral reading is an art that requires rehearsal after rehearsal to perfect it. It cannot be whipped into shape over night. A Director who has some training in oral interpretation would be most helpful. It is possible by reading, interest, and research to become familiar with speech and interpretative pausing, emphasis, enunciation, inflections, and voice projection. While it is true training would greatly enhance the leadership quality, it is also true that a person who has an appreciation for, and an understanding of good reading skills himself, has the potential of a good director.

The Director should have imagination, enthusiasm, personality, color aliveness, and genuine desire to lead choral speech.

A Director must sincerely study the passage to be used. He should endeavor to feel the author's meaning and try to creatively interpret the same. He should be able to convey the interpretation to the group and yet not superimpose it upon them. He must seek to share the group's "best" interpretation of the passage so that together they can build, color, and shade meanings into a harmonious whole. No individual should control the group, nor should the group be just an imitation of the Director's reading skills.

A beginning group should above all, endeavor to achieve a unity of expression. The Director or leader must constantly guard against mechanical utterance and seek for freshness and spontaneity of delivery. It is by no means easy for a group speaking together to give value and impassioned feeling to words, but it can be done as the director quickens the perception of the speaking ensemble.

The Director should strive to create enthusiasm for choral speech and for excellence of performance. The leader always desires individual satisfaction and pleasure for the Choral Speaking Ensemble. It must also be understood that the leader can only lead the speaking ensemble into a meaningful WORSHIP and INTERPRETATION experience as he himself comprehends and appreciates the selection.

SELECTION OF MATERIAL
AND TONE RANGE

In starting choral speech with any group, the leader should work for flexibility and clarity. To do this, the group must give attention to:

1. Selection of the material.

The selected passage should be suited to the group in relation to their age, spiritual, emotional, and intellectual maturity; their experience in choral speaking and their understanding of the art, together with drama and stage sense.

2. Range of Tone.

This should include both pitch and volume. While individual members should aim at increasing the range of tone from low to high notes with good resonance, consideration must also be given to the range of tone within the group such as low, medium, and high voices. Some leaders will classify tone as dark (low), light (high) with voices difficult to classify as either, being a plus or minus of the dark or light voices. It is best to achieve a fairly even balance.

Each leader arrives at a grouping method of his own preference, but the following is an easy one based on comparison:

On the blackboard, write:

LOW   MEDIUM   HIGH

a. Ask the choral speaking members to give their name, address, and birthdate. As they finish speaking, the Director will list them in the proper grouping (L) (M) (H) according to their speaking voices.

b. When all members have been placed in their respective voice divisions, each division should speak together, "We belong to the 'low', 'medium', or 'high' division."

c. As each division speaks, the Director will listen for voice differences within the group. He should also be certain there is a marked difference in the voice range of the two or three divisions he has arranged.

d. It should be remembered, as suggested earlier, that the division may be so arranged as to have a balanced range of tone within the group. This arrangement is particularly effective when you have solo, duet, trio, and quartet speaking parts.

VOICE QUALITY
AND EXERCISES

THE

DIRECTOR

1. Quality of Voice.

In the development of the Speaking Ensemble, the Director should also give consideration to the quality of the voice, to breathing, to force, to pleasantness, to bodily action, i.e., communication with eyes or any posture or gesture that might be clues to interpretation.

Because most readers fail to realize how much we read with our bodies, what Bishop Kennedy suggests as a goal for the preacher standing before his congregation aptly applies to the participant in choral speech:

"A preacher (reader) ought to be able to stand before people and give the impression of perfect control over his whole body; or better yet, to give the impression that every muscle is the servant of the message." [8]

The Director could utilize the Songsters' or Vocalists' method of "warm up" at the beginning of rehearsal.

Exercises in pitch variety, by saying a word like "OH" in may different ways:

OH - pleasure

OH - surprise

OH - pain

OH - disappointment

and as many other expressions as you or the group can develop.

Exercises in emphasis with phrases or sentences emphasizing different words:

Are "YOU" going?   Are you "GOING"?

"HE" gave me the keys.   He "GAVE" me the keys.

He gave "ME" the keys.   He gave me the "KEYS".

Exercises in exclamations or commands:

Ow! Sh. .hh! Ah! Forward March! Halt! [9]

For smoothness in voice changes, use the word "AH" and glide up and down in pitch, volume, and breathing.

It is also good to use words with a variety of inflections to change the meaning or interpretation, such as using the word:

GO. GO? GO! GO --

For good enunciation and articulation, let them practice the following:

Ah, ee, oo, aw with good lip movement - or

Boo, Bah, Bow, Bee - or you could use the old rhyme,

"She sells sea shells by the sea shore" - or

"Peter Piper picked a peck of pickled peppers".

There are many such exercises available in voice and speech books at your local library that will give the Director added suggestions in this and other areas of voice development.

In conclusion, the Director should aim his leadership so that the speaking ensemble will be heard, what they speak will be understood, and that it also shall be felt. In other words, understand the thought, keep the thought, and share the thought.

TECHNIQUES OF INTERPRETATION

Many of the techniques have been alluded to in connection with subjects covered in previous chapters. In this chapter, a very brief definition of the various techniques will be considered. The skillful use of these will certainly result in a facility of thought and speech as well as creative interpretation and performance.

| **V** |
| **O** | The use of the voice is not just for hearing only, it is for interpretation so that there will be understanding and empathy or a feeling for the hearer. Therefore, the voice must be free to respond to the content of the selection, spontaneously expressing the thought and mood. In brief then, we must develop an "audience ear" so we can hear ourselves as others hear us. When we aim for this in our presentation, we will eliminate a tense, strained voice; a weak, fatigued voice; a tight, constricted voice; or a slurred, thick voice. Developing the voice will take time, patience, practice, and knowledge of how to go about it. |
| **I** |
| **C** |
| **E** |

In referring to the voice, let us consider three relative characteristics which are pitch, quality, and volume.

| **P** |
| **I** | Pitch is a term applied to the variations of sound. It is the highness or lowness of sound. It could be called the musical scale of the voice. In reading or talking, it has been determined that the voice range is approximately two octaves. Therefore, pitch is the movement of the voice up and down the musical scale. We could speak then, of high pitch as in the tenor clef range and low pitch as in the bass clef range. |
| **T** |
| **C** |
| **H** |

The use of pitch has untold possibilities. For instance, take the word "YES" and use it with different pitch patterns to express various moods. You could identify the movements of pitch with an arrow up ↗ for higher, and down ↙ for lower, and horizontal ⟶ for sustained. It is possible you might also like to glide up or down in pitch to express a given mood. Here are some moods you might work with in a rehearsal. The use of a blackboard would accentuate the various changes.

EXAMPLE: acceptance ⟶

                 joy ↗

                 sadness ↙

YES . . . . . .   resignation

Expressed as   grief

                 concern

                 agreement

                 enthusiasm

You might like to try   "NO"

                      "GOOD"

                      "HELLO"

                      "GOOD MORNING" with some of the suggested emotions.

Melody, by pitch, with all its modulation, is necessary for adequate expression of meaning.

Q	How often we have heard it said, "He has a good voice, naturally." This, no
U	doubt, is a true statement but certainly not a limiting statement. It is true that
A	each person has a normal voice quality that is suggestive of his individuality.
L	However, good voice timbre or quality can be developed.
I	Voice quality is unique, and it sets a person apart as "YOU". It is the "quality"
T	of voice by which one is recognized. The developing of voice quality will never
	take away the individuality but will only enhance, improve, release, and give
Y	color to the existing voice quality.

Quality, then, is the identifying character of the sound of the voice. It could be compared to that of the distinguishing sounds of the trumpet, from the trombone, or the voilin, from the harp.

Quality of voice is closely related to emotion and can be a clue to the personality. Think for a moment about the quality of the voice of people you know. There is the soft voice, the hard voice, the heavy voice, and the light voice; a bold voice or a timid voice; and what about the gruff voice and the "oh, so pleasant" voice? Of course, we know of the harsh, hoarse, rough, smooth, full or thin voice all as identifying qualities. Listen to speech on TV or Radio; analyze the speaker's voice, then analyze your voice. Listen to it critically. It will be very helpful. A sensitive, expressive tone quality is very important in communicating moods and ideas. It is a well-known fact we must all work to improve this aspect of the voice.

EXAMPLE:

Why not try contrasts of tone quality in the following readings:

"A merry Christmas, Uncle! God save you!" cried a cheerful voice. . .

"Bah!" said Scrooge, "Humbug!" Dickens, CHRISTMAS CAROL

Pilate saith unto them, "What shall I do then with Jesus which is called Christ?" They all say unto him, "Let Him be crucified." And the governor said, "Why, what evil hath He done?" But they cried out the more, saying, *"Let Him be crucified."* (Matthew 27: 22,23,24)

V	Loudness, force, strength, or intensity are descriptive terms of volume. They
O	refer to the carrying power or projection of the voice. It is also the product of
	the energy with which the original tone is created and the degree of vocal force
L	and resonance given to the sound.
U	Vocal force may be associated with syllables, words, phrases, or an entire
M	sentence. The improper use of force is confusing to the hearer, and this fault
	is also a cause of listener fatigue. Certainly, the continued use of force or
E	volume will dampen the listener's attentiveness.

Volume or tone must be based on good voice production. The speaking ensemble must be able to give any amount of power needed without stiffening or hardening the voice. Exercises in volume should be practiced with "lipping", gradually increasing power and articulation. However loudly we speak, we must not raise our pitch to a shout. Try it with these words, increasing the volume with each word. Imitate a drum or a bell.

"Boom! Boom! Boom! Boom! Boom!"

"Ding, dong, ding!"   "Ding! Ding! Dong!"

In achieving an effortless production of volume, we also will achieve variety, pleasantness, and flexibility. Conversely, we will not create boredom, dullness, or monotony.

D **U** **R** **A** **T** **I** **O** **N**	Duration is the length of time that a sound lasts and has a great deal to do with the rate of speaking. In Choral Speech, rate of speaking adds life, vitality, brilliance, and resonance. Whether the rate of speaking is fast, moderate, or slow depends upon the length of time an individual sound, phrase, or word-cluster is held. The sustaining of certain sounds in words or phrases produces overtones. It is like plucking the violin string and hearing the vibrations of all the parts of the whole string making a rich sound. The duration of pauses between words and phrases can also contribute to the harmony of speech duration. Duration of sound and rate of reading, when effectively employed, will provide new insights, new pleasure, and a naturalness and spontaneity to the selection being spoken.

EXAMPLE:

Say with long held vowels and long pauses:

> In the beginning, God . . .and in the end,
>
> And in the in-between, forever He
>
> Is the insistent power, the constant friend,
>
> The steadfast hope of all eternity. [10]

> Come out into the sunlight,
>
>   Heart of mine;
>
> Why linger in the shadows
>
>   And repine!
>
> In the blue, the birds are singing
>
>   Up above;
>
> Throw away thy gloom and sadness,
>
>   All is love!   - Ralph S. Cushman [11]

> Lord God of Hosts, be with us yet,
>
> Lest we forget-lest we forget.   - Rudyard Kipling [12]

P **H** **R** **A** **S** **I** **N** **G**	Clusters of words, or word groupings that form units of thought related to the main idea are referred to as phrases. Thus, phrasing in reading becomes extremely important to communicating the meaning. A word belonging to one thought cluster should never be linked with a thought pattern that is not related to the sentence content. For instance, note how the meaning is changed when the name Jesus is associated with the following two phrases:

> Is not this Jesus -- the son of Joseph?

> Is not this -- Jesus, the son of Joseph?

In the first instance, we are referring to more than one Jesus; and in the second instance, one named Jesus.

We must take care to phrase by thought structure to convey the correct meaning. Good phrasing is determined by weighing the proper relationship of words and groups of words to the main idea.

Sometimes words or clusters of words are placed in unusual positions within the sentence structure, making it difficult to grasp the meaning. Phrasing, then, becomes the key to interpreting the passage.

We should note here that punctuation used in writing is not always an indication of phrasing. Punctuation is designed for the eye and phrasing for the ear and comprehension. As a result, a phrase may be indicated where there is no punctuation and disregarded when it is punctuated. Every choral speaking group must be aware of the differences between written and oral punctuation so that the variations of their phrasing will be effective.

EXAMPLE:

Read the following verses with variations of phrasing:

> Oh let me grow!
> About me buds are bursting
> And greening trees are yearning toward the sky,
> And everywhere is God's good power worsting
> The stagnant earth and lifting life on high.
> Then let me grow!
> This world is mere beginning;
> Soul, thou art born for larger things than this:
> Eternal mansions wait thy ardent winning,
> Adventures high, the battlements of God, thy Master's kiss?
>
> -Ralph S. Cushman [13]

"Hurry, hurry is the greatest enemy of literary appreciation and enjoy ment."-Clark [14] The way in which the choral speaking group uses the factor of time influences the ease with which listeners hear and understand. In considering timing for interpretative reading, there are three techniques or principles to follow:

1. Tempo

2. Pause

3. Rhythm

TEMPO

While tempo of speech is, in many aspects, an individual matter related to the personality (Southerners speak more slowly - an Easterner much faster), a person may be deliberate, excited, enthusiastic; but in choral speech, there is a need to continuously adjust the rate of speaking to the given selection. Some factors to consider in determining the tempo:

a. Nature of the material

b. Mood of material will influence the tempo

c. Emotional intensity or solemnity of the interpretation

d. Size of the auditorium

e. Ease of audience comprehension

Remember, there is no "fixed" tempo; but considering all factors, the rate and speed of speaking should vary. It should always be what is deemed best for naturalness of expression and listener comprehension. Audience interest is sustained through changes of tempo.

EXAMPLE:

Note the possible changes of tempo in the following:

AFTON WATER
Robert Burns

Flow gently, sweet Afton, among thy green braes;
Flow gently, I'll sing thee a song in thy praise;
My Mary's asleep by thy murmuring stream,
Flow gently, sweet Afton, disturb not her dream.
Thou stock-dove whose echo resounds through the glen,
Ye wild whistling blackbirds in yon thorny den,
Thou green-crested lapwing, thy screaming forbear,
I charge you disturb not my slumbering fair.

Psalm 105: 41, 42, 43, 45

He opened the rock, and the waters gushed out;
They ran in the dry places like a river.
For He remembered His holy promise
And Abraham His servant.

And He brought forth His people with joy,
His chosen with gladness:
That they might observe His statutes
And keep His laws. Praise ye the Lord!

THE PAUSE

The pause very definitely affects the tempo. The pauses between words or phrases may be long or short; the longer the pause, the slower the tempo. The number of pauses will also affect the timing. Pauses should never be so short the audience gets the feeling of being rushed. It is better for pauses to be long and unhurried. A long pause before a significant idea creates suspense. An abrupt pause after an idea strengthens the effect of the words.

A pause may do one of several things:

   a. Suggest completion of thought

   b. Set a phrase or word apart.

   c. Separate units of thought.

   d. Make an idea distinct.

   e. Suggest great emotion.

   f. Indicate emphasis.

The importance of the pause cannot be overestimated for it always gives the listener an opportunity to respond more fully to what he is hearing.

EXAMPLE:

The reader's sense of timing should be his guide in deciding how long to hold a pause in support of an idea. These verses give unusual opportunities for pausing:

ALL YOUR ANXIETY

Is there a heart o'erbound by sorrow?

Is there a life weighed down by care?

Come to the Cross, each burden bearing,

All your anxiety, leave it there.

All your anxiety, all your care,

Bring to the Mercy Seat, leave it there;

Never a burden He cannot bear,

Never a friend like Jesus.

-Salvation Army Song Book #246

54

A STEWARDSHIP HYMN

Awake, my soul, the night is spent

And day is calling o'er the hill;

Almighty Christ, take Thou my hand

And strengthen me to do Thy will.

Ambassador of God to men,

Help us to live Thy love again.

-Ralph S. Cushman

THINK ON THESE THINGS

Finally, brethren, whatsoever things are true,

Whatsoever things are honest,

Whatsoever things are just

Whatsoever things are pure,

Whatsoever things are lovely,

Whatsoever things are of good report;

If there be any virtue, and if there be any praise,

Think on these things!

-Philippians 4:8

R **H** **Y** **T** **H** **M**	Rhythm is the means by which other aspects of timing: i.e. the tempo and the pause, may be unified to contribute to a total audience impression.
	
	To cultivate the use of rhythm, we must:
	  a. Work through word meanings.
	  b. Focus on mood and emotion.
	  c. Invigorate with imagination: create images in the minds of our hearers, both of sight and of sound.
	  d. Adventure with meter so as to sense the cadence and find the rhythm patterns.

While it is true that the use of rhythm must not be "overdone" or be "mechanical", rhythm purposely employed not only fulfills an artistic quality, but it supports, enhances, and reinforces the meaning and the mood of the selection. The communication of rhythm is enjoyable to the listeners as well as to the speech choir.

In carrying the thought, in conveying the meaning, the relative significance of techniques such as projection, enunciation, empathy, diction, and breathing should always be our concern.

EXAMPLE:

Read the following in a sing-song manner, then as if they were written in prose, not poetry. Now read them in rhyme considering tempo and rhythm.

SWEET AND LOW

Sweet and low, sweet and low,
Wind of the western sea!
Low, low, breathe and blow,
Wind of the western sea!
Over the rolling waters go,
Come from the dying moon, and blow,
Blow him again to me:
While my little one, while my pretty one
Sleeps.

-Alfred Tennyson

CLIMBING UP THE GOLDEN STAIRS

O, my heart is full of music and of gladness
As on wings of love and faith I upward fly;
Not a shadow-cloud my Saviour's face obscuring
While I'm, climbing to my homestead in the sky.
O, I'm climbing up the golden stair to Glory,
O, I'm climbing with my golden crown before me;
I am climbing in the light,
I am climbing day and night,
I shall shout with all my might when I get there!
I am climbing up the golden stair!

-Salvation Army Song Book #369

PRAISE YE THE LORD!

Praise God in His sanctuary;
Praise Him in the firmament of His power.
Praise Him for His mighty acts;
Praise Him according to His excellent greatness.
Praise Him with the sound of the trumpet;
Praise Him with the psaltery and harp.
Praise Him with the timbrel and dance;
Praise Him with stringed instruments and organs.
Praise Him upon the loud cymbals;
Praise Him upon the high-sounding cymbals.
Let every thing that hath breath
Praise the Lord.
Praise ye the Lord!

-Psalm 150

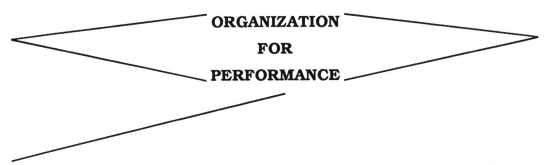

ORGANIZATION
FOR
PERFORMANCE

The Speaking Ensemble, in its organization, must give consideration to the following essential procedures:

1. Membership with respect to age, sex, voice quality, and an appreciation of the media.

2. A sense of the potential meaning for listeners through this media.

3. Desire to be well trained and effective in performance.

4. A willingness to prepare and identify with the selection in this worship experience.

5. A knowledgeable awareness that this media is adaptable to various groups:

   a. Corps Cadets

   b. Junior Soldiers

   c. Sunday School Classes

   d. Home League

   e. Young Married Couples

   f. Mixed Groupings

It is best to keep the age groupings within a given age range.

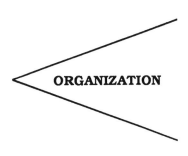

ORGANIZATION

There is a difference of opinion as to how many should compose the group. It is generally agreed, however, that it should not be less than ten and not more than twenty. The voices of a large group speaking in unison can easily sound muddled and the enunciation indistinct. It is true that in a large measure the material, the purpose, and the place of the reading as well as the age and the ability of the speaking ensemble should decide the total number in the group.

The V-shaped arrangement or an adaption of it is the most preferred because of the visibility it gives to all the functioning parts of the speaking group. It also assists the Director in leading and control of the speaking ensemble. The arrangement would be similar to this:

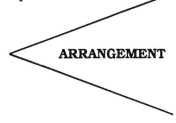

ARRANGEMENT

	DIV I					DIV II
SOLO I (M)	X	X	X	X	X	SOLO II (M)
QUARTET		X	X	X	X	
TRIO			X	X	X	
SOLO I (W)			X	X		SOLO II (W)

Solo or --   **O**   Director if he is part of the group

ARRANGEMENT

It is easy to see from this diagram that the speaking parts are easily identified as well as serving to assist in the leadership of the group. The Divisions are split down the middle in this arrangement. If there should be other solo parts, they are generally minor and can be chosen from any area of the group.

This arrangement makes for good balance and groups the speaking parts according to performance participation. It is best if the ensemble can be on risers. However, in case this is not possible, the arrangement should be such that no one stands directly in front of another member of the group. This is necessary for good voice projection.

Mixed voices are best for most readings, but any reading can be adapted to women's voices or for the use of children. Voices should be considered according to pitch such as high, low, or medium. In forming combinations like a quartet, the leader should combine in equal balance low and high voices with considerable range and select voices that blend well in tone and texture. They also should have sufficient distinctive quality that each voice will be heard. Enunciation, diction, force, and the ability to communicate an interpretation must be considered when selecting a soloist. Solo I and Solo II should be voices of varying range also, the one high and the other low. You will find that the writers of choral readings generally give consideration to this in preparing the material. It then becomes the leader's responsibility to follow through accordingly.

Enunciation, diction, emphasis, stress, and expression are skills that can be developed. Therefore, the significant requirement in organizing and arranging a group is a sincere willingness by all to work in this area. Pure speech, clear enunciation, lovely resonant voices in a Scriptural speaking ensemble is the result of HOURS OF APPLICATION AND TRAINING.

In one of his verses, Walt Whitman writes of the greatness of language.

LANGUAGE

Great is Language - it is the mightiest of the sciences;

It is the fulness, color, form diversity of the earth;

And of men and women and of all qualities and processes,

It is greater than wealth - it is greater than buildings, ships, paintings, music.[15]

The secret of a productive rehearsal is the Director. While the participants are the channel through which the interpretation flows, it is the Director that makes the channel deep, keeps it free of obstructions, pushes back the banks of thought and understanding and, in very essence, directs the course of the flow and movement to the audience. In the Director's attempt to keep the channel open and to assist in

REHEARSAL

the flow of thought, he must never be guilty of self-promotion, or self-intrusion that would impede the current of meaningful expression. The ultimate is accomplished as the Director and the Ensemble UNITE in a stream of interpretation that communicates a single impression.

How is this accomplished during the rehearsal?

SHARING

As suggested earlier, both the Director and the participants in the group, the readers, must become students of the selection i.e. study and share its mood, something of its history and background, relationship to readers and listeners, its emphasis, its concerns, and perhaps some insights representing life experiences. They might also share ways by which they can effectively communicate and interpret the selection to their listeners. This sharing will create appreciation for their text, for the Director, and for each other. It will give them pleasure and stiumlate appreciation and pleasure in their hearers.

While the Director or leader may command attention and guide specific parts of the reading, each member of the group must sense his importance as a reader. He must honestly desire and endeavor to become an able reader and consciously believe in this craft and more specifiically, HIS craft as a vital, significant part of worship. Each reader should. above all, in rehearsal and in worship services, have a sense of the rare and wondrous privilege choral speech is in communing with God and the exciting possibility of helping worshipers to experience the same.

PERSONAL COMMITMENT

While the above is a personal commitment of attitude, there is also a personal responsibility of action. Each individual of the group or brigade must have a sense of personal responsibility to be in attendance at scheduled rehearsals. This is important, for one missing member can influence the effectiveness of the rehearsal time in a given area.

GOOD READING COPY

Many regard the copy, text, or manuscript for the readers as a minor matter, and consequently, they exercise little time in preparation and use of it.

If the reading group has poor copy, their reading will definitely be affected in many ways. There certainly will be a loss of eye contact; facial expressions will not be as articulate; posture may be poor which always promotes lazy speech; focus will not be on the listener; body movement will be inhibited; vitality and enthusiasm will not be reflected; timing, rhythm, vocal quality, and projection may be sacrificed; con fidence be crippled; naturalness will be wilted; and the total interpretation will be threadbare, frayed, and faded. GOOD COPY IS IMPORTANT!

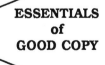

ESSENTIALS of GOOD COPY

   a. Easily readable

   b. Clear type, well spaced

   c. Double spaced always

   d. Speaking parts and divisions clearly indicated

e. Indentation for phrases with special emphasis

f. Paper should not be thin, slick, slippery, or hard to turn, and especially not rattle. If more than one page is to be turned, it is helpful to partially bend the lower corner of the page.

Hold copy at good reading level so you do not choke off your voice. Hold copy with one hand, allowing a free hand for gesture. Watch Billy Graham and note how he gestures with his Bible in his hand; even so, we can gesture with prepared copy. In a group, all must do the same thing unless it is during the reading of the parts, - solo, etc. Bodily action such as the use of hands, arms, face may be helpful in transition of thought from a mood of joy to a mood of sorrow; a mood of disappointment to a mood of contentment; a mood of failure to a mood of success; or any of the varied emotions within the reading.

At the time of rehearsal, all material should be in readiness. Every member of the group should have an individual copy of the selection. It is helpful in reading as well as attractive at the time of performance if the selection is in a binder. Never clip sheets together.

MARKING FOR READING In preparation for reading during the rehearsal, time should be given for <u>each person to individually mark his copy</u>. This, of course, is done after the discussion period regarding the selection to be read. The markings should be at the suggestion of the Director and be uniform so that the interpretation will speak but one message.

Any method of marking that is helpful can be used. the following suggestions are markings that you might find useful and that might prompt similar markings of your own:

a. For a short pause...... a short double bar //

For a long pause...... a long double bar //

<u>Example:</u>

Butterfly asleep folded soft on temple bell.

"Ho, everyone that thirsteth Come ye to the waters.

Come ye, buy and eat." Isaiah 55:1

EXAMPLES

b. For emphasis or strong.... <u>a straight underline</u>

For a secondary stress ...... a wavy line

<u>Example:</u>

<u>See</u> the heavy leaf on this <u>silent</u>, <u>windless</u> day.

"There is <u>no</u> searching of His <u>understanding</u>.

<u>He</u> giveth <u>power</u> to the <u>faint</u>, and to them that have <u>no</u> understanding,

He <u>increaseth strength</u>." Isaiah 40:29

c. For raising or lowering the voice ......   an arrow up ↗ or down ↙

For quick movement in speech ......   a long straight arrow ⟶

For deliberate movement ......   short, staccato arrows
→   →   →

Example:

Listen↗ with faint, dry sound the leaves break from the trees and fall. ↙
→ → → → →
"But they that wait upon the Lord ↙shall renew their strength

They shall mount up↗ with wings as eagles ↗

They shall run and not be weary

They shall walk and faint not."↙ Isaiah 40:31
→ → →

d. For sustaining word...... a straight line following the word —

Example:

In ending rain — the house-pent boy is fretting

With his brand — new — kite.

"Seek — ye the Lord while He may be found

Call — ye upon Him — while He is near." Isaiah 55:6

e. Words that are to be articulated, attacked, or accented might be "pinged" or hit hard. Use an inverted v with a dot over the word to be "pinged". ⋏

When a word or phrase is to have overtones, or a duration of sound which is the opposite of a "pinged" or accented word, we might call it "ponged" and mark it accordingly with a spread-out v and a curved line above it. this would suggest lengthening the sound ⌄̃

Example:

Hey, there! Stóp!

I will never lay down my arms! Never! Never! Never!

"Behold your God!"

"Behold, the Lord your God will come with a strong hand."

"The grass withereth - the flower fadeth

But the word of our God shall stand forever."

"Ho, everyone that thirsteth, come ye to the waters."

f. With respect to volume, intensity, rate, retard, etc., music markings can be used most effectively, such a "p" for piano; "ff" for loud;; "mf" for moderate loud; "mp" for moderate piano; "ret" for retard; "cres" for crescendo; for volume increase and diminish; and any others you would desire to use.

It has also been suggested that stress syllables be capitalized within the word or the entire word if it is to be stressed.

EXAMPLES:

"Oh God, thou art MY God." Psalm 63:1
"Does the road wind UPhill all the way?
YES to the VERY end." -Rosetti

61

 **TESTING** Early in the first rehearsal, if it has not been done previously, the Director should test each voice for pitch volume, resonance, range and then, according to the quality, assign the Solo parts, form the Duets, Trios, and Quartets as well as separating the group into two well-balanced Divisions.

The first rehearsal will be spent mostly in briefing members on choral speech for this is the pivot on which the whole future of the Speaking Ensemble will turn. This should include: **BRIEFING**

a. Definition of Choral Speech

b. Purposes

c. Interpretation of reading

d. Permanent position of readers for the reading in V-shape arrangement. This may change with each selection.

e. Explanation of symbols and marking of selection.

f. Assigning of all parts.

g. Schedule of rehearsals and instructions regarding the same.

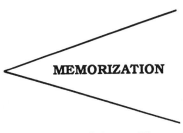 **MEMORIZATION** Memorization of lines is important to a colorful, meaningful presentation. Complete or even partial memorization may not always be possible, but certainly it should be one of the goals for special presentations. While all the lines may not be totally memorized in every performance, the members should be so familiar with the lines that they are NOT READ. However, we should note that some lines must be memorized, particularly SOLO lines. This achievement will be most rewarding for all participants as well as for the listeners. As you know, some listeners will be critics, self-styled or otherwise; so that every visual factor and emotional or intellectual complement must be employed. It is always a good idea to read the entire passage and then work on difficult passages.

The goal of the Scripture Speaking Ensemble is to transmit an experience that they have come to understand through the Word of God or literature. While the significant function of the Scripture Speaking Ensemble is one of interpretation, it must also be realized this group can be very effective in establishing moods, setting the tone and atmosphere of worship. **CONCLUSION**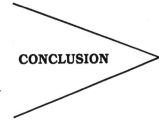

Let us share the beauty, the pleasure, the intrinsic values, and the growing possibilities of choral speech in our worship experiences in every activity of Salvation Army ministries.

> Be not like a stream that brawls
> Loud with shallow waterfalls,
> But in quiet self-control
> Link together soul and soul.
>
> - Longfellow

Part III

Worship Resources

Worship Resources

and

Program Enrichment

"SHARED EXPERIENCE IS THE GREATEST OF HUMAN GOODS."
John Dewey

THE CALL TO WORSHIP

The Call to Worship is frequently perceived as a verse of scripture read by the leader of the worship service. However, projecting the essence of the scripture thought may not be the result.

While the Call to Worship should be related to the general theme of the worship service, its main function is to bring the worshiper into the atmosphere of worship. The effective Call to Worship will involve the worshiper in the expression of worship, and it will secure the attention, the thinking, the feelings, and the thoughts of the worshiper.

The Call to Worship always has the unique quality of suggestion, which unconsciously binds spirit to spirit in achieving the experience leading to worship.

It is a *call* to worship and should involve the audience not only in listening, but in expressions of unison and response.

PRAISE TO GOD

CALL TO WORSHIP

I was glad when they said unto me,
    Let us go into the house of the Lord.

Therefore will I offer in His tabernacle sacrifices of joy
    I will sing, yea, I will sing praises unto the Lord.   *Psa. 122:1; Psa. 27:6*

CALL TO WORSHIP

O give thanks unto the Lord; for He is good
    Magnify Him with thanksgiving.

Praise the Lord for His goodness
    For His wonderful works to the children of men.   *Psa. 107:8*

CALL TO WORSHIP

Blessed is the nation whose God is the Lord;
    Righteousness exalteth a nation,
    But sin is a reproach to any people.

O praise the Lord all ye nations,
    Praise Him all ye people.   *Psa. 33:12*

CALL TO WORSHIP

Think about all you can praise God for
    and be glad about

Fix your thoughts on what is true,
    and good and right

Think about things that are lovely and pure,
    and dwell on the fine, good things in others.   *Phil. 4:8* LB

CALL TO WORSHIP

There are different kinds of service to God,
    but it is the same Lord we are serving.

God has given each of you some special abilities
Be sure to use them to help each other,
Passing on to others God's many kinds of blessings.   *1 Cor 12:5,28* LB

CALL TO WORSHIP

Oh, that we might know the Lord!
    Let us press on to know Him

And when we obey Him every path He guides us on
    Is fragrant with His lovingkindness and His truth.

CALL TO WORSHIP

Give thanks to the Lord, call on His name;
 Let the hearts of those who seek the Lord rejoice.

Sing to Him, sing praise to Him;
 Talk ye of all His wondrous works

Look to the Lord and His strength;
 Seek His face always.   *1 Chron. 16:8,9,11*

CALL TO WORSHIP

Sing joyfully to the Lord
 It is fitting for the upright to praise Him

Compose new songs of praise to Him
 For all God's words are right
And everything He does is worthy of our trust

Sing joyfully to the Lord;
 He loves whatever is just and good;
 The earth is filled with His tender love.   *Psa. 33:1,3,4,5*

CALL TO WORSHIP

I will praise Thee, O Lord, with my whole heart;
 I will show forth all they marvelous works.

I delight to do thy will, O my God;
 Yea, thy law is within my heart.

I will lift up my hands in thy name,
 Doing service as to the Lord.   *Psa. 9:1; 138:1; Psa. 40:8; Psa. 119:48*

CALL TO WORSHIP

What shall we render unto the Lord
 For all His benefits toward us?

We will offer to Him the sacrifice of thanksgiving,
 And will call upon the name of the Lord;

Now therefore shall we serve the Lord with gladness,
 And show how great things God hath done unto us.
          Psa. 116:12 Psa. 100:2 Psa. 126:3

CALL TO WORSHIP

Thank God for all His love and grace
Thank God for this His holy place
Thank God for patient loving care
Thank God and all His goodness share.

From The Salvation Army Song Book

Consecration and Service

Call to Worship   (#513)

Saviour, dear Saviour, draw nearer,
    Humble in spirit I kneel at Thy Cross;
Speak out thy wishes still clearer,
    And I will obey at all cost.

Call to Worship   (#438)

God of almighty love,
    By whose sufficient grace
We lift our hearts to things above,
    And humbly seek Thy face.

Call to Worship   (#480)

Come, Saviour Jesus from above,
    Assist us with Thy heavenly grace;
Empty our hearts of earthly love,
    And for thyself prepare the place.

Call to Worship

O let our hearts for ever be
    The home in which Thou lov'st to dwell;
Renewed and filled with love to Thee,
    Endued with power that love to tell!

Call to Worship   (#451)

O that in us the mind of Christ
    A fixed abiding-place may find,
That we may know the will of God,
    And live in Him for lost mankind.

Call to Worship   (#445)

Lord, send thy Spirit from above
    With light and love and power divine;
And by His all-constraining grace
    Make us and keep us ever Thine.

Call to Worship   (#434)

Lord, we come to Thee beseeching
    For a heart-renewing here;
Up to Thee our hands are stretching,
After Thee our hearts are reaching;
    Saviour, in thy power draw near.

Call to Worship　　　　　(#527)

It is not with might to establish the right,
　　Nor yet with the wise to give rest;
The mind cannot show what the heart longs to know
　　Nor comfort a people distressed.
O Saviour of men, touch my spirit again,
　　And grant that Thy servant may be
Intense every day, as I labor and pray,
　　Both instant and constant for Thee.

Call to Worship　　　　　(#729)

Through every fear our soul doth climb
Above the things of passing time,
And to my eyes the sight is given
Which makes my earth a present Heaven.

Call to Worship　　　　　(#772)

Renew our will from day to day;
Blend it with Thine, and take away
All that now makes it hard to say:
　　Thy will be done.

Call to Worship　　　　　(#756)

Spirit of faith, come down,
　　Reveal the things of God,
And make to us the Godhead known,
　　And witness with the Blood.

The faith that conquers all,
　　And doth the mountain move,
And saves who'er on Jesus call,
　　And perfects them in love.

Call to Worship　　　　　(#669)

This is the day of prayer;
　　Let earth and Heaven draw near;
Lift up our hearts to seek Thee there,
　　Come down to meet us here.

Call to Worship　　　　　(#662)

Help us to help each other, Lord,
　　Each other's cross to bear;
Let each his friendly aid afford,
　　And feel his brother's care.

Help us to build each other up,
　　Our little stock improve;
Increase our faith, confirm our hope,
　　And perfect us in love.

Call to Worship   (#619)

O God, if still the holy place
    Is found of those in prayer,
By all the promises of grace
    We claim an entrance there.

Call to Worship   (#612)

O fill us with Thy fullness, Lord,
    Until our very hearts o'erflow
In kindling thought and glowing word
    Thy love to tell, Thy praise to show.

Call to Worship   (#603)

Present we know Thou art;
    But, O Thyself reveal!
Now, Lord, let every waiting heart
    Thy mighty comfort feel!

Call to Worship   (#581)

Come, then to us reveal Thy love,
And pour the Spirit from above,
That we with holy motives may
The impulse of His will obey.

Call to Worship   (#557)

As pants the hart for cooling streams,
    When heated in the chase,
So longs our soul, O Lord for Thee,
    And Thy refreshing grace.

Call to Worship   (#626)

Revive Thy work, O Lord,
    Exalt Thy precious name;
And by the Holy Ghost, our love
    For Thee and Thine inflame.

Call to Worship   (#615)

Mid all the traffic of the ways,
    Turmoils without, within,
Make in our hearts a quiet place,
    And come and dwell therein.

Call to Worship   (#616)

O let Thy grace inspire
    Our soul with strength divine!
Let all our powers to thee aspire,
    And all our days be Thine.

Call to Worship   (#657)

The Spirit breathes upon the Word,
    And brings the truth to sight;
Precepts and promises afford
    And sanctifying light.

Call to Worship   (#655)

Lord, Thy word abideth,
    And our footsteps guideth;
Who its truth believeth
Light and joy receiveth.

Call to Worship   (#217)

Spirit divine, attend our prayers.
    And make this house Thy home;
Descend with all Thy gracious powers;
    O come, great Spirit, come.

Call to Worship   (#213)

Holy Ghost, we bid Thee welcome,
    Source of life and power Thou art,
Promise of our Heavenly Father,
    Now thrice welcome in our heart.

"ALONGSIDE ME"

I've found a friend
Oh, such a friend
He loved me 'ere I knew Him.
He drew me with the cords of love
And thus He bound me to Him.

-James G. Small

Happy is the person who loves Jesus
    and stays close to Him.
    who enjoys conversation with Him
    who allows His arms of love
        to comfort
            to encourage
                to console
                    to bear your burden
                        to hold you as His friend
                            to clasp you to Him and feel
                              his tenderness and strength.

For Jesus said, "I have called you friends,
    And you are my friends
    If you love and obey me."
            Hymn "I found a Friend"
            John 15:14,15

"SONG OF LOVE"

If love flows in
Love will flow out.

And every day the Lord will enlarge
    your capacity for love.

You will love God above everything
You will be prepared to face anything.

Love is not only   good and great
Love is active: -
    Kind, long suffering
      Gentle
        Patient,
          Never rude, or selfish,
            Not touchy, haughty or fretful.

Love knows no bounds, no limits;
Love is happy, joyous, free
Love transforms the thing it loves,
Love abides forever!
           I Corinthians 13 (L.B.)

"THE APPROACH"

We look to Thee in every need
"Ask and it shall be given you."

We seek thy help in burdens we carry
"Seek and ye shall find."

We pray for courage, strength and grace.
"Before they call I will answer
While they are yet speaking I will hear."

We give ourselves to loving thee alone.
"God is love and he that dwelleth in love
Dwelleth in God
And God in him."

Matt. 7:7 - Isa. 65:14 - I John 4:16

"BLESS THE LORD"

Let not mercy and truth forsake you
Bind them about your neck;
Write them upon the table of your heart.

Don't forget to be merciful to me, O Lord
Fill my heart with your grace.

The Lord is merciful and gracious,
Very tender to those who don't deserve it,
And full of kindness and love.

Bless the Lord oh my soul,
All that is within me
Bless His holy name.
Bless the Lord! My soul would shout
I will bless you Lord because you are my God.
You are very great!

Prov. 3, Psa 10, Psa 103 (L.B.)

"CHOSEN"

But thou art My servant....
Whom I have chosen....
Whom I have taken hold of.

I have called thee...
I have chosen thee...
I have summoned thee.

Fear thou not, for I am with thee.
Be not dismayed, I am thy God.
I will strengthen thee
I will help thee
I will hold thy hand.

Isa. 41:10

"SOMETHING HAPPENS"

Let us therefore, come boldly unto
      the throne of grace,
That we may obtain mercy
And find grace to help in time of need.

You can ask God for anything
      using the name of Jesus,
And God will do it.
And we are sure of this
That He will listen to us,
Whenever we ask Him for anything
In line with His will.

And if we really know He is listening to us
Then we can be sure He will answer us.

      Heb. 4:16 - John 14:13,14 - 1 John 5:14,15 (LB)

"DELIGHT OF PRAISING"

Bless the Lord, O my soul
Everything inside me shouts
Bless the Lord!

I can never forget the glorious
      things He does for me.
Every morning I praise Him
      and thank Him.
And every evening I rejoice in
      His faithfulness.

I am so refreshed by His blessings;
I will praise God to my last breath.
I will praise Him forever.
      Hallelujah!

      Selections Psa. 103:1; 92:2; 104:33

"ALWAYS PRAISING"

Let the people praise Thee, O God
Let all the people praise Thee.
We will be glad and sing for joy;

      With our voice we will praise Thee
      With our works we will praise Thee
      With our prayers we will praise and adore
      With our life we express our praise
      With our love we share Thy praise

That our love may abound yet more and more,
That we may approve things that are excellent,
      and be sincere.
Being filled with the fruits of righteousness,
Unto the glory and praise of God.

      Psa. 67:3 Phil. 1:9-11

"ENLIGHTENMENT"

Take away, oh Lord, the veil
Of my heart while I hear the
Scriptures,

Teach me Thy statutes
Touch my heart

Enlighten my understanding
Open my lips and fill them with thy praise.
Selection adapted Bishop Lancelot Andrewes 1555-1626

"FREE US!"

Oh God, of earth and altar
Bow down and hear our cry;
Our earthly rulers falter
Our people drift and die.

The walls of gold entomb us
The swords of scorn divide
Take not thy thunder from us
But take away our pride.

From all that terror teaches
From lies of tongue and pen
From sleep and from damnation
Deliver us good Lord.

Lead us from hate to love
From war to peace.
Let peace fill our hearts
Our homes, our world, our universe.

Selection adapted G.K. Chesterton 1874-1936

"GOD'S WORD AND YOU"

Thy Word have I hid in my heart
That I might not sin against Thee.
I will delight myself in Thy statutes
I will not forget Thy Word.

Oh how I love Thy law
It is my meditation all the day.
The entrance of Thy words giveth light
It giveth understanding unto the simple.

Thy Word is a lamp to my feet,
And a light unto my path.
Open thou mine eyes
That I may behold wondrous things out of Thy love.
Psa. 119:11, 16, 77, 130, 105, 18

"HONORING FATHER"

(Father's Day)

Men in the congregation sing the first verse of "Faith of Our Fathers"

"FAITH OF OUR FATHERS"

Faith of our fathers, living still,
　　In spite of dungeon, fire and sword,
O how our hearts beat high with joy
　　Whene'er we hear that glorious word!
Faith or our Fathers, holy faith,
　　We will be true to Thee 'till death.

The first verse of "Rise up O men of God" is also appropriate.

"HOLY IS HIS NAME"

Thus saith the high and lofty one that inhabiteth eternity
Whose name is Holy;

I dwell in the high and holy place
With Him also that is of a contrite and humble spirit.

To revive the spirit of the humble
To revive the heart of the contrite ones.

I the Lord your God am holy
Sanctify yourselves, therefore,
　　　and be ye holy.

Isa. 57, Lev.19, Lev 20

"THE HOUSE OF THE LORD"

Surely the Lord is in this place
This is none other than the house of the Lord.
And the gate to heaven.

One thing have I desired of the Lord
That will I seek after.

That I may dwell in the house of the Lord,
To behold the beauty of the Lord
And to inquire in His temple.

Enter into His gates with Thanksgiving
And into His courts with praise.

Gen.28, Psa. 27, Psa. 100

"IMAGE OF GOD"

LEADER: Great is the Lord, and greatly to be praised;
and His greatness is unsearchable.
I will speak of the glorious honor of thy majesty,
and of thy wondrous works.

PEOPLE: Praise the Lord for His goodness, and for His
wonderful works to the children of men.
Blessed be the Lord, who daily loadeth us with benefits,
even the God of our salvation, who hath called us
out of darkness into His marvelous light.
Psa. 145:3- Psa.145:5- Psa. 107:8- Psa.68:19

"IN US"

Father give to us your Holy Spirit
Fill us with your fullness today
In us, through us, and around us
Hold us in your love we pray.

"LET US WORSHIP"

Let us worship the Lord our maker
WORSHIP IN HUMILITY;
 For the proud cannot receive the blessing of Lord.
WORSHIP IN CONFIDENCE:
 For there hath not failed one word of all His good promise.
WORSHIP EXPECTANTLY:
 For whatsoever we ask the Father, in Christ's name
 He will give it.
WORSHIP IN FAITH:
 For he that cometh to God must believe that He is,
 And that He is a rewarder of them that diligently seek Him.
1 Kings 8:56- John 14:13- Heb. 11:6

"OPEN OUR HEARTS"

As a pearl dewed flower in the early morning
 opens its petals to receive
 the life giving warmth of the sun
So may we in this moment of worship
 open our hearts to receive
 the life-giving warmth of the Son of God.

"REVERENCE"

In the sacredness of this moment
We echo the dedication of the Psalmist David:
But I, by your great mercy,
Will come into your house;
In reverence will I bow down
Toward your holy temple.

Psalm 5:7

"JOY OVERFLOWS"

Worship the Lord with a shout of joy,
Enter His presence singing with joy.

There is great uplifting power in joy

>Express joy in your gratitude,
>Express gladness in your faith,
>Express happiness in your service.

Yes, dance for joy in all your living
And let a bird of joy sing in your tree.

Rejoice in the Lord always -
Be inexpressibly joyous under
all circumstances,
For the joy of the Lord is your strength.

Believing:

>He is always with you,
>He is always near you,
>He is always loving you.

Rejoice with joy unspeakable and full of glory
Let your cup of joy overflow!

Phil. 4:4; Neh. 8:10; I Peter 1:8 LB

"HUSH! DRAW NEAR"

Hush! for this hour is holy
Let us draw near to Him
Who hears our prayer
Let us remember He listens
More to our hearts
Than to our words.

"MEDITATION"

We come to thee with quiet mind.
Thyself to know
Thy will to find
In Jesus' steps our steps must be.
We follow Him
To follow Thee.

Catherine Baird

"QUEST"

Give thanks unto the Lord,
> Call upon His name
Make known His deeds among the people

Sing unto Him
> Sing psalms to Him
Talk ye of all His wondrous works

Seek the Lord
> And His strength
Seek His face at all times.
>> I Chron. 16: 8-11

"JOYFUL WORSHIP"

O come, let us worship;
> Let us kneel before the Lord our maker.
Worship the Lord in the beauty of Holiness
> Bow down before Him, His majesty proclaim
With love, and in lowliness,
> Kneel to adore and honor His name
For God is a spirit, and they that worship Him
> Must worship Him in spirit and in truth.

>> Psa. 95:6- Psa.96:9- John 4:24

"TAKING TIME"

Hear, oh my people, and I will speak.

I will not hurry through this day.
I will listen by the way.*

I will hear what God the Lord will speak.

I will not hurry through this day
I will take time to think and pray.*

Incline your ear and come unto me
Hear and your soul shall live.

Speak Lord for thy servant heareth.
Make me to hear joy and gladness.
> Psa.50:7- Psa.85:8- Isa. 55:3- Psa. 51:8- 1 Samuel 3:9
> *Ralph Spaulding Cushman; Hilltop Verses and Prayers;
> Abingdon-Cokesbury Press; New York, page 73

"OUR CONFIDENCE"

God is our refuge and strength
A very present help in trouble
Therefore, will not we fear.
In God have we put our trust
We will not be afraid.

Great is the Lord and greatly to be praised.
> Psalms 46, 56, 48

"GIVE US AWARENESS"

I will mention the lovingkindness
                                    of the Lord
And the praise of the Lord.
I will recount the Lord's acts of unfailing love;
All that the Lord had done for us
      All He has done in tenderness
      By His many acts of love.

                                    Isa. 63:7

"INSISTENT SOUNDS"

Hush! for the day is holy
Let all within you be hushed
This is the day which the Lord hath made
We will rejoice and be glad in it.

Let my mouth be filled with Thy praise
And with Thy honor all the day long.
O how I love thy law
It is my meditation all the day.
Every day will I bless thee
And I will praise Thy name forever and ever.
            Nehemiah 8:11 Rotherham Translation
            Psa. 118:24; Psa. 71:8; Psa. 119:97; Psa. 145:2

"A PRAISING HEART"

Whoso offereth praise, glorifieth me.
O Lord, open thou my lips;
And my mouth shall show forth Thy praise.

I will praise the Lord according to His righteousness,
I will sing praise to the name of the Lord most high.
I will sing forth the honor of His name,
I will make His praise glorious.

Let my mouth be filled with thy praise,
And with thy honor all the day,
For I shall yet praise thee more and more.
For the Lord is great; and greatly to be praised.
            Psalms 50:23; 51:15; 7:17; 66:2; 71:8,14; 96:4

87

"DISCOVERY"

Leader: O Lord our God, in whom we live, and move,
        and have our being,
        Open our eyes that we may behold thy fatherly
        presence ever about us.

All: Draw our hearts to thee with the power of
        thy love.
        Teach us to be careful for nothing.

Leader: When we have done what Thou has given us to do
        Help us to leave the issue to Thy wisdom.

All: Take from us all distrust and doubt,
        Lift our thoughts up to Heaven

Leader: And make us to know all things are possible to us,
        Through Jesus our Redeemer.

Adapted - Bishop Brooke Westrott 1825-1901

"UNHURRIED TIME"

Let us find some unhurried time
To ponder upon God Himself
To withdraw from things,
        idle talk, or busy tasks
Let us discipline ourselves to quietness
As we listen and talk to Jesus, our friend;
Anointed, strengthened and renewed, so
From our inner room, we return to the
        outer plains of living.

He that dwelleth in the secret place
        of the most High
Shall abide under the shadow of
        the Almighty.

Set your affections on things above
Not on things of the earth -
For your life is hid
With Christ and God.

In stillness and in staying quiet
There lies your strength.

Psa. 91, Col.3, Isa.30 (NEB)

"WHAT GREAT LOVE"

We thank you Lord, for all the things you have
      done to make us happy
But we are most grateful for the lavishing of
      your love.

    A love too great for us to understand
    A love too high for us to reach unto
    A love so bright all the world shines
        with its glory.

This great love is God expressed in our salvation.

    Redeeming us,
        Delivering us,
            Protecting us,
                Guiding us,
                    Supporting us.

All this your love does for us.
Yes, herein is love, not that we loved God,
But that He loved us.
and sent His only son into the world that we might
    live through Him.

God is love!
    In us,
        Around us,
            Enfolding us.

For He that dwelleth in Love
    Dwelleth in God
    And God in Him!

                              I John 4: 9,10,16

"PRAISE HIM"

I will rejoice in the Lord
I will joy in the God of my salvation
I will sing to the Lord for He has
    triumphed gloriously.
The Lord is my strength and my song,
And He has become my salvation.
This is my God, and I will praise Him
I will exalt Him!
My God, you are 100% dependable;
You are the same yesterday, today and forever.
I know you never change.

      Hab. 3:18 Ex. 15:1,2 Heb. 13:8 LB

WORSHIP THE LORD IN THE BEAUTY OF HOLINESS

(A CALL TO WORSHIP)

Words and Music
James Curnow

Wor - ship the Lord in the beau - ty of Hol - i - ness,

Wor - ship the Lord in the spir - it of praise.

Bow down be - fore Him, Love and a - dore Him, Come let us

wor - ship in spir - it and truth. spir - it and truth.

**O come,
let us worship and bow down:
let us kneel before the Lord
our maker.**

Psalm 95:6

Choral Speech

Selections for Interpretation
and for
Presentation

ABIDING IN HIM

ALL	He that dwells in the secret place of the Most High shall abide under the shadow of the Almighty.
SOLO I (M)	I will say of the Lord, He is my refuge and my fortress:
SOLO II (W)	In Him will I trust.
DIVISION I	Surely He shall deliver you from the snare of the fowler,
DIVISION II	And from the noisome pestilence.
SOLO I (M)	He shall cover you with His feathers,
SOLO II (W)	And under His wings shall you trust:
TRIO	His truth shall be your shield and buckler.
QUARTET	You shall not be afraid for the terror by night,
DIVISION I	Nor for the arrow that flies by day,
DIVISION II	Nor for the pestilence that walks in darkness;
ALL	It shall not come nigh you.
SOLO I (W)	Because you have made the Lord, which is my refuge, your habitation,
DIVISION I	There shall no evil befall you,
DIVISION II	Neither shall any plague come nigh your dwelling.
SOLO II (W)	He shall give His angels charge over you
SOLO I (M)	To keep you in all your ways.
ALL	Dwell in the secret place ... Abide under the shadow of the Almighty.

Selections from Psalm 91

CALL TO DECISION

QUARTET	And it came to pass, when Ahab saw Elijah,
SOLO I (W)	*(spoken as if in parenthesis)* Ahab, king of Israel
SOLO II (W)	*(spoken as if in parenthesis)* Elijah, the prophet of God,
QUARTET	When Ahab saw Elijah, Ahab said unto him,
SOLO II (M)	Are you he that troubleth Israel?
QUARTET	And Elijah answered,
SOLO I (M)	I have not troubled Israel, but you
QUARTET	But you - but you - but...you *(increase intensity)*
SOLO I (M)	You have forsaken the commandments of the Lord.
ALL	Forsaken the commandments of the Lord. *(Deliberately)*
SOLO I (M)	You have followed Baalim. Now, therefore, send --
QUARTET	Send...send
SOLO I (M)	*(begin speaking while the quartet enunciates the "d" on Send)* Send and gather all Israel unto Mount Carmel, and the prophets of Baal 450.
DIVISION I	So Ahab sent unto all the children of Israel,
DIVISION II	And gathered the prophets of Baal 450.
ALL	They gathered together unto Mount Carmel.
QUARTET	And Elijah came unto all the people, and said,
SOLO I (M)	How long halt you between two opinions?
DIVISION I	How long?
DIVISION II	How long?
SOLO I (M)	If the Lord be God follow Him, but if Baal, then follow him.
QUARTET	*(spoken slowly and softly)* And the people answered him not a word.
	PAUSE

(Two members of the Quartet speak:)

	Then Elijah said unto the people
SOLO I (M)	I only remain a servant of the Lord, but Baal's prophets are 450 men. Let them choose a bullock, lay it on wood, and put no fire under it.
DIVISION I	One bullock on the altar for the prophets of Baal.
SOLO I (M)	I will dress the other bullock, lay it on wood, and put no fire under it.

96

DIVISION II	One bullock on the altar for the prophet of God.
SOLO I (M)	Call you on the name of your gods, and I will call on the name of the Lord. The God that answers by fire, <u>let him be God!</u>
QUARTET	And all the people answered and said,
ALL	It is well spoken.
QUARTET	And the prophets of Baal called to their god, from morning even until noon.
SEVERAL VOICES	*(Pleading)* Baal! Baal! Send fire! Oh, Baal, Baal. Hear us Baal!
DIVISION I	Hear us, Baal!
DIVISION II	Baal, Baal, hear us!
QUARTET	*(Deliberately)* But there is no voice, nor any that answered.

<u>MEDITATIVE PAUSE</u>

	(Solo from the Quartet:) And they leaped upon the altar. *(spoken with force)*
QUARTET	And it came to pass at noon that Elijah mocked them, and said,
SOLO I (M)	Cry aloud, for he is a god. He is talking, or he is on a journey, or perhaps he is asleep, and must be awakened.
QUARTET	And they cried aloud,
SEVERAL VOICES	*(crying loudly and separately as well as together, with ever increasing intensity)* Baal! Baal! Baal you are god. Send fire Baal. You must hear us Baal.
SOLO VOICE	*(very pronounced)* Baal, see we sacrifice our life - Hear us now - O Baal.
ALL	<u>B-A-A-L</u>! <u>B-A-A-L</u>! BAAL HEAR US! *(Pause)*
QUARTET	At the time of the evening sacrifice there was neither voice, nor answer. And Elijah said unto the people,
SOLO I (M)	Come, near unto me.
DIVISION I	And Elijah repaired the altar that was broken down.
DIVISION II	And with twelve stones he built an altar in the name of the Lord.
QUARTET	And he made a trench about the altar. and laid the sacrifice thereon.
	(One member of the Quartet:) And Elijah, the prophet of God, said
SOLO I (M)	Fill four barrels with water.
ALL	Four barrels! *(slowly)* Four...barrels...with water?

QUARTET	And Elijah said,
SOLO I (M)	Pour the water on the sacrifice and the wood.
DIVISION I	And Elijah, the prophet of God, said a second time,
SOLO I (M)	Fill four barrels with water. Pour it over the altar.
QUARTET	And they poured four more barrels of water on the sacrifice.
SOLO I (W)	Eight barrels of water they poured on the sacrifice.
DIVISION II	And the prophet of God said, a third time,
SOLO I (M)	Fill four barrels with water. Pour it upon the altar.
SOLO I (W)	Four barrels of water?
ALL	Once.
SOLO II (W)	Four barrels of water?
ALL	Twice.
SOLO III (W)	Four barrels of water?
ALL	Thrice.
DIVISION I	Twelve barrels? Twelve barrels of water?
DIVISION II	Twelve barrels! They poured twelve barrels of water upon the altar.
QUARTET	And the water ran <u>round</u> about the altar -
DIVISION I	A-round - a-round - a-round - a-round. *(a rhythmic second part starting on the word "Round" and continuing through the Quartet's last word "Water")*
QUARTET	*(continuing)* and filled the trench also with water.
ALL	And it came to pass at the time of the evening sacrifice, Elijah the prophet came near.
QUARTET	And Elijah the prophet of God, prayed,
SOLO I (M)	*(spoken as a prayer)* Lord God of Abraham, Isaac, and of Israel, let it be known this day that you are God. *(Pause)* Hear me, oh Lord, hear me! Hear me, that this people may know you are God. and will turn their heart to you.
QUARTET	Then the fire of the Lord...<u>fell</u>.
ALL	The fire <u>fell</u>!
QUARTET	And consumed the burnt sacrifice, and the wood, and the stones, and the dust, and licked up the water that was in the trench!
SOLO II (W)	And when the people saw it, they fell on their faces. And the people said,
ALL	The Lord, he is <u>God</u>! The Lord, <u>he is God</u>!

DIVISION I	Great is our God above all gods.
DIVISION II	O Lord you are our God. It is nothing with you to help, whether with many or with few.
SOLO III (M)	Who is a God like unto you?
DIVISION I	That pardons iniquity?
DIVISION II	That delights in mercy?
ALL	Great is thy faithfulness!

Note to Director:

(On the word "consumed" an echo part could be arranged for a soprano or tenor voice. The word would be spoken as an echo might sound during the remaining parts of the QUARTET assignment.)

Scripture: I Kings 18:17-39; II Chronicles 2:5; II Chronicles 14:11; Micah 7:18; Lamentations 3:23

CALLED AND ENLISTED

NARRATOR	Moses stared unbelievingly. The bush blazed with a blinding brightness.
MOSES	This is no ordinary bush--it is burning, but not burning up. A brush fire in the desert is nothing, but this bush is different. What is it?
NARRATOR	Quickly Moses kicked his sandals aside and flung himself to the ground, burying his face in the sand. Thoughts tumbled through his mind--words rolled, leaped and whirled about him but nothing made sense.
MOSES	Am I having a heat stroke? No! No! I _feel_ as if I'm standing on holy ground. Hallucinations would be a pleasure compared to facing a holy God.
NARRATOR	Moses suddenly felt dirty, mean, and completely unfit for the majestic presence of God. Then came the voice. Moses detected an indescribable sadness as God spoke.
VOICE	"I have surely seen the affliction of My people, and have heard their cry...for I know their sorrows."
NARRATOR	It made Moses feel good that God knew all about it, and he thrilled as the Lord spoke further.
VOICE	"I am come down to deliver them."
NARRATOR	Moses was so lost in rapture, he scarcely caught the importance of the words he was hearing, but as their meaning became clear, he was shocked into reality.
VOICE	Moses! Moses! Come now, therefore, and I will send thee unto Pharaoh.
MOSES	Surely God, you do not mean me?
NARRATOR	Moses cringed.
MOSES	Me, God? Go to Pharaoh?
NARRATOR I	Moses wanted to crawl away but he didn't have the strength.
NARRATOR II	He thought he saw Pharaoh towering above him, leering at him with a sinister smile.
PHARAOH	Let your people go? Ha! Ha! And what will you do for me, little man?
NARRATOR	Will you topple Pharaoh from his throne, Moses?
MOSES	Please, Pharaoh. Please understand.
PHARAOH	Ah! I understand all right. You and your God have something up your sleeve, eh Moses?

NARRATOR	Pharaoh jeered.
PHARAOH	Come now, Moses. I've got a bigger sleeve--and I've got plans too. So long, Moses. Come back when you and your God have found a bigger sleeve.
NARRATOR	Moses screamed.
MOSES	I can't! I can't!
NARRATOR	God's voice brought him back to reality. Its tone was insistent.
VOICE	Moses, I am the God of thy fathers. Certainly I will be with thee.
MOSES	But who am I? I'm nobody! Why, even my own people won't believe you have sent me--how could Pharaoh? Send someone else--not me.
NARRATOR	Moses made every excuse he could think of--He told God all the things he couldn't do. But God knew what he could do if only he would.
VOICE	Go, Moses! I AM that I AM! I will bring thee out of Egypt.
MOSES	I can't! I can't! Send someone else.
NARRATOR I	Suppose God had taken Moses at his word. Some of God's "greatest" have felt inadequate, incompetent, unqualified, untalented, ineffective. But God saw qualities in them--powerful beyond description.
NARRATOR II	You are going to have opportunity for some God-given, spirit-directed service. Will you march forward against the powers of darkness? Behold the door is open--no man can shut it. You can be mighty! You can join the fight of faith.
NARRATOR III	Don't think you can do everything--you can't! You won't even do everything you'd like to do. But you can do many things. It is not what you can do, but what you will do that is the deciding factor. Be willing, and strong in the strength which God supplies.

Scripture Selection: Exodus 3

CARRY ON!

ALL	Carry on! Carry on!
DIVISION I	Though the records of the past high are looming,
DIVISION II	To the winds all doubting cast,
ALL	Keep on booming,
SOLO (M)	Let every effort bring to man God's great salvation,
SOLO (W)	With inspiration, perspiration, desperation,
ALL	Carry on! Carry On!
QUARTET	We must Carry On!
DIVISION I	Nothing ever has been gained idly sitting;
DIVISION II	Soldiers never have been trained in ways of quitting.
SOLO (W)	Then forward, comrades, with grim determination!
SOLO (M)	With inspiration, perspiration, desperation
QUARTET	We must Carry On!
ALL	Yes, we will carry on, and raise the flag of Blood and Fire,
SOLO (M)	We'll keep it waving
ALL	Breaking all records, we'll never tire,
SOLO (M)	Battles braving......
DIVISION I	The enemy is dragging souls to degradation,
DIVISION II	With inspiration, perspiration, desperation,
ALL	We will Carry on! Carry on, for God and The Salvation Army.

Adapted from: *More Poems of a Salvationist* by Irena Arnold

CLOTHED WITH STRENGTH

ALL	The voice of Him that crieth in the wilderness,
SOLO I (M)	Prepare ye the way of the Lord.
SOLO II (M)	Make straight in the desert a highway for our God.
ALL	The Voice said,
SOLO I (M)	Cry
ALL	And he said,
SOLO II (M)	What shall I cry?
MEN	All flesh is grass,
WOMEN	And all the godliness thereof is as the flower of the field:
DIVISION I	The grass withereth,
DIVISION II	The flower fadeth
ALL	The Word of our God shall stand forever.
MEN	Behold your God!
SOLO I (W)	Hast thou not known?
SOLO II (W)	Hast thou not heard?
DIVISION I	The everlasting God--the Lord
DIVISION II	The Creator of the ends of the earth
WOMEN	Fainteth not
MEN	Neither is weary.
ALL	There is no searching of his understanding.
WOMEN	He giveth power to the faint;
MEN	And to them that have no might, He increaseth strength
WOMEN	Even the youths shall faint and be weary,
MEN	And the young men shall utterly fall;
SOLO I (W)	They shall mount up with wings as eagles;
DIVISION I	They shall run,
SOLO I (M)	And not be weary
DIVISION II	They shall walk
SOLO I (W)	And not faint.
ALL	They are traveling in the greatness of His strength.

Selected from Isaiah 40 and 63

CONTENTMENT

This Choral Speech is for three persons.

SPEAKER 1	The Lord is my Shepherd, I shall not want!
SPEAKER 2	Not want?
SPEAKER 3	Not want?
SPEAKER 1	I shall not want!
SPEAKER 1	He maketh me to lie...*(interrupted by 2 & 3)*
SPEAKERS 2-3	TO LIE?
SPEAKER 1	He maketh me to lie down in green pastures *(assuringly)*
SPEAKER 2	He r<u>estoreth</u> my soul
SPEAKER 3	He restoreth <u>my</u> soul
SPEAKER 1	He restoreth my <u>soul</u>
ALL	He leadeth me in the paths of righteousness for His name's sake.
SPEAKER 2	Yea, though I walk through the valley of the shadow of death...
SPEAKER 1	I will fear no evil
SPEAKER 3	For thou art with me
ALL	Thy rod and thy staff they comfort me.
SPEAKER 1	Thou preparest a table before me in the presence of mine enemies;
SPEAKER 2	Thou anointest my head with oil
SPEAKER 3	My cup runneth over
ALL	SURELY GOODNESS AND MERCY SHALL FOLLOW ME ALL THE DAYS OF MY LIFE
SPEAKER 3	And I will dwell in the house of the Lord forever
SPEAKERS 1-2	And I will dwell in the house of the Lord, <u>forever</u>
ALL	I WILL DWELL IN THE HOUSE OF THE LORD FOREVER.

PSALM 23

A DIVINE COMMISSION

ALL	Listen!...Listen!...Listen!
SOLO I (M)	"I will listen to what the Lord is saying"
ALL	Listen quietly...listen carefully
SOLO I (W)	I am listening...listening inside me.
ALL	"I will hear what God, the Lord, will speak"
DIVISION I	The voice outside of me says you have no time to listen
DIVISION II	The inward voice whispers truth
QUARTET	Listen...the Lord is speaking
ALL	"Speak Lord for thy servant heareth"
SOLO II (M)	"Holy"
SOLO III (M)	"Holy"
SOLO IV (M)	"Holy"
SOLO II (W)	Holy, Holy, Holy, Lord God of Hosts
ALL	"The whole earth is full of Thy glory."
SOLO II (M)	"Whom shall I send?"
SOLO III (M)	"Who will go for me?"
ALL	Who will go?
DIVISION I	But I am not called, Lord
DIVISION II	I haven't really heard your voice
SOLO I (M)	Have you ever put your ear to the Word of God and listened?
DUET	Have you ever put your ear to the hurting, lonely, burdened, sin-weary heart of mankind?
SOLO II (M)	The Lord God hath opened my ears
DIVISION I	"And thine ears shall hear a word behind thee, saying
DIVISION II	"This is the way, walk ye in it"
QUARTET	Whom shall I send?
SOLO I (W)	You want me to do something now Lord?
SOLO II (W)	You mean I'am to keep on doing it?
DIVISION I	Get up! Never stop doing it.
DIVISION II	Act! Do whatever you can do, and don't spare yourself!

SOLO I (M)	Then said I, Here am I; Send me!
VARIOUS VOICES	HERE AM I! Here am I! Here am I! Here am I! Here am I!
DIVISION I	We believe! We hear!
DIVISION II	We accept! We go!
VARIOUS VOICES	Send me!
	Send me!
	Send me!
	Send me!
SOLO I (M)	"And the Lord said, Go and tell this people unto them a child is born...a Saviour is given."
DUET	"That they may see with their eyes"
TRIO	"And hear with their ears"
QUARTET	"And understand with their hearts"
ALL	"And be healed" I'll go where you want me to go, dear Lord.

Selections from Isaiah 6 and 30, Psalm 85:8, I Samuel 3:9

GO FOR GOLD!

(For use during the Olympics)

ALL	GO FOR GOLD!
SOLO I	Gold?
SOLO II	Silver?
SOLO III	Bronze?
ALL	NO! Go for the Gold!
DIVISION I	Not everyone merits gold
DIVISION II	Silver or Bronze may be their best.
SOLO	Then what is the gold?
ALL	The reward of excellence!
DUET	It is being happy in a special kind of way.
SOLO	Happy in what?
DUET	In this clear and complete conviction
SOLO	The God who is all-powerful..
SOLO VOICES	All wise...all-gracious...Governor over all
ALL	Loves us!
SOLO	But love is muted as the world cries, "Go for Gold"
QUARTET	Men say, "Gold is power"
ALL	Power! Power!
QUARTET	Capitalists say, "Gold is money"
ALL	Invest..stocks...bonds...Make money!
QUARTET	Educators say, "Gold is knowledge"
ALL	Knowledge...Understanding...Wisdom.
QUARTET	Scientists cry, "Gold is nuclear energy"
ALL	Neutrons! Protons! Atoms!
SOLO	Where, oh where is the voice of God?
SOLO	Where, oh where is the voice of love? the love of God?
ALL	The happiness of God is gold!
DUET	Happy, yes, very happy are the ears which listen
DIVISION I	Not to the outside world
DIVISION II	But to the inside voice, teaching gold truth within.

SOLO	Something great happens inside you when you believe this.
ALL	You are happy from the bottom of your feet to the top of your head.
SOLO I	Jesus said, "Go for the Gold" when he said,
SOLO II	"Go ye into all the world and preach the Gospel."
ALL	Go ye! Go with the gold of love into the highways and the byways.
DIVISION I	Highways are crowded
DIVISION II	Noisy and dangerous
ALL	Byways are rough
DIVISION I	Dusty and lonely
DIVISION II	Depressing and discouraging
SOLO	Go and compel them to come in. GO YE!
DIVISION I	And as you go witness
DIVISION II	Let love compel you!
SOLO	Go for the Gold of Peace!
SOLO	Go for the Gold of Faith!
ALL	Go for the Gold of the Spirit!

GOD STEPPED INTO THE WORLD

ALL	In the beginning God created male and female In His own image and His own likeness.
DIVISION I	But man marred the image of God
DIVISION II	Sin was born!
ALL	But God so loved the man and woman He created
SOLO	God stepped into the world!
DIVISION I	"The WORD became flesh and dwelt among us, and we beheld His glory."
DIVISION II	"Glory as of the only begotten of the Father - full of grace and truth."
ALL	Truth? Truth! What is truth?
DIVISION I	We search; we seek; we reach out for truth.
DIVISION II	Sometimes we follow blind leaders of the blind.
ALL	We see things happen, but there is no truth.
DUET	The Life, the Truth, the Way came to man, and man knew Him not.
TRIO	He WAS despised and rejected of men! *(FAITH enters)* *(Perhaps in ancient soldier costume)*
FAITH	Awake! Awake!
	He IS despised and rejected of men.
ALL	No, not today. Calvary was 1900 years ago.
FAITH	Yes, 1900 years ago, and today...1988. Calvary is happening every day. Men crucify the Son of God by rejecting His way of life. Awake! Awake! I say.
ALL	Who are you?
FAITH	I am the voice that sounds in every street, in every town, city or hamlet. I am the voice in calamity, in every trouble, in war and peace, in life and death.
ALL	Why do you cry, "Awake"?
FAITH	I cry for righteousness...for truth I cry for goodness and honor... I come to disturb the Christian and wake him from his slumber.
DIVISION I	Truth...Truth...Truth... *(Syncopated whisper)*

DIVISION II	Truth...Truth...Truth... *(As above getting faster and louder)* *(Truth in costume enters quietly during the above)*
TRUTH	" I AM THE WAY, THE TRUTH, AND THE LIFE." Thus spake Jesus of Himself as He declared His purpose. John said of Him, "That was the true light, which lighteth every man that comes into the world."
ALL	Sin is darkness! Our sin sends the Son of God to Calvary.
DIVISION I	The sin of our enormous pride
DIVISION II	The sin of indifference and hardness of heart
DIVISION I	The sin of compromise and expediency
DIVISION II	Sin of ordinary people; sin of respectable citizens
MEN	Sin of parents
WOMEN	Sin of children
MEN	Sin of races
WOMEN	Sin of nations
ALL	God stepped into our world because He loved us and laid on Him the sin of us all.
SOLO	God stepped into our world with His love By a child in a stable
DIVISION I	By the ministry of a God-man
DIVISION II	By the cross of Calvary
ALL	By a joyous resurrection and a blessed Holy Spirit.
FAITH	"For God so loved the world that He gave His only begotten Son...
TRUTH	That whosoever believeth in Him, should not perish
ALL	But have everlasting life."

Scripture: John 1:14, 14:6, 5:16

GO MOSES! GO TODAY

ALL	O God, who are we?
SOLO (M)	Tell us God, what is our name?
DIVISION I	Is this where we belong?
DIVISION II	Tell us, God, why are we here?
SOLO (M)	Our God, tell us, please tell us,
SOLO (W)	Hold out your hand to us; give us a sign.
DIVISION I	Are we slaves ?
DIVISION II	Born to be slaves?
SOLO (M)	I suspect we are slaves.
QUARTET	Slaves in the mud pits of Egypt,
DIVISION I	Where Israelites must trample straw all day in the mud pits;
DIVISION II	To mix the clay and mold the bricks.
ALL	0 God, why? Will we never be set free?
DUET	We're a young, creative, determined people
QUARTET	Why must we be forced to slavery?
DIVISION I	Without hope we cannot dream,
DIVISION II	Without a plan we cannot scheme,
DUET	We cannot chart tomorrow
ALL	O Lord God, will we ever be free?
SOLO (M)	Do you hear the groans of our people?
SOLO (W)	Do you see them leaning against the mud pits--
ALL	Scraping mud from their arms, their legs, and splattered faces, or wiping dried blood from the back of a friend or brother--
DIVISION I	Where the whip cut deep,
DIVISION II	And the smart was of the heart, knowing no one cares.
ALL	Hardly anyone talked about the promise. The old, old promise God made to Abraham.
DIVISION I	Of a land rich and prosperous
DIVISION II	Flowing with milk and honey
ALL	Where we, a people; God's people would worship Him as Lord of all.
SOLO (M)	O God, the God of yesterday, Are you the God of today?

ALL	Do you have a plan for Israel?
QUARTET	We can't wait another day!
ALL	We feel quite justified to yell,
SOLO (W)	To scream
SOLO (W)	To cry
ALL	Why? Why? Why, O Lord?
DIVISION I	Will we ever escape from this mess?
DIVISION II	These mud pits of Egypt?
ALL	These holes of slavery and despair? Will we finally, forever, be free?
SOLO (M)	Oh, God give us a sign!
SOLO (M)	Today, not tomorrow.
DIVISION I	A dry bush glows; a flickering flame in its branches.
DIVISION II	Burning... Burning, but not consuming
SOLO (M)	What a vision - I must be dreaming! A burning bush. I must see this great sight! Why is the bush not burnt?
DIVISION I	Moses! Moses! The ground on which you stand is holy!
DIVISION II	Moses! Moses! Take off your shoes!
ALL	Moses! Moses! I am your father's God. The God of Israel.
SOLO (M)	I see my people suffering; I hear my people cry; I am come to deliver them; to set them free.
DIVISION I	You will do it for me Moses; NOW!
DIVISION II	You will go to Egypt's king!
ALL	Go Moses! Go to Pharaoh and bring my people out of Egypt.
SOLO (M)	Me, God? Who am I, to go?
QUARTET	Who am I? I'm just a shepherd!
DIVISION I	Who am I? A murderer; I killed an Egyptian and hid him in the sand.
DIVISION II	Who am I? A deserter who fled the courts of Egypt.

ALL	Who am I?
	Unqualified Untutored,
	   Untrained Uninformed,
	   Unskilled Unfit
	(these could be spoken in quick succession as a solo)

ALL	UNABLE AND UNCONVERSANT .....I CANNOT SPEAK!
SOLO (M)	But I AM with you!

DIVISION I	Are you really God?
DIVISION II	Are you for sure, God?
ALL	Yes, Yes, I AM! I AM!
SOLO (M)	But how can I know they will believe me?
ALL	Because I AM! I AM! I AM!
DIVISION I	I AM the El Shaddai
	I AM the Lord God, Almighty
	I AM the God of Abraham and Isaac.
SOLO (M)	I AM! It is true. I AM!
ALL	Say, I AM has sent you.

(A few bars of music.)

ALL	Is not this a symbol of our times?
QUARTET	All around us are people just like the Israelites.
ALL	People who are bound
DIVISION I	Fathers...Mothers...Teachers...Students...Coaches...Athletes...
DIVISION II	Teenagers...and young adults...yes, children, the kids, we say...
ALL	They're everywhere; these people who want to be free.
SOLO (W)	They walk the sidewalks of our towns,
DUET	They drive the highways of our country,
TRIO	They're in our homes, our schools, our theatres, our shops, our playgrounds.
ALL	They are everywhere; bound, broken, hopeless, despairing, burdened,frustrated, scared.
DIVISION I	There they are in bondage, enslaved, captives...
DIVISION II	To sin, drugs, alcohol, pornography, pseudo religions, dishonesty, hatred, prejudice
ALL	Under the lash of Satan!
DIVISION I	A slave, a subject of the evil power of this world
DIVISION II	Held captive by peer pressure, gang pressure, conformity, and an empty void.
ALL	Enslaved by habits, by uncontrollable desires.
DIVISION I	They're waiting...they're hurting...desperate, hoping against hope.

113

DIVISION II	They're crying, screaming, groaning, sobbing... They're expecting...
ALL	Help! Help! Help!
SOLO (M)	Then the glowing, burning, radiant face of God appears
SOLO (W)	Gleaming in the sun - a rich red, fireless flicker
QUARTET	The reflection of God's face
ALL	The Glory!
DIVISION I	And out from the brilliant glowing
DIVISION II	Came the lightning voice
ALL	I AM! I AM!
DIVISION I	The Christ, the Son of God!
DIVISION II	The Lamb of God which takes away the sin of the world.
ALL	And who the Son makes free, is free indeed!
SOLO (M)	Christian, you must GO for me, and bring my people out of bondage.
ALL	But I can't speak!
DIVISION I	Please send someone else
DIVISION II	They'll not believe me
DIVISION I	They won't listen to me
DIVISION II	My heart says, "YES" My mind says, "NO"
ALL	Please listen and hear; they need you - YOU must Go!
SOLO	I AM! I AM! will be with you. I AM the way, the Truth, the Life.
DIVISION I	I AM is sending you the call to serve and to go.
DIVISION II	I AM needs you to free a world of slaves.
DIVISION I	I AM will be with you!
DIVISION II	I AM gives you Himself, His Holy Spirit, His Power.
ALL	I AM! I AM! I will be with you. GO!

From the Bible: Exodus 3 - 5; John 1:36; John 8:36 John 14:6

A GREAT COMMISSION

ALL	GO....GO into all the world and preach the Gospel to every creature.
DIVISION I	Into all the world?
DIVISION II	Preach the Gospel?
SOLO (M)	Go? Why should I?
SOLO (W)	Contentment is here!
SOLO (M)	Position and power are here!
DUET	Fame and earthly recompense are here.
SOLO (W)	I am satisfied!
ALL	Go into all the world and preach - Go preach the Kingdom of God.
SOLO (M)	Why should I? The world is not my concern.
SOLO (W)	It's just too much.
DIVISION I	Business commands
DIVISION II	Success fascinates.
ALL	To spread the Gospel abroad is a staggering task for man or God.
QUARTET	Go! Go out into the highways and byways and compel them to come in.
ALL	Into the highways and byways?
DIVISION I	Highways are crowded, noisy and dangerous; confusing and frustrating.
DIVISION II	Byways are rough, dusty, lonely, depressing, discouraging.
SOLO (M)	Compel them to come in?
QUARTET	Every man must choose his own way; no man must be forced.
TRIO	GO...NOW...TODAY. The love of Christ constrains you.
ALL	Love is muted by the voices of the world;
QUARTET	Leadership demands:
ALL	POWER! POWER!
QUARTET	Business babbles:
	MAKE MONEY! MAKE MONEY! MAKE MONEY!
QUARTET	Educators insist:
ALL	KNOWLEDGE! DEGREES!

QUARTET	Researchers chatter;
ALL	NEUTRONS! PROTONS! ATOMS! COMPUTERS!
QUARTET	The world prattles and parrots:
ALL	PROGRESS! PROGRESS! PROGRESS!
TRIO	Where, oh where is the voice of God?
ALL	And Jesus said, "I am the Way, the Truth, and the Life."
QUARTET	Go to this people and say:
DIVISION I	Hearing you shall hear, and shall not understand,
DIVISION II	Seeing you shall see, and not perceive;
QUARTET	But be it known unto you that the Gospel of Christ is the power of God unto salvation to every one that believeth.
TRIO	Go...Go quickly and tell...
DIVISION I	Wanted! Hearts to take up the faith.
QUARTET	Walk the dismal paths of tensions, strains, and pressures.
DIVISION II	Wanted! Hearts to keep the faith.
QUARTET	Bring the peace of God so deep and penetrating.
DIVISION I	Wanted! Hearts to project the faith.
QUARTET	Wherever sin abounds - the market, shop, the home, or school.
DIVISION II	Wanted! Hearts baptized with BLOOD AND FIRE.
ALL	We are "Blood and Fire" Salvationists. We will GO.
DIVISION I	Not by might,
DIVISION II	Nor by power...
ALL	We will GO by and with God's Spirit.
DIVISION I	We will preach Christ
DIVISION II	We will practice compassion
DIVISION I	We will denounce sin
DIVISION II	We will declare salvation.
ALL	The Salvation Army will go into all the world to preach the Gospel to every creature.

Scripture Selections: Matthew 16:15; Luke 14:23; John 14:6; Romans 1:16

HAPPINESS IS..........GOD WITH US!

ALL	I will bless the Lord at all times
DIVISION I	My soul shall be joyful in the Lord
DIVISION II	I will rejoice in thy salvation
SOLO (W)	As a Christian I am happy in a special kind of way
ALL	Inexpressibly happy!
SOLO (M)	Happy in what?
QUARTET	In this clear and complete persuasion
TRIO	The God who is all powerful
SOLO I	All-wise
SOLO II	All-gracious
SOLO III	Governor over all
ALL	LOVES ME!
DIVISION I	Behold, what manner of love the Father hath bestowed upon us
DIVISION II	That we should be called the Sons of God
SOLO I	In this was manifested the love of God toward us
ALL	Because that God sent His only begotten Son into the world, that the world might live through Him.
SOLO I	Herein is Love
SOLO II	Not that we loved God
ALL	But that He loved us
DUET	If God so loved us we ought also to love one another
DIVISION I	This God is always with me
SOLO II	Is never absent
SOLO III	No, not for a moment
DIVISION II	I am eternally linked together with God
ALL	Linked together with God?
SOLO	Yes, Jesus said, Lo, I am with you alway
QUARTET	God is <u>really</u> with us!
DIVISION I	We need His presence
DIVISION II	To stand by our side
DIVISION I	To walk with us

117

DIVISION II	To hold our trembling hands
ALL	God really is with us--REJOICE!
SOLO I	He walks with us
SOLO II	He shares the long, weary road
DIVISION I	Let us love, not merely in theory or words
DIVISION II	Let us love in sincerity and in practice
SOLO II	We are linked together with God eternally
SOLO III	We are called to BE the love of Jesus
ALL	REJOICE! Happiness is...God with us! REJOICE!

Scripture Selections: Isa. 34:1; Psa. 35:9; I Jn. 3:1;
I Jn. 4:1,9,10; Matt. 28:20; I Jn. 3:16 (Phillips)

A HEART OF COMPASSION

ALL	The Saviour of men came to seek and to save
SOLO I (M)	The souls who were lost to the good
ALL	His spirit was moved
DIVISION I	For the world which He loved
DIVISION II	With the boundless compassion of God
SOLO I (W)	And still there are fields where the laborers are few
DUET (M-W)	And still there are souls without bread
TRIO (W)	And still eyes that weep where the darkness is deep
QUARTET	And still straying sheep to be led.
ALL	"When Jesus saw the multitudes
SOLO I (M)	He was moved with compassion on them
DUET (M-W)	Because they were scattered abroad as sheep having no shepherd"
DIVISION I	"His compassions fail not.
DIVISION II	They are new every morning
ALL	Great is His faithfulness"
VOCAL SOLO	Except I am moved with compassion How dwelleth thy Spirit in me In word and in deed Burning love is my need I know I can find this in Thee.
ALL	O, Saviour of men touch my spirit again
DIVISION I	Let thy compassion move among us
DIVISION II	Let thy compassion speak to us
ALL	O Saviour of men touch my spirit again
SOLO I (M)	And grant that thy servant may be, Intent every day as I labor and pray
SOLO I (W)	Both instant and constant for Thee.
ALL	"Go...Go...Go ye into all the world and preach the gospel to every creature"
SOLO II (M)	Will you go?
SOLO III (M)	Do you hear their cry?
SOLO IV (M)	Can you feel their need?

VOCAL SOLO	O is not the Christ 'midst the crowd of today Whose questioning cries do not cease?
DIVISION I	Then Jesus called His disciples unto Him and said,
DIVISION II	Have compassion on the multitude
VOCAL SOLO	And will He not show to the hearts that would know The things that belong to their peace?
ALL	"And God, being full of compassion
DIVISION I	Forgave their iniquity
DIVISION II	Destroyed them not
ALL	Yea, many times, He turned His anger away!"
VOCAL SOLO	But how shall they hear if the preacher forbear Or lack in compassionate zeal? Or how shall hearts move with the Master's own love Without His anointing and seal?
ALL	Oh, Christian do you not hear? Will you not listen?
QUARTET (mixed)	Away with such babblings! We're busy! Can't you see? We have no time!
SOLO I	They are your brothers -- they need you... Won't you help them?
QUARTET	Let someone else do it - what about the missionaries - they can do it!
SOLO I (M)	Missionaries need your help Missionaries need your support
SOLO II (W)	You can go...You can give...
DIVISION I	Money...time...talent...skills
DIVISION II	Care...concern...love...prayer
SOLO I (M)	You can open your heart to compassion
DUET	You can hear their cry and dry their tears
SOLO I (W)	You can be moved by compassion
DIVISION I	They are starving...You can feed them
DIVISION II	They are naked...You can clothe them
DIVISION I	They are sick..You can visit them
DIVISION II	They are in prison...You can go to them
DIVISION I	They sit in darkness...You can bring light
DIVISION II	They are fallen...You can lift them up
DIVISION I	They are bound...addicted...You can loose them
DIVISION II	They are lonely...forsaken...You can bring hope

ALL	They need a friend... tell them of the love of Jesus
SOLO I (M)	"In this was manifest the love of God toward us, because God sent His only begotten son into the world, that we might live through Him."
VOCAL SOLO	Oh Saviour of men, touch my spirit again And grant that thy servant may be Intense every day, as I labor and pray Both instant and constant for Thee
Chorus	Except I am moved with compassion
Song	S.A. Song Book #527

Scripture: Matt. 9:36; Lam. 3:22; Matt. 15:32; Psa. 78:38; 1 John 4:9

Words of Song: Albert Orsborn

A HOLY STANCE

ALL	*(Quickly - somewhat staccato, but not choppy)* The earth is the Lord's and the fullness thereof; the world, and they that dwell therein. For He hath founded it upon the seas and established it upon the floods.
SOLO I	The earth is the Lord's
SOLO II	The earth is the Lord's
SOLO III	The earth--
ALL	And the fullness thereof *(Pause)*
DIVISION I	The world is the Lord's
DIVISION II	And they that dwell therein.
SOLO I	(Slow) For He hath founded it upon the seas
SOLO II	*(Interrupt Solo I in quick succession)* Founded it upon the seas
SOLO III	Founded it upon the seas
SOLO IV	Founded it upon the seas
ALL	And established it upon the floods.
SOLO I	Who shall ascend into the hill of the Lord?
SOLO III	Who?
SOLO IV	Who?
SOLO II	He that hath clean hands
SOLO III	And a pure heart.
SOLO IV	Who?
ALL	He that hath clean hands and a pure heart.
SOLO I	Who shall stand in His holy place?
DIVISION I	Who?
DIVISION II	Who?
DIVISION I	He that hath not lifted up his soul unto vanity
DIVISION II	Nor sworn deceitfully
ALL	He shall receive the blessing from the Lord, and righteousness from the God of his salvation.

Selections from Psalm 24

KNOW THE TRUTH

ALL	"Take heed that your heart be not deceived, and ye turn aside and serve other gods and worship them."
SOLO	"Let no man deceive you
DIVISION I	With vain words
ALL	Be not deceived
DIVISION II	By evil men and seducers
ALL	Who wax worse and worse."
DUET	"...and being deceived"
SOLO	"Be no more tossed to and fro,
QUARTET	...and carried about
DIVISION I	With every wind of doctrine,
DIVISION II	By the sleight of men."
ALL	"Let no man deceive you
QUARTET	...with cunning craftiness"
SOLO	Take heed...they lie in wait to deceive
ALL	"Be not deceived These are they that rebel against the light... and the truth is not in them."
SOLO	Jesus said, "I am the way, the TRUTH, and the life. And ye shall know the truth and truth shall make you free."

Scripture Selections: Duet. 11:6; Eph. 5:6; 2 Tim. 3:13;

Eph. 4:14,15; Job 24:13; John 8:32

LIFE'S DESIRE AND DESIGN

ALL	Our Father, listen to the confession of our hearts as we think about life.
SOLO	Life is abounding and enriching.
DUET	We are surrounded by appliances, gadgets, calculators, and computers.
TRIO	And instant nourishment, time savers, miracle fabrics and micro-wave ovens,
ALL	Still we are empty; BREAK TO US THE BREAD OF LIFE.
SOLO	Life is enlightening and enabling.
DIVISION I	We have technology, psychiatry, medicine, psychology, and motivational research,
DIVISION II	We have the power of positive thinking to help ourselves
ALL	Still we are confused; BREAK TO US THE BREAD OF LIFE
SOLO	Life is satisfying and pleasing.
DIVISION I	We have television,
DIVISION II	Transistor radios,
DIVISION I	Cassettes,
DIVISION II	Stereos, videos,
DIVISION I	Movies, sit-coms,
DIVISION II	Time, time, -- leisure time,
DUET	Automobiles, boats, planes,
TRIO	Spectator sports and participating sports,
ALL	Still we are dissatisfied; BREAK TO US THE BREAD OF LIFE.
SOLO	Our Father, we admit that life is desire and life is design, but it is not what it should be.
DIVISION I	Forgive us for unworthy and selfish desires.
DIVISION II	Forgive us for thinking that a man's life consists in the abundance of things he possesses.
ALL	Dear God, turn us from self to you, so that we in turn may turn others to you.

LIFE SERVICE

STRANGER	God is too slow! We cannot wait upon His everlasting time.
SALVATIONIST	God is too slow?
STRANGER	We are troubled by darkness
SALVATIONIST	God gives us light
STRANGER	We are troubled by hunger
SALVATIONIST	God gives us bread
STRANGER	We are poor...we are dying...there are too many of us.
SALVATIONIST	God loves you all
STRANGER	Hear us! Hear us!
SALVATIONIST	We hear you; we know you are weary
VOICE	Weary of falsehood..
VOICE	hypocrisy
VOICE	corruption
VOICE	slogans
SALVATIONIST	Weary of striving
VOICE	hoping
VOICE	trying
VOICE	struggling
VOICE	sighing
STRANGER	Hear us! Hear us! Give us bread!
SALVATIONIST	"The bread of God is that which comes down from heaven and giveth life to the world" "Man shall not live by bread alone." We must get INVOLVED. WE MUST GET INVOLVED!
VOICE	But it may be inconvenient
VOICE	There will be self-denial
VOICE	Shouldering burdens
VOICE	Tasting bitterness
SALVATIONIST	We need a new life-style. INVOLVEMENT! "And Jesus went forth and saw a great multitude of people, and was moved with compassion towards them, and began to teach them many things." *(Continue reciting: Mark 6:31-44)*

VOICE	We are sent together into the world
VOICE	To serve our brothers everywhere
VOICE	To hear their cry
VOICE	To meet their needs
SALVATIONIST	We will bring bread. Jesus said, "I am the bread of life. He that comes to me shall never hunger." Let us go and give the service of our lives.

Scripture: John 6:33, Matt. 4:14, John 6:35

LIVING JOYFULLY

ALL	All the land...All the land...Make a joyful noise unto the Lord, All the land.
DIVISION I	Make a joyful noise unto the Lord,
DIVISION II	Serve the Lord with gladness:
SOLO I (W)	Come before His presence with singing
SOLO II (M)	Know you that the Lord, He is God
QUARTET	It is He that has made us, and not we ourselves;
ALL	We are His people, and the sheep of His pasture.
DIVISION I	Enter into His gates with thanksgiving
DIVISION II	And into His courts with praise;
TRIO	Be thankful unto Him, and bless His Name,
SOLO I (M)	For the Lord is good,
SOLO II (W)	His mercy is everlasting,
ALL	And His truth endures...His truth endures...His truth endures to all generations.

Selections from Psalm 100

LIVING WATER

SOLO I (M)	Save me, oh God, for the waters are come in unto my soul.
SOLO II (M)	I am weary of my crying: my throat is dried: mine eyes fail while I wait for my God.
DIVISION I	They that hate me without a cause are more than the hairs of my head.
DIVISION II	They that would destroy me are mighty.
DUET (W)	For Thy sake I have borne reproach.
ALL	Reproach hath broken my heart.
QUARTET (M)	I am full of heaviness
DUET (W)	I looked for some to take pity - but there was none.
DIVISION I	They gave me also gall for my meat;
DIVISION II	In my thirst they gave me vinegar to drink.
SOLO II (M)	Ho, everyone that thirsteth, come ye to the waters.
SOLO II (W)	My soul thirsteth for God, for the living God.
DIVISION I	Whosoever drinketh of the water that I shall give him shall never thirst.
DIVISION II	The water that I shall give him shall be in him a well of water.
ALL	A well of water springing up into everlasting life.
SOLO I (M)	Give me this water, that I thirst not.

Selections from Psalm 69, Isaiah 55, Psalm 42, John 4

MARCH ON! SALVATION SOLDIER

SCRIPTURE SOLO (M or W)

    Finally, my brethren, be strong in the Lord, and in the power of His might.

MEN   Our Soldiers are a happy host

TRIO   Equipped with the power of the Holy Ghost

SOLO (M)   Amen!

SCRIPTURE SOLO   Put on the whole armor of God, that ye may be able to stand against the wiles of the devil.

ALL   Amen! Amen!

SOLO (W)   While others sleep, we're wide awake

DUET (M)   To rescue souls from the burning lake.

SCRIPTURE SOLO   For we wrestle not against flesh and blood, but against principalities, against powers, against the rulers of the darkness of this world, against spiritual wickedness in high places.

    Wherefore take unto you the whole armor of God, that ye may be able to withstand in the evil day, and having done all, to stand.

ALL   Amen! Amen! Amen!

SCRIPTURE SOLO   Stand therefore, having your loins girt about with truth, and having on the breastplate of righteousness; and your feet shod with the preparation of the Gospel of peace.

MEN   March On, Salvation Army. March On! March On!

WOMEN   Amen! Amen! Amen! Amen!

SCRIPTURE SOLO   Above all, taking the shield of faith, wherewith ye shall be able to quench all the fiery darts of the wicked.

MEN   Rush to the fight and spread the Light

WOMEN   Claim victory in Jehovah's might.

SCRIPTURE SOLO   And take the helmet of salvation, and the sword of the Spirit, which is the Word of God.

SOLO (M)   MARCH ON!

WOMEN   MARCH ON!

MEN   MARCH ON!

ALL   MARCH ON Salvation Army. MARCH ON!

Selections from Ephesians 6
Combat Songs - Page 36

A MODERN PRAYER AND THE PSALMS

QUARTET	As the hart pants after the water brooks,
SOLO (W)	So pants my heart after You, O God.
SOLO (M)	Inside me there's a deafening scream, and I'm crying, Lord.
SOLO (W)	I feel so alone; so completely alone.
QUARTET	My God, my God, why have You forsaken me? Why are You so far from helping me?
ALL	I feel uprooted. like a tree in a storm
TRIO	O, my God, my soul is cast down within me:
SOLO (M)	Why are You disquieted in me?
DIVISION I	My life is in turmoil, the upheaval possesses me.
DIVISION II	I am trying to be composed, I don't want to make waves.
ALL	From the end of the earth will I cry to You.
SOLO (M)	When my heart is overwhelmed, lead me to the rock that is higher than I.
DUET	This moment presses in on me
TRIO	This moment consumes me - it has power over me. It is my moment!
ALL	Hide not Your face from me in the day when I am in trouble;
DIVISION I	Incline Your ear unto me;
DIVISION II	In the day when I call, answer me speedily.
SOLO (W)	I want to hold on to the past; I want to cry, to weep tears of self-pity.
SOLO (M)	I am confused when I look at tomorrow. Tomorrow is despair, distress, destruction, dis...everything.
DIVISION I	When my spirit was overwhelmed within me,
DIVISION II	Then You, O God, knew the way I must go.
SOLO (M)	In the way wherein I walked have they privately laid a snare for me.
ALL	You are here in the road with me. I hear Your voice; calling me to love, life, and responsibility. You have work for me; a job I must do.
DIVISION I	Sing unto the Lord, bless His Name;
	Show forth His salvation from day to day.
DIVISION II	Declare His glory among the heathen, His wonders among the people.

QUARTET	My senseless thinking, my burning torch of self-affection has made my life touchy, grumpy, and resentful.
DUET	Know you that the Lord, He is God;
TRIO	It is He that has made us, and not we ourselves;
QUARTET	We are His people, and the sheep of His pasture.
ALL	Lord, I am listening. I know You are kindness, and mercy. You are freedom and peace.
SOLO (M)	I was almost lost, Lord, but in this dark moment, you found me. I looked for help, and You were there.
ALL	My soul, wait only upon God; for my expectation is from Him 0 give thanks to the Lord; call upon His Name Make known His deeds among the people.
SOLO (W)	I remembered, Your love goes on, and on, I was released; God's power really works, I know too, faith goes on and on I am safe and sound. Thank you God, I am healed and whole.
DIVISION I	I waited patiently for the Lord; And He inclined unto me, and heard my cry.
DIVISION II	He brought me up also out of an horrible pit, Out of the miry clay,
ALL	And set my feet upon a rock, and established my goings.

Psa. 42; 22; 102; 96; 100; 40.

A MOMENT TO DECIDE

ALL	Once to every man and nation--comes the moment to decide
SOLO I	Every Man!
SOLO II	Every Nation!
ALL	Every man and every nation must decide.
MEN	In the strife with truth or falsehood.
ALL	We must decide. We must all decide.
WOMEN	For the good or evil side.
DIVISION I	Some great cause.
DIVISION II	Some great decision
ALL	Some great cause or decision
	Offering each the bloom or blight.
DIVISION I	And the choice goes on forever.
SOLO I (W)	Choose ye!
SOLO II (W)	Today you must choose!
DIVISION II	Twixt that darkness and that light.
SOLO I	Every man and every nation must decide.
ALL	Choose ye light! Decide for the right!
DIVISION I	(syncopated whisper) - truth...truth...truth...
DIVISION II	EVIL! OR TRUTH!
ALL	Though the cause of evil prosper--yet, truth alone is strong!
SOLO I	TRUTH!
MEN	Forever on the scaffold?
SOLO II	WRONG!
WOMEN	Forever on the throne!
ALL	Ah! The scaffold sways the future.
MIXED QUARTET	Truth cannot fail!
DIVISION I	Behind the dim unknown
DIVISION II	Standeth God!
MIXED QUARTET	Truth will triumph!
WOMEN	God is standing within the shadows.
MEN	Keeping watch above His own.
ALL	Truth is strong.
	Truth will triumph over wrong.

From the poetry of James Russell Lowell "A MOMENT TO DECIDE""

ON TO CONQUER

SOLO I	On to Conquer!
ALL	On to Conquer!
DIVISION I	On to conquer every nation,
DIVISION II	With a mighty two edged sword,
SOLO I	Who are these with colors waving Sweeping forward through the land?
DIVISION I	Toil and strife and dangers braving,
DIVISION II	Daring for the right to stand.
SOLO II	Who are these in town and city With their music song and drum?
QUARTET	Lifting up the name of Jesus In the city, street, and slum?
ALL	'Tis the Army of Salvation 'Tis the Army of the Lord.
SOLO I	On to Conquer!
SOLO II	On to Conquer!
DIVISION I	Who are these in love united?
QUARTET	Going forth the lost to win, Saving souls by evil blighted,
DIVISION II	From the depths of grief and sin.
ALL	'Tis the Army of Salvation.
SOLO I	From the power of sin set free,
SOLO II	Saved from fear and condemnation,
QUARTET	Serving God with liberty.
ALL	'Tis the Army of Salvation 'Tis the Army of the Lord.
SOLO I	On to conquer every nation
SOLO II	With a mighty two edged sword.
ALL	On to Conquer! On to Conquer!

From the Army Song Book #707 1953 Edition

133

OUR WORLD

SOLO I	The world is mine!
SOLO II	The world is yours!
ALL	The world is "US"
QUARTET	What a world we have made!
SOLO I	A world of problems-
DIVISION I	Of hate, anger, and despair
SOLO II	A world darkened by evil
DIVISION II	Violence, crime, pornography, permissiveness, pseudo religions, dishonesty.
ALL	AND..... AND...... AND....SIN
QUARTET	A world of pleasure, of things we can measure
DIVISION I	A world that is OURS, but a world in NEED.
DIVISION II	A world that is wanting for faith and a creed.
ALL	We are the world!
SOLO I	You are the world!
SOLO II	I am the world!
ALL	If it is our world; we've got problems.
SOLO I	Wake up to a world in need
SOLO II	Wake up and start to lead
DIVISION I	Wake up and see what you can give
DIVISION II	Wake up to your world, and make it live!
ALL	Our world can be changed by you
SOLO I	Why not find out what you can do.
ALL	HOW? WHEN? WHERE?
QUARTET	Hand in hand with the God above You can give our world His love.
ALL	God loved the world and sent His Son If you believe this, it can be done.
SOLO II	Take to the world what you have heard From the Bible, His truth and word.
ALL	You WILL change the world.
DIVISION I	Don't worry about the problems you meet

DIVISION II	Face them; God's love knows no defeat.
ALL	You will change the world!
DIVISION I	Live, tell, show the world the man of Galilee
DIVISION II	He will help you change the world, and set men free.
SOLO I	The world is yours!
SOLO II	The world is mine!
SOLO I-SOLO II	The world is us!
ALL	God's world is for man When we accept His loving plan.

THE SALVATION ARMY BEGINS IN AMERICA

ALL	The Salvation Army invades the United States of America.
SOLO (M)	March 11, 1880 eight Salvationists arrive by the steamship *Australia* from London, England; one man Commissioner Railton.
SOLO (W)	With seven Hallelujah lassies dressed in long skirts and frock coats. They had a red band around their hats with gilt letters reading The Salvation Army.
ALL	They came down the gangplank singing hymns and waving a red, yellow and blue flag.
QUARTET	They attracted much attention as they knelt and prayed and declared war on sin.
DIVISION I	First in Castle Garden, New York City
DIVISION II	Then on March 21st, in Newark, New Jersey at the Odeon theatre.
ALL	Their prayers at that first meeting place Are being answered yet,
SOLO (M)	In blessing on our Army work, For God does not forget,
DIVISION I	Yes, in little old New York they stood, Seven women and one man;
DIVISION II	Religionists departing from The ordinary plan.
SOLO (W)	The women jingled tambourines,
SOLO (M)	The man, he beat a drum;
QUARTET	The text of all their simple talks Was found in one word,"Come!"
DIVISION I	'Twas "Come with us, we'll do you good!" 'Twas "Come and start to pray!"
DIVISION II	'Twas "Come and get your sins forgiven!" "Come and walk the narrow way!"
TRIO	Some scoffed and sneered, some boldly jeered,
QUARTET	Some listened to the word,
SOLO (W)	And hooting children followed them, And all the street was stirred.
SOLO (M)	But some of those who criticized Soon learned the worth of prayer,

ALL	From this peculiar little band,
	Possessed with courage rare.
DUET	These pioneers have passed away,
	But still their work goes on;
TRIO	Now President and people praise
ALL	The good that has been done.
DIVISION I	Today they number thousands strong,
DIVISION II	Redeemed through Jesus' blood,
ALL	Salvation Army all alive
	To do the people good.
DIVISION I	And still the keynote of their text,
	The magic message, "Come!"
DIVISION II	As silver bands accompany
	The tambourine and drum.
SOLO (M)	They have not brought their standards down,
SOLO (W)	The Bible all their plea,
ALL	They honored God, - God honored them,
	With power and victory.

Adapted from "More Poems of a Salvationist"
Irena Arnold

THE SEARCH

ALL	O Lord, You have searched me, and known me.
DIVISION I	You know my downsitting and my uprising;
DIVISION II	You understand my thought afar off.
SOLO I (M)	You compass my path and my lying down,
SOLO II (W)	You are acquainted with all my ways,
TRIO	For there is not a word in my tongue, but, lo, O Lord, You know it altogether.
DIVISION I	You have beset me behind and before,
DIVISION II	You have laid Your hand upon me,
ALL	Such knowledge is too wonderful for me;
TRIO	It is high, I cannot attain unto it.
SOLO I (W)	Whither shall I go from Your Spirit?
SOLO II (M)	Whither shall I flee from Your presence?
DIVISION I	If I ascend up into Heaven, You are there;
DIVISION II	If I make my bed in Hell, behold, You are there.
QUARTET	How precious also are Your thoughts to me, O God!
ALL	How great is the sum of them!
SOLO I (W)	If I should count them,
ALL	They are more in number than the sand.
DIVISION I	Search me, O God, ... Search me
DIVISION II	Search me and know my heart;
SOLO I (M)	Try me ... Oh, God, try me ...
QUARTET	Try me and know my thoughts
SOLO II (W)	See if there be any wicked way in me
ALL	Lead me in the way everlasting. Savior, lead me lest I stray. Lead me...Lead me all the way.

Selections from Psalm 139

THE SEARCH ENDS

ALL	Man is still the hunter. *(Pause)* He has searched from generation to generation.
SOLO I (M)	For that elusive Shangri La,
SOLO II (W)	That unreachable star,
TRIO	That undefinable thing that makes life tolerable.
ALL	His search has taken him
DIVISION I	To space,
DIVISION II	To the depths of the earth,
DIVISION I	To the complexities of science,
DIVISION II	To the simplicities of the commune,
ALL	And still he searches.
SOLO (M)	For what he pursues is what every man has sought for before him...
DIVISION I	A sense of completeness,
DIVISION II	And wholeness,
ALL	And a world that has a sense of sanity and order.
TRIO	So now, that search unrewarded, he narrows down the path, from the haunts..
DIVISION I	Of immorality and permissiveness
DIVISION II	Of materialism, drugs, pseudo-religions, and greed
ALL	And war!
DIVISION I	He now turns inward, to age-old questions
DIVISION II	Of self-realization and self-esteem
DUET	To purpose
TRIO	And direction
ALL	And to find the answers to these, he turns
DIVISION I	To people around him,
DIVISION II	To the Bible, and to God-esteem,
SOLO I	To the ONE who has said to mankind everywhere "Ye shall seek me, and find me, when you shall search for me with all your heart."
ALL	The search ends...
DIVISION I	For he has found God..
DIVISION II	Through Jesus Christ.
ALL	"Ask and it shall be given you.. seek and ye shall find."

Scripture: Jer. 29:13 Matt. 7:7

A STORM AT SEA

ALL	And Jesus with His disciples entered into a ship
DIVISION I	And behold there arose a great tempest in the sea
DIVISION II	Insomuch that the ship was covered with the waves
SOLO I (W)	But Jesus was asleep
ALL	And the disciples came to Him saying
DIVISION I	Lord! Save us
DIVISION II	Master, carest thou not that we perish?
SOLO II (M)	Lord, we perish?
ALL	Lord, save us! We perish!
TRIO (W)	And Jesus said unto them,
SOLO I (M)	Why are you fearful, O you of little faith?
TRIO (W)	And Jesus arose, and rebuked the wind and said unto the sea
SOLO I(M)	Peace be still! Peace be still!
DIVISION I	Peace be still?
	(Note: This must be asked as a question for effective interpretation. This represents the group of disciples who witnessed the miracle. They asked the question in amazement - could this really have happened?)
DIVISION II	Peace be still?
SOLO I (M)	Peace . . . . .
SOLO II (M)	Peace . . . . .
SOLO III (M)	Peace . . . . .
DIVISION I	Peace . . . . . *(Softly)*
DIVISION II	Peace . . . . . *(Softly)*
ALL	Peace be still! *(Softly)*
	(The disciples have seen the miracle happen, and they affirm the miracle. Pause between the three words.)
TRIO (W)	And the wind ceased and there was a great calm.
VOCAL CHORUS	"Peace Be Still"

Scripture Selections: Matt. 8:23; Luke 8:22

TIME IS LIFE

	(Organ tolls the clock chimes 1-2-3-4-5-6-7-8-9-10)
DIVISION I	Ten seconds have just passed.
DIVISION II	Time is not hidden from the Almighty.
ALL	In the beginning, God created
SOLO	God created... (tumbling) the earth, the sun, the moon, the stars
ALL	The world!
DIVISION I	God made of one blood all peoples
DIVISION II	To dwell upon the face of the earth
Organ chimes	1-2-3-4-5-6-7-8-9-10
DIVISION I	Ten seconds just passed
DIVISION II	Sixty-six people died and went into eternity!
ALL	There is an appointed time for everything.
DIVISION I	To everything there is a season
DIVISION II	And a time to every purpose under the heaven.
WOMEN	A time to be born
MEN	A time to die
SOLO I	A time to plant
SOLO II	And a time to reap
DUET	A time to tear down
TRIO	And a time to build
DIVISION I	A time to weep
DIVISION II	And a time to laugh
ALL	A time to mourn, and a time to dance
SOLO I	A time to keep silence
SOLO II	And a time to speak
DIVISION I	A time to love
DIVISION II	And a time to live
ALL	A TIME TO LIVE!
SOLO I	Remember how short time is
SOLO II	Our time is in His hand.

DIVISION I	What time I am afraid, I will trust in Thee.
DIVISION II	He hath made everything beautiful in His time.
SOLO	Time...it is the gift of God...
DIVISION I	To use or employ...
DIVISION II	To enjoy and convert
DIVISION I	To manage...or manipulate
DIVISION II	To discipline or innovate
DIVISION I	To direct or control
DIVISION II	To command or regulate
ALL	Time is life! There is a time to LIVE!
SOLO	For to me to live is Christ...for Christ liveth in me, and the life I now live, I live by the faith of the Son of God who loved me and gave Himself for me.

Scripture Selections: Gen. 1; Acts 17:26; Ecc. 3; Psa. 31:15; Psa. 56:3; Gal. 2:20

UNMERITED MERCY

SOLO I (M)	Seek the Lord while He may be found,
SOLO II (W)	Call upon Him while He is near.
TRIO	Let the wicked man forsake his way,
QUARTET	And the unrighteous man his thoughts;
ALL	Let him return unto the Lord...Return...Return...Return unto the Lord
SOLO I (W)	He will have mercy upon him
ALL	He will pardon...He will abundantly pardon.
DIVISION I	For My thoughts are not your thoughts
DIVISION II	Neither are your ways My ways
TRIO	Says the Lord.
ALL	For as the heavens are higher than the earth
SOLO I (M)	So are My ways higher than your ways
SOLO II (W)	And My thoughts than your thoughts.
DIVISION I	For as the rain comes down, and the snow from heaven,
SOLO I	And returns not thither,
DIVISION II	But waters the earth, and makes it bring forth and bud,
TRIO	So shall My Word be that goes forth out of My mouth
DIVISION I	It shall not return unto Me void
DIVISION II	But it shall accomplish that which I please
QUARTET	And it shall prosper in the thing whereto I sent it.
ALL	Seek...Seek...Seek the Lord...Seek and you shall find. You shall find the Lord.

Selections from Isaiah 55

143

WAIT ON THE LORD

ALL	Wait on the Lord, be of good courage, and He shall strengthen thy heart.
MEN	Hast thou not known?
WOMEN	Hast thou not heard?
ALL	That the everlasting God, the Lord, the Creator of the ends of the earth, fainteth not, neither is weary.
DUET	There is no searching of His understanding.
DIVISION I	He giveth power to the faint
DIVISION II	And to them that have no might He increaseth strength
SOLO I (M)	Behold, I am with thee
SOLO I (W)	And will keep thee in all places whither thou goest
ALL	I will not leave thee,
DUET	Until I have done that which I have spoken to thee of.
DIVISION I	As the mountains are round about Jerusalem
DIVISION II	So the Lord is round about his people from henceforth even forever.
DUET	Even the youths shall faint and be weary
QUARTET	And the young men shall utterly fall;
ALL	But they that wait upon the Lord,
SOLO I (M)	Shall renew their strength
DUET	Shall mount up with wings as eagles
TRIO	Shall run and not be weary
QUARTET	Shall walk and faint not
ALL	Wait on the Lord.

Scripture Selections   Psa. 27:14; Isa. 40; Genesis 28; Psa. 125

WEAPONS OF FAITH

(Background Music - Marching Song - "Onward, Christian Soldiers")

SOLO I (M)	Onward! Salvation Soldier.
SOLO II (M)	*(Marching tempo)* March onward with blood and fire unfurled.
QUARTET	*(These words are spoken in march tempo during the words of Solo II. The timing should be such that the QUARTET speaks the last "on-ward" on the word "unfurled" and "Christian Soldier".)*
	On-ward On-ward On-ward
ALL	Onward Christian Soldiers! March onward into all the world and preach the Gospel to every creature.
DIVISION I	Be strong in the Lord,
DIVISION II	And in the power of His might.
SOLO I (M)	March onward against all the hosts of Hell!
SOLO II (M)	Stand against the wiles of the devil!
ALL	Stand your ground forever---*(sustained - big swell)*
DUET (W)	Never give in
ALL	No, never yield the field
DUET (W)	Never compromise
ALL	No, never, never waver.
SOLO I (M)	Put on the whole armour of God,
ALL	Part of the armour will not do.
SOLO II (W)	Evil penetrates the mind half-committed.
ALL	Wholeness is holiness.
QUARTET	Sin weakens the heart half-submitted.
SOLO I (M)	Wherefore, take the whole armour of God.
ALL	Holiness is able to withstand all the powers of darkness.
QUARTET	Put on the whole spiritual armour, Christian Soldier:
DIVISION I	The girdle of truth
DIVISION II	The breastplate of righteousness
ALL	The shoes of peace
DIVISION I	The shield of faith -
SOLO I (W)	It will quench all the fiery darts of the wicked -

ALL	The helmet of salvation
DIVISION II	The Sword of the Spirit -
SOLO II (M)	It is the Word of God -
SOLO III (W)	Sharper than any two-edged sword.
ALL	Onward Christian Soldiers armed with the spiritual weapons of your warfare,
QUARTET	For the weapons of our warfare are not carnal, but mighty
ALL	Mighty through God to the pulling down of strongholds
QUARTET	Casting down imaginations, and every high thing that exalts itself against the knowledge of God
DIVISION I	And brings into captivity every thought
DIVISION II	To the obedience of Christ.
ALL	Onward Christian Soldier--This is the victory that overcomes the world--even your faith!
Chorus:	"On We March!" (Salvation Army Song Book #700)

Selections from Ephesians 6

WHAT IS A FAMILY?

ALL	Behold, the Lord our God hath showed us His glory and His greatness.
SOLO	Go thou near, and hear all that the Lord Our God shall say.
SOLO II	Stand thou here by me, and I will speak unto thee.
ALL	Ye shall observe to do as the Lord your God commanded you.
SOLO	O that there were such an heart in them that they would keep all my commandments always; lest there be among you man or woman, or family whose heart turneth away from the Lord.
ALL	A family? What is a family?
DIVISION I	Why do you ask?
DIVISION II	Everyone knows what a family is.
DUET	Oh do they?
TRIO	Of course...a family is...a family is...
QUARTET	A family is...
DUET I	A family is...
DUET II	A family is...
SOLO I	There is a fabric that binds together a family
DUET I	A family is...
DUET II	A family is...
DUET I	A family is people!
ALL	That's it...A family is people.
TRIO	Who cares when you are sad
DIVISION I	Who shares in your achievements, and your failures
DIVISION II	Who understands when your head aches, and your nerves are edgy, and you feel so irritable.
QUARTET	Who remembers you are not perfect, just human.
ALL	Who respects your limitations and all your growing Who loves...
SOLO II	Large heartedly,
SOLO III	Freely,
DIVISION I	A love that shoulders burdens, and never grows weary
DIVISION II	A love that is courageous, patient, tender and wise
ALL	A family is a school

147

SOLO I	Where we learn honor and integrity,
SOLO II	Where we learn to listen and share ideas
SOLO III	Where we learn to like ourselves because we are special
DIVISION I	Where we learn the rules of living
DIVISION II	Where we learn discipline and responsibility
DUET	Where we learn to make good decisions and profit by unwise decisions
ALL	Where we learn about God with a happy, excited spirit
SOLO I	A family is a garden
SOLO II	To run and play in
SOLO III	To walk and rest in
ALL	A family is a comfortable place
TRIO	To ask for help
QUARTET	To express our frustrations
DIVISION I	To talk about our problems, to laugh, to cry, to nurse our bruises
DIVISION II	To even yell when we stumble, fall, or are hurt
ALL	A family is a garden, yes, where we can be happy, sing, pray, and say thank you.
SOLO I	And thou shalt love the Lord thy God with all thy heart, with all thy soul and with all thy might.
ALL	And these words shall be in thy heart, and thou shalt teach them diligently to thy children
DUET	Thou shalt talk of them when thou sittest in thine house
TRIO	When thou walkest by the way
QUARTET	And when thou liest down and when thou risest up.
ALL	Hear therefore, and observe to do, that it may be well with thee and thy family.
ALL	A family is
	...people
	...a school
	...a garden

Scripture: Deut. 6:5, 6, 7

WHO WILL GO?

ALL	"In the year that King Uzziah died I saw also the Lord sitting upon a throne, high and lifted up, and his train filled the temple. Above it stood the seraphims; each one had six wings; with twain he covered his face, and with twain he covered his feet; and with twain he did fly. And one cried unto another, and said:
SOLO I (W)	'Holy,
SOLO II (W)	'Holy,
DIVISION I	'Holy is the Lord of Hosts.
DIVISION II	'The whole earth is full of His glory.'"
QUARTET	"And the posts of the door moved at the voice of him that cried, and the house was filled with smoke. Then said I:
SOLO I (M)	"Woe is me! For I am undone; because I am a man of unclean lips; and I dwell in the midst of a people of unclean lips; for mine eyes have seen the king, the Lord of Hosts."
QUARTET	"Then flew one of the seraphims unto me, having a live coal in his hand, which he had taken with the tongs from off the altar; and he laid it upon my mouth, and said:
SOLO I (W)	'Lo, this hath touched thy lips and thine iniquity is taken away, and thy sin purged.'
ALL	"Also I heard the voice of the Lord, saying:
SOLO (M)	"Whom shall I send, and who will go for us?"
QUARTET	"Then said I,
SOLO I (M)	"Here am I; send me."
QUARTET	"And he said,
ALL	"Go!" *(spoken clearly and loudly)*
DIVISION I	Centuries after the prophet Isaiah, yet with the same spirit of consecration and dedication, came William Booth
DIVISION II	A youthful son of Nottingham, whose fiery, compassionate soul was stirred by the need of the sin-stricken, drink-sodden crowds of nineteenth century England.
QUARTET	From that compassion sprang the will to accomplish; and, by the grace of God, The Salvation Army came into being. Nations of the world felt the glow of it and opened their doors in welcome and invitation. Today, the Army work is known in all parts of the globe.

SOLO Il (M)	We salute the Salvationism of the pioneers who went into the unknown that they might carry the light of the knowledge of the glory of God in the face of Jesus to the uttermost parts of the earth.
ALL	They bore hardship and loneliness. They knew suffering and heartache.
DIVISION I	But they endured with patience
DIVISION II	They toiled until the closing of the day.
ALL	Theirs is the glory.
QUARTET	Ours the heritage. We will not shirk, nor falter, but enter proudly into our heritage. For we too, the youth of this day and generation, have heard the voice which said:
SOLO I (M)	"Whom shall I send, and who will go for us?"
ALL	And we have answered:
	(Appoint members of group to do these Solos)
SOLO	Here am I...
SOLO	And I...
SOLO	And I...
SOLO	And I...
SOLO	Send me...
SOLO	And me...
ALL	Here am I...send me!

Scripture Selection: Isaiah 6:1-7

WITNESS TO THE LIGHT

ALL	And darkness was upon the face of the deep.
SOLO (M)	Darkness - deep, black darkness!
ALL	And God said, "Let there be light!"
SOLO (W)	And there was light!
DIVISION I	Light! Penetrating the darkness.
DIVISION II	Light! Dispelling the darkness.
ALL	And God saw the light that it was good.
DIVISION I	But men loved darkness -
DIVISION II	Men loved darkness.
SOLO	Kings loved darkness
SOLO	Nations loved darkness
SOLO	Leaders loved darkness
SOLO	The World loved darkness
DIVISION I	And the light shineth in the darkness
DIVISION II	And the darkness comprehended it not
QUARTET	And this is the condemnation that light is come into the world.
DIVISION I	And men loved darkness rather than light
DIVISION II	Because their deeds were evil
SOLO	Evil
SOLO	Hateful
SOLO	Dishonest
SOLO	Lustful
SOLO	Jealous
SOLO	Envious
SOLO	Disbelieving
QUARTET	Behold darkness covered the earth, and gross darkness the people
ALL	But the people that walk in darkness have seen a great light
SOLO	Revealing the way
DIVISION I	Arise and shine for thy light is come
DIVISION II	And the glory of the Lord is risen upon thee.

SOLO	Then spake Jesus, "I am the light of the world; he that followeth me shall not walk in darkness, but shall have the light of life"
DUET	Walk as children of the light; walk worthy of the Lord.
TRIO	Who hath delivered us from the power of darkness
ALL	Walk in the light as He is in the light
QUARTET	Let your light shine before men that they may see your good works and glorify your Father which is in Heaven.
DIVISION I	Witness to the light!
DIVISION II	Speak for the light!
ALL	Live in the light. For the Lord is our Light.

Scripture: Genesis 1:2,3,18; John 3:19; John 1:5; Isa. 60:1; Isa. 9:2; John 8:12; Eph. 5:8; Col. 1:10,13; 1 John 1:7; Matt. 5:16

THE WORSHIPER

QUARTET (M)	One day a man went from his home, his office, his factory, his fields, his school, to express his faith, and commune with his God, in the house of the Lord.
TRIO (W)	As he was worshiping the world the thought he had left out-side was not out-of-mind.
QUARTET (M)	Voices kept calling him; interrupting, disrupting, arresting, pulling the check string of his worship.
TRIO (W)	To worship in spirit and truth is not easy in our world.
ALL	It is never easy to meditate in worship. Always there are the voices of the world.
SOLO I (Worshiper)	Lord, you are in your holy temple. Lord, let the world keep silence before you.
QUARTET	Voices fill the silence and trigger one thought after another.
VOICES	Watch the time you haven't got all day... Sally's dental appointment... Telephone Andy... A 20 page term paper... Pick up the cleaning... Write a letter to mother... Will they lower the taxes... I forgot to take my aspirin... And...on...and on..and ON
QUARTET	"Be still and know that I am God!"
SOLO I (Worshiper)	Quiet my mind, Lord. Keep me still...don't let the clatter of my mind rob me of the stillness. Voices! Voices! Will they never stop calling?
VOICES	Tonight is the Little League game... You promised Ralph to go bowling... I'd rather go to McDonald's... The church finance committee meets tomorrow... I must make the bank deposit this afternoon... Mary needs the car... There's a good TV program tonight...
SOLO I	It's happening again. All these lesser things are pushing you out Lord. Will the voices never be still?
QUARTET	This book of the law shall not depart out of thy mouth, but thou shalt meditate therein day and night.
ALL	It isn't easy to worship, to pray in our world...it never was easy.

DIVISION I	You can't stop the mental motion
DIVISION II	The mind loves to flit from one thing to another.
QUARTET	You can control the jumps!
TRIO	You can channel your thoughts.
QUARTET	Take a new approach!
TRIO	Take corrective measures!
DIVISION I	Jot down your intrusions and return to your reading and praying. Develop prayer habits.
DIVISION II	Make a prayer list and let it pull you back when your mind begins to wander.
QUARTET	"In quietness and confidence shall be your strength."
SOLO I	The world is ever present with us. Yet, the world is a Christian's concern.
ALL	"Pray without ceasing!"
	"The effectual fervent prayer of a righteous man availeth much."
	"Wait on the Lord, be of good courage, and He shall strengthen thy heart."
SOLO I	One tries to get away from the world...and the worshiper cries out.
ALL	*(This could be a vocal solo)* There is a place of quiet rest Near to the heart of God A place where all is joy and peace Near to the heart of God. O, Jesus, blest Redeemer Sent from the heart of God, Hold us who wait before Thee Near to the heart of God.

(C.B. McAfee - Salvation Army Song Book #973)

Scripture Selections: Psa. 46:10; Joshua 1:8; Isaiah 30:15;

1 Thess. 5:17; James 5:16; Psa. 27:14

Choral Speech

Selections for
Special Occasions

BUT HE CAME

ALL	And the Word became flesh and dwelt among us.
SOLO	Christ became a human being and lived here on earth among us, and was full of forgiveness and truth. (L.B.)
ALL	He didn't have to come.
DIVISION I	He didn't have to come.
DIVISION II	But He came!
ALL	He came because He loved a lost humanity.
TRIO	I am come a light into the world.
QUARTET	That whosoever believeth in me shall not walk in darkness.
ALL	But shall have the light of life!
SOLO	He didn't have to come.
ALL	He was the Father's Son.
SOLO	This is my beloved son in whom I am well pleased.
ALL	He didn't have to come.
QUARTET	But He came to die that you and I might be set free.
DUET	If the Son of man therefore shall make you free--
TRIO	Ye shall be free indeed!
DIVISION I	He didn't have to be born of Mary,
DIVISION II	He didn't have to leave His Father's house,
ALL	He didn't have to come,
SOLO	But He came to die that you and I might be set free.
DIVISION I	The Son of man is come ....
DUET	To seek ....
TRIO	And to save ....
DIVISION II	That which is lost.
ALL	He didn't have to come.
SOLO	But He took upon Himself the form of sinful man,
DIVISION I	Born in a cattle stall,
DIVISION II	He was the Lord of all;
QUARTET	But with humble birth He came to earth.
SOLO	In Bethlehem

Christmas

DIVISION I	He didn't have to be laid in a manger
DIVISION II	He didn't have to be a carpenter's boy.
SOLO I (M)	For unto you is born this day in the city of David a Saviour which is Christ the Lord.
SOLO II (W)	And ye shall find the babe wrapped in swaddling clothes and lying in a manger.
ALL	He didn't have to come. He was the Father's Son.
DIVISION I	But He came to sacrifice His life for you and me.
DIVISION II	He didn't have to die.
QUARTET	But He freely gave Himself a ransom for our sin.
TRIO	Such love the Saviour shared, more precious than pure gold,
DUET	For He suffered, died, and bore the shame of guilty men.
ALL	The Son of man came to give His life a ransom for many.
SOLO	He didn't have to come,
ALL	But He came!
DIVISION I	He didn't have to be born of Mary,
DIVISION II	He didn't have to leave his Father's house,
ALL	He didn't have to come. He was the Father's Son....
SOLO (W)	His only Son
DIVISION I	He didn't have to come!
DIVISION II	He didn't have to come!
ALL	But He came!!
SOLO (M)	I am come that ye might have life and that ye might have it more abundantly.

Selections from the Gospels

Adapted from the Anthem "He Didn't Have To Come" (Boelinger)

158

CHRISTMAS IS OVER!

ALL	It's over! Christmas is over.
SOLO	The little town of Bethlehem is quiet.
DIVISION I	The travelers have all gone home.
DIVISION II	The stable is empty, the glory is gone.
WOMEN	The sky echoes no glad refrain.
MEN	The shepherds have returned to their sheep.
SOLO	Was it all a crazy dream, or could it be the shepherd's wild imagination?
ALL	It's over! Christmas is over.
MEN	Has the prophecy really been fulfilled?
WOMEN	Has anything really changed?
SOLO	After a night with the angels, it isn't easy to return to being "just" a shepherd.
QUARTET	"Just" a shepherd, you say; we will never be just shepherds again.
SOLO	Can one be touched by a heavenly glory, and life remain unchanged?
ALL	It's over! Christmas is over.
DIVISION I	We have taken down the Christmas tree.
DIVISION II	We have carefully wrapped each precious decoration.
DIVISION I	We have put away the manger scene.
DIVISION II	We have tenderly enfolded in soft cotton, the baby Jesus.
SOLO	Is it all over? Is Christmas over? Is Christmas something we wrap up, and put away until next year?
ALL	No, it's not all over! Christmas is not over.
DIVISION I	Christmas is an essence you carry with you every day.
DIVISION II	It is a divine experience that pervades our living.
QUARTET	It is a spirit of loving, of sharing, of giving.
SOLO	Christmas is never over!
ALL	For Christmas is wrapped up and put away in the heart!

EMMANUEL

ALL	Emmanuel! God is with us!
DIVISION I	Emmanuel! We are not alone.
DIVISION II	Emmanuel! God is really with us.
Vocal Solo	O come, O come Emmanuel, and ransom captive Israel That mourns in lonely exile here Until the Son of God appears
ALL	Emmanuel - what wonderful news; God came down to us.
DIVISION I	God really cares!
DIVISION II	Cared enough to send his only Son.
ALL	Emmanuel! A Jesus of flesh and blood came down to us.
DIVISION I	Emmanuel - a presence to walk beside us.
DIVISION II	Emmanuel - real enough to hold my trembling hands.
ALL	Jesus - God - Emmanuel; a warm companion, a living friend.
Vocal Solo	Rejoice! Rejoice! Emmanuel Shall come to thee, O Israel.
SOLO (M)	Rejoice! The good news is that "God with us" is for all time.
SOLO (W)	Rejoice! It is true; Emmanuel lives in our hearts today!
DIVISION I	Emmanuel is always with us.
DIVISION II	Emmanuel is never absent, no not for moment.
ALL	Emmanuel! He loves, he cares, he understands, he comforts. He is everywhere. He is in all things. Emmanuel, the one-alongside-us.
Vocal Solo	O come, O come Emmanuel, and cheer Our spirits by Thine advent here Disperse the gloomy cloud of night And death's dark shadows put to flight. Rejoice! Rejoice! Emmanuel Shall come to thee, O Israel
QUARTET	Arise, shine, for thy light is come!
DIVISION I	God in us is calling us to healing light.
DIVISION II	God in us is calling us to share His bright light.
SOLO (M)	A world in darkness needs His light and love.
DIVISION I	We must not only love the God in us
DIVISION II	We must be the love of God in us.

Christmas

ALL	God comes! Praise Him! He is here. Declare Him!
SOLO (W)	He has made us like himself. He has stamped his image on our hearts.
ALL	Emmanuel has come again. Rejoice! He comes now.
DIVISION I	God is still with us!
DIVISION II	We will honor him with our body, mind, and spirit.
ALL	Emmanuel! He is with us. He lives in us.
SOLO (M)	We will live for him!
SOLO (W)	We will do His will!
ALL	Rejoice! Rejoice! Emmanuel He comes. He is here. Praise Him!

REJOICE! MESSIAH COMES

ALL	Comfort ye, comfort ye my people, saith your God.
DIVISION I	Speak ye comfortably to Jerusalem.
DIVISION II	Cry unto her that her warfare is accomplished, that her iniquity is pardoned.
SOLO (M)	The voice of him that crieth in the wilderness, "Prepare ye the way of the Lord, make straight in the desert a highway for our God."
DIVISION I	Every valley shall be exalted, and every mountain and hill made low.
DIVISION II	The crooked shall be made straight, and the rough places plain.
ALL	And the glory of the Lord shall be revealed, and all flesh shall see it together; for the mouth of the Lord hath spoken it.
QUARTET	And he shall purify the sons of Levi, that they may offer unto the Lord an offering in righteousness.
SOLO (W)	Behold, a virgin shall conceive, and bear a Son, and shall call his name EMMANUEL, God with us.
DIVISION I	O thou that tellest good tidings to Zion, get thee up into the high mountain.
DIVISION II	O thou that tellest good tidings to Jerusalem, lift up thy voice with strength.
QUARTET	Lift it up, be not afraid; say unto the cities of Judah, behold your God!
ALL	Arise shine, for thy light is come, and the glory of the Lord is risen upon thee.
SOLO (W)	For unto us a Child is born, unto us a Son is given, and the government shall be upon His shoulder.
SOLO (M)	And His name shall be called Wonderful Counselor, the Mighty God, the Everlasting Father, the Prince of Peace.
ALL	Rejoice greatly, O daughter of Zion; shout, O daughter of Jerusalem: behold thy king cometh unto thee.
QUARTET	He is the righteous Saviour, and He shall speak peace unto the heathen.
DIVISION I	Then shall the eyes of the blind be opened, and the ears of the deaf unstopped;
DIVISION II	Then shall the lame man leap as an hart, and the tongue of the dumb shall sing.

Christmas

DIVISION I	He shall feed His flock like a shepherd; and He shall gather the lambs with His arm,
DIVISION II	And He shall carry them in His bosom, and gently lead those that are with young.
SOLO (M)	Come unto Him, all ye that labour and are heavy laden, and He shall give you rest.
SOLO (W)	Take His yoke upon you, and learn of Him; for He is meek and lowly of heart and ye shall find rest unto your souls.
ALL	HALLELUJAH! For the Lord God omnipotent reigneth.
QUARTET	The kingdom of this world is become the kingdom of our Lord, and of His Christ and he shall reign for ever and ever.
ALL	KING OF KINGS, AND LORD OF LORDS, HALLELUJAH!

Scripture: Isa. 40; Isa. 7:14; Isa. 60:1; Isa. 9:6; Zech. 9:9,10; Isa. 35:5,6; Matt. 11:28; Rev. 19:6,16; Rev. 11:15

NO ROOM

MIXED VOICES	In the days of Caesar Augustus a decree went out that all the world should be taxed. And all went to be taxed every one to his own city.
SOLO (W)	So Joseph, who was a carpenter, went up from Galilee, out of the city of Nazareth into Judea, unto the city of David which is called Bethlehem.
SOLO (M)	And Mary, his wife, went with him. It was evening when they came to the Inn at Bethlehem.
	(Enter Joseph and Mary - Mary sits on stool- Joseph goes to door - Inn keeper appears - Shakes his head "NO" and points for Joseph to be gone) SOLO No Room!
TRIO (Men slowly)	No room, no room! Sorry, there is no room!
DUET	No room, no room! The Inn is full.
SOLO	No, no room for Mary or the carpenter, Joseph.
	(Joseph helps Mary to rise and supports her as they exit right)
WOMEN	The Inn is full.
MEN	No, no room.
TRIO	There is no room.
MEN	No, no room!
SEVERAL SOLOS	Try somewhere else... This Inn is full... Don't you see the crowd... Go on to the next town... No room here, just move on... There isn't room for one more person Move on...move on... No! no room No room...unless? There is the stable It is clean...
SOLO (W)	Mary brought forth her first born son and wrapped him in swaddling clothes and laid him in a manger. And she called his name "JESUS" for he shall save the people from their sins.
SOLO (M)	If in our world today Joseph walked our way looking for a place where the Christ could be born, would he find many of us saying, "There is no room - no room for anyone else..."?
DUET	No room for anything more
DIVISION I	Christmas is just so much rush...

Christmas

SOLO	Cards, presents, ribbons, candles, candies, tinsel, trinkets, turkey, cranberries
DIVISION II	There just isn't any room, for anything more!
TRIO	Busy, busy, busy!
MEN	Rush, rush, rush
DUET	Hurry, hurry, hurry.
SOLO	There is no time for the Christ of Christmas.
ALL	No room, no room, for the Child of Bethlehem.
SOLO	No room for the spirit of love - No room for the spirit of Christ.
ALL	No room, no room, there is no room today for Jesus
SOLO	No room, for the message of Faith in this weary, sin-sick world.
ALL	No room, no room for the Faith of Christmas
TRIO	No room for faith!
MEN	No room for the hope and goodwill the Christ Child brings.
DIVISION I	No, no room today for Love, for Faith, for Hope or Goodwill.
DIVISION II	No room for the peace, the calm, the quietness of Christmas...
ALL	No room today. Is there no room for Jesus?
Sing Chorus	"Room for Jesus, King of Glory Hasten now His Word obey Swing your heart's door widely open Bid Him enter while you may.

Song Book #241
(Daniel W. Whittle)
Scripture Selection: Luke 2

WHY, A STAR?

ALL	"For God so loved the world that He gave His only begotten Son that whosoever believeth in Him, should not perish but have everlasting life."
SOLO I (M)	"In Him was life and the life was the light of men."
TRIO	Love and light came down at Christmas
SOLO (W)	Love so lovely...
SOLO (M)	Light Divine!
DIVISION I	Ever since God created man in His own image...
DIVISION II	God has longed for man to know Him
SOLO (W)	Truly know Him...
DUET	And love Him...
TRIO	And commune with Him...
QUARTET	And be His very own.
ALL	"And the light shineth in the darkness, and the darkness comprehended it not."
SOLO (M)	"And the Light came unto His own, and His own received Him not."
ALL	Again and again man has turned aside...
DIVISION I	And closed his ears
DIVISION II	And hardened his heart
DIVISION I	And disobeyed
DIVISION II	And gone away from God.
SOLO (M)	"The people that walked in darkness have seen a great light."
SOLO (W)	"For God who commanded the light to shine out of darkness, hath shined in our hearts."
SOLO (M)	No, God never becomes discouraged!
DIVISION I	Amid all the clamor and confusion
DIVISION II	Of people seeking selfish goals
SOLO (M)	God spoke!
DUET	"And when the fulness of time was come
TRIO	God sent forth His son"
QUARTET	"And the light became flesh and dwelt among us."
SOLO (W)	And Lo, a star appeared in the East

Christmas

DIVISION I	"Arise and shine for the light is come
DIVISION II	And the glory of the Lord is risen upon thee."
ALL	"The Dayspring from on high hath visited us."
SOLO (W)	Why, a Star?
ALL	To herald the Prince of Light!
DIVISION I	"We have also a more sure word of prophecy
ALL	Whereunto ye do well that ye take heed,
DIVISION II	As unto a light that shineth in a dark place,
SOLO (W)	Until the day dawn
SOLO (M)	And the Day Star arise in your heart.
ALL	Following a star is never easy
DUET	We're so self-willed...
TRIO	So self-determined...
QUARTET	So self-scheming...
DIVISION I	One never knows what will happen when one follows a star.
DIVISION II	But follow it we must!
SOLO (M)	"For they that be wise shall shine as the brightness of the firmament
ALL	And they that turn many to righteousness as the stars forever and ever."
SOLO (M)	For Jesus said, "I am the light of the world: he that followeth me shall not walk in darkness, but shall have the light of life."
SOLO (W)	"Behold what manner of love the Father hath bestowed on us."
ALL	Love and Light came down at Christmas!

Scripture Selections: John 3:16, John 1:3, John 1:5, John 1:11, Isa. 9:2, 2 Cor. 4:6, John 1:14, Isa. 60:1, Luke 1:78, 2 Peter 1:19, Daniel 12:3, John 8:12, I John 3:1

THE BLESSING

SOLO I (M)	The earth is the Lord's
ALL	And the fullness thereof;
SOLO I (M)	The world,
ALL	And they that dwell therein.
DIVISION I	For He hath founded it upon the seas _
DIVISION II	And established it upon the floods.
SOLO I (W)	Who shall ascend into the hill of the Lord?
SOLO II (W)	Who shall stand in His holy place?
DIVISION I	He that hath clean hands
DIVISION II	And a pure heart;
QUARTET	Who hath not lifted up his soul unto vanity,
TRIO	Nor sworn deceitfully.
DIVISION I	He shall receive the blessing of the Lord,
DIVISION II	And righteousness from the God of His salvation.
SOLO I (M)	Lift up your heads, oh ye gates;
SOLO II (M)	Be ye lifted up ye everlasting doors.
ALL	And the King of Glory shall come in!
SOLO I (M)	Who is this King of Glory?
DIVISION I	The Lord strong and mighty!
DIVISION II	The Lord mighty in battle!
SOLO II (M)	Lift up your heads, oh ye gates!
QUARTET	And the King of Glory shall come in!
SOLO I (M)	Who is this King of Glory?
ALL	The Lord of hosts, He is the King of Glory!

Selections from Psalm 24

GOLGOTHA

SOLO I (W)	Then Pilate...took Jesus...and scourged Him.
QUARTET	And the soldiers platted a crown of thorns and put it on His head, and they put on Him a purple robe, and said,
MEN	Hail, King of the Jews!
QUARTET	And they smote Him with their hands.
SOLO I (W)	Then said Pilate to the Chief Priests, and the people,
SOLO II(M)	I find no fault in this man.
ALL	Blasphemer! King of the Jews!
SOLO I (M)	He stirreth up the people!
ALL	He stirreth up the people!
SOLO II (M)	I will chastise Him, and release Him.
DIVISION I	Away with this Man!
SOLO I (W)	He is good and holy.
DIVISION II	Away with this Man!
SOLO I (M)	He would destroy the temple!
DUET (M)	Release unto us Barabbas!
ALL	Release unto us Barabbas!
SOLO II (M)	What shall ye then that I shall do unto Him whom ye call King of the Jews?
SOLO I (M)	Crucify Him!
SOLO I (W)	He healed our sick
SOLO II (M)	Crucify Him!
SOLO III (M)	He made me see
ALL	Crucify Him! Crucify Him!
SOLO III (M)	Why? What evil hath He done?
SOLO II (M)	He is a deceiver!
DIVISION I	Crucify Him!
DIVISION II	Crucify Him!
QUARTET	Then came Jesus forth, wearing the crown of thorns and the purple robe.
SOLO I (W)	And Pilate said unto them,
SOLO II (M)	Behold, your King!

Easter

DIVISION I	Away with Him!
DIVISION II	Away with Him!
SOLO I (M)	Come on soldier, use that whip!
ALL	Crucify Him! Crucify Him!
SOLO II (M)	Shall I crucify your King?
DIVISION I	We have no King but Caesar!
DIVISION II	Bah! Look at Him - He said he could call a legion of angels,
ALL	We have no King but Caesar!
SOLO I (M)	Away with this man!
SOLO II (M)	Crucify Him!
SOLO 3,4,5	(Spoken in rapid succession) Crucify Him! Crucify Him! Crucify Him!
DIVISION I	Crucify Him!
DIVISION II	Crucify Him!
ALL	Crucify Him!
TRIO	And they took Jesus and led Him away.
QUARTET	And He bearing His cross went forth unto a place of a skull, which is called in the Hebrew, Golgotha.
ALL	For God commendeth His love toward us in that while we were yet sinners Christ died for us.

Scripture Selections: Matt. 27; Luke 23; John 19

THE LAMB OF GOD

SOLO I (M)	Who hath believed our report?
SOLO I (W)	To whom is the arm of the Lord revealed?
MEN	He is despised and rejected of men;
WOMEN	A Man of sorrows and acquainted with grief.
DUET	He was despised and we esteemed Him not.
TRIO	He was wounded for our transgressions,
QUARTET	He was bruised for our iniquities,
DIVISION I	The chastisement of our peace was upon Him,
DIVISION II	And with His stripes we are healed.
MEN	He was oppressed
WOMEN	And He was afflicted
SOLO II (M)	Yet He openeth not His mouth.
DIVISION I	He is brought as a lamb to the slaughter
DIVISION II	And as a sheep before her shearers is dumb
SOLO II (M)	So He openeth not His mouth.
ALL	All we like sheep have gone astray,
SOLO I (M)	We have turned every one to his own way.
ALL	The Lord hath laid on Him the iniquity of us all.
QUARTET	For God so loved the world
SOLO I (W)	That He gave His only begotten Son
DIVISION I	That whosoever believeth in Him
DIVISION II	Should not perish
ALL	But have everlasting life.

Selections from Isaiah 53; John 3

OUR SAVIOR

ALL	And there shall come forth a Rod out of the stem of Jesse
SOLO I (M)	And a Branch shall grow out of its roots.
DIVISION I	And the Spirit of the Lord shall rest upon Him.
TRIO	The spirit of wisdom and understanding
QUARTET (M)	The spirit of counsel and might -
TRIO	The spirit of knowledge and the fear of the Lord.
DIVISION II	And He shall not judge after the sight of His eyes, neither reprove after the hearing of His ears.
SOLO II (M)	But with righteousness shall He judge
SOLO II (W)	And reprove with equity.
ALL	Then said Jesus,
SOLO I (M)	Father, forgive them for they know not what they do.
SOLO I (W)	Behold, the day of the Lord cometh.
QUARTET	In that day there shall be a fountain opened in the house of David for sin and for uncleanness.
DIVISION I	God hath made Him, Who knew no sin, to be sin for us,
DIVISION II	That we might be made the righteousness of God in Him.
ALL	We pray you, in Christ's stead, be ye reconciled to God.

Selections from Isaiah 11; Zechariah 13 and 14; Luke 23; II Corinthians 5

HEARTFELT THANKSGIVING

DIVISION I	Though I offer my Thanksgiving in November
DIVISION II	But forget that each day merits my thanks,
ALL	I am at heart ungrateful.
SOLO I (W)	And though I praise Thanksgiving as a noble tradition
SOLO I (M)	And desire it should be observed by all
SOLO II (W)	But by my life express no devotion to God or thoughtfulness to others
ALL	I am not really grateful.
DIVISION I	And though I have a great family feast
DIVISION II	And share a bit with the needy,
SOLO II (M)	But my heart is dutiful or smug,
ALL	I am still ungrateful.
DIVISION I	Thanksgiving of the heart doth magnify the Lord,
TRIO (W)	Is never an occasion for pride or idle boasting.
DIVISION II	Thanksgiving of the heart is not selfish,
QUARTET (M)	Nor unmindful of the needs of others;
SOLO I (M)	Never wearies of service,
TRIO (W)	Thanksgiving of the heart is not fretful, but always glad,
SOLO I (W)	Lightens our burdens,
SOLO II (M)	Deepens our joys,
SOLO I (M)	Sustains our faith,
SOLO II (W)	Heals our sorrows.
ALL	Thanksgiving of the heart never fails,
DUET	But whether there be possessions, they shall fail;
TRIO	But whether there be privileges, they shall cease;
QUARTET	But whether there be freedom, it may vanish away;
ALL	But Thanksgiving of the heart always triumphs!
DIVISION I	For what worldly goods denied
DIVISION II	Thanksgiving of the heart offered greater happiness.
SOLO I (M)	What life made seem futile
QUARTET (M)	Thanksgiving of the heart made purposeful.
SOLO I (W)	What circumstances made insurmountable,

Thanksgiving

QUARTET (M)	Thanksgiving of the heart gave conquering power.
ALL	And now abideth
DUET	Thanksgiving of the Mind,
TRIO	Thanksgiving of the Purse,
QUARTET	Thanksgiving of the Heart...
ALL	But the greatest of these is Thanksgiving of the Heart!

A Paraphrase of I Corinthians 13

THANKSGIVING

SOLO I (M)	O give thanks unto the Lord, for He is good,
TRIO	For His mercy endures forever.
SOLO I (M)	O give thanks unto the God of gods
SOLO II (W)	Forever -
DUET	For His mercy endures.
SOLO I (M)	O give thanks to the Lord of lords - to Him Who alone does great wonders -
SOLO II (W)	Forever
DUET	His mercy endures
SOLO II (M)	Forever.
SOLO I (W)	To Him that stretched out the earth above the waters,
TRIO	For His mercy endures forever.
	(Background TRIO - Softly)
TRIO	Mercy...Forever.
SOLO I (W)	To Him that stretched out the earth above the waters - To Him that made great lights - The sun to rule by day, the moon and stars to rule by night -
ALL	*(Crescendo)* For His mercy endures forever!
SOLO I (M)	O magnify the Lord with me and let us exalt His Name
ALL	Forever.
SOLO II (W)	I will bless the Lord at all times,
SOLO III (W)	His praise shall continually be in my mouth.
SOLO IV (W)	My soul shall make her boast in the Lord,
ALL	For His mercy endures
SOLO I (W)	Forever -
TRIO	*(Background)* Mercy...Forever.
SOLO I (M)	Bless the Lord, oh my soul; and all that is within me, bless His Holy Name.
	Bless the Lord, oh my soul; and forget not all His benefits, Who forgives all your iniquities, Who heals all your diseases, Who redeems your life from destruction, Who crowns you with lovingkindness and tender mercies -
TRIO	For His mercy endures forever.

Thanksgiving

SOLO I (W)	Bless the Lord, all servants of the Lord - which by night stand in the house of the Lord. Lift up your hands in the sanctuary
SOLO III (W)	And bless...and bless
SOLO II (M)	The Lord -
SOLO IV (W)	And bless the Lord -
TRIO	For His mercy endures forever.
SOLO I (W)	The Lord -
TRIO	Forever -
SOLO I (M)	That made Heaven and earth
TRIO	Forever -
SOLO I (W)	Bless Him...Bless the Lord
TRIO	Forever!
ALL	Bless the Lord...He is good. Bless the Lord, forever.

Selections from Psalms 136; 34; 103

AN OVERFLOWING HEART

ALL	Bless the Lord, O my soul: Bless the Lord,
SOLO I (M)	And all that is within me
ALL	Bless His Holy Name.
DIVISION I	Bless the Lord, O my soul
DIVISION II	And forget not all His benefits
SOLO I (M)	Who forgives all our iniquities,
QUARTET	Who heals all our diseases,
SOLO I (W)	Who redeems our life from destruction,
QUARTET	Who crowns us with lovingkindness and tender mercies,
SOLO I (W)	Who satisfies our mouth with good things;
ALL	Bless...Bless...Yes, Bless the Lord!
QUARTET	So that our youth is renewed like the eagle's.
QUARTET	The Lord executes righteousness
TRIO	And judgment for all that are oppressed.
DIVISION I	He made known His ways to Moses,
DIVISION II	His acts to the children of Israel.
TRIO	The Lord is merciful and gracious,
SOLO I (M)	Very gracious...and slow to anger,
SOLO II (W)	Very merciful...and plenteous in mercy.
DIVISION I	He will not always chide,
DIVISION II	Neither will He keep His anger forever.
DIVISION I	He has not dealt with us after our sins,
DIVISION II	Nor rewarded us according to our iniquities
TRIO	For as the heaven is high above the earth,
ALL	So great is His mercy toward them that fear Him;
TRIO	As far as the east is from the west.
ALL	So far has He removed our transgressions from us.

Selections from Psalm 103

PRAISE HIM IN HIS SANCTUARY

ALL	Praise ye the Lord.
SOLO (M)	Praise God in His sanctuary.
DIVISION I	Praise Him in the firmament of His power.
DIVISION II	Praise Him for His mighty acts;
ALL	Praise Him according to His excellent greatness.
SOLO (M)	Praise Him with trumpet sound.
SOLO (W)	Praise Him with psaltery and harp.
TRIO (W)	Praise Him with timbrel and dance;
SOLO (W)	Praise Him with loud cymbals,
ALL	Make a joyful noise unto the Lord, all ye lands.
DIVISION I	Serve the Lord with gladness;
DIVISION II	Come before His presence with singing.
SOLO (M)	Know ye that the Lord He is God.
DIVISION I	It is He that hath made us
DIVISION II	And we are His.
ALL	Praise ye the Lord.

Scripture Selection: Psalm 150

The Litany

THE LITANY

The repetition of an idea or the balancing of one idea against another, as is achieved in the litany, adds beauty and variety to our worship.

This antiphonal form of expression will add a dimension to the interpretation of a thought or scripture passage that is not achieved in other forms of worship. The rhythm, the emphasis, the contrast of a phrase or a sentence in the refrain strengthens meaning.

The litany, then, is a series of statements or scripture by a leader which is followed by a repetitive response from the congregation.

When preparing a litany the element of effectiveness is achieved by securing a sincere, convincing response concept which although it is repetitive, it will not be monotonous.

A litany can take the following forms:
    A Litany of Supplication
    A Litany of Praise
    A Litany of Adoration
    A Litany of Confession
    A Litany of Thanksgiving
    A Litany of Faith
    A Litany of Gratitude
    A Litany of Compassion or Social Concern

There are many resources for the Litany:
    Literature
        Poetry
            The Salvation Army Song Book
                The Bible
                    Hymns
                        Books of prepared litanies.

Some of the songs in the Salvation Army Song Book that are adaptable to this form of responsive worship are listed below. The Leader reads the statement in the verse and the congregation responds with the repetitive phrase or line.
Songs - 28, 56, 243, 247, 300, 460, 571, 608, and 973

ARRANGING TOMORROW

LEADER	Let us resolve in this New Year to look ahead and go forward with faith.
ALL	Help us Lord, as we resolve to reach up to you.
LEADER	Closing the gate on the past we will not worry about what is past and gone.
ALL	Help us Lord as we resolve to reach up to you.
LEADER	Learning something new every day will enrich our mind and spirit; a verse of scripture, an inspirational poem, a sentence of a new truth.
ALL	Help us Lord, as we resolve to reach up to you.
LEADER	A good Christian should excel in all virtues. May Christ be the pattern for our life style so that we may be like him, in outward practice and appearance each day.
ALL	Help us Lord, as we resolve to reach up to you.
LEADER	Forgiving old grudges and those who have hurt and wronged us, we will seek to heal the breach.
ALL	Help us Lord, as we resolve to reach out to others.
LEADER	Expressing appreciation more often, we will say "thank you" and not take services for granted. Writing little thank you notes will help us and help others.
ALL	Help us Lord, as we reach out to others.
LEADER	Most of us talk too much and listen too little. For people who are burdened, anxious, hurting, lonely make us a good listener.
ALL	Help us Lord, as we resolve to reach out to others.
LEADER	Foregoing some personal pleasure, we will go out of our way to do something to help others and make their day brighter.
ALL	Help us Lord, as we resolve to reach out to others.

AWARENESS

LEADER   Dear Son of God, because you came into the world to reveal to us the Father,

RESPONSE   Open our eyes that in Thy life we may see God, the Father.

LEADER   We believe that you are the Revealer of Truth

RESPONSE   Open our minds that we may be aware of your presence and be strangely drawn to You.

LEADER   We are glad that you walked the highways and byways of Galilee, and knew the weariness of the journey,

RESPONSE   Open our hearts and make us sensitive to your invitation "Come unto Me, and I will give you rest."

LEADER   We rejoice that you were not a stranger to toil and labor.

RESPONSE   Open our spirits to the strength and courage we can find in You.

LEADER   We praise you, dear Son of God, that your voice still echoes through all time, "If I be lifted up, I will draw all men unto me."

RESPONSE   Open our lives, make us aware, help us to catch Your Spirit, and pattern our lives after the Truth you came to reveal.

COME, MY LORD

LEADER   O disclose Thy lovely face!
            Quicken all my drooping powers;
            Gasps my fainting soul for grace
            As a thirsty land for showers.

RESPONSE   Come my Lord, no more delay.

LEADER   Dark and cheerless is the morn
            Unaccompanied by Thee;
            Joyless is the day's return
            Till Thy mercy's beams I see,

RESPONSE   Come my Lord, with inward light.

LEADER   Visit then, this soul of mine,
            Pierce the gloom of sin and grief;
            Fill me, Radiance divine,
            Scatter all my unbelief;

RESPONSE   Come my Lord, Thyself display.

Salvation Army Song Book #412

CREATION

LEADER   All things bright and beautiful,
             All creatures great and small,
             All things wise and wonderful,

RESPONSE   The Lord God made them all.

LEADER   Each little flower that opens,
             Each little bird that sings,
             He made their glowing colors,
             He made their tiny wings;

RESPONSE   The Lord God made them all.

LEADER   The purpleheaded mountain,
             The river running by.
             The sunset, and the morning
             That brightens up the sky.

RESPONSE   The Lord God made them all.

LEADER   The cold wind in the winter
             The pleasant summer sun
             The ripe fruits in the garden,
             He made them every one.

RESPONSE   The Lord God made them all
             All things bright and beautiful
             All things wise and wonderful
             The Lord God made them all.

Salvation Army Song Book #25

A COMMITTED HEART

LEADER   O for a heart to praise my God,
A heart from sin set free,
A heart that always feels the Blood
So freely spilt for me!

RESPONSE   Give me a heart to praise my God

LEADER   A heart resigned, submissive, meek,
My great Redeemer's throne;
Where only Christ is heard to speak,
Where Jesus reigns alone.

RESPONSE   Give me a heart that talks to God.

LEADER   A humble, lowly, contrite heart,
Believing, true and clean;
Which neither life nor death can part
From Him that dwells within.

RESPONSE   Give me a committed, faithful heart.

LEADER   A heart in every thought renewed,
And full of love divine
Perfect and right, and pure and good,
A copy, Lord, of Thine.

RESPONSE   Give me a growing, loving heart.

Salvation Army Song Book #444

DISCIPLES IN THE MAKING

LEADER   In our doubts and uncertainty, grant us grace to ask what you would have us to do.

ALL   Mold us into well-formed disciples.

LEADER   In our darkness, may we see the light and walk in the path where your light is shining,

ALL   Mold us into well-formed disciples.

LEADER   Grant us quietness, confidence, and refreshment in your strength when we feel weary, tired, or burdened.

ALL   Mold us into well-formed disciples.

LEADER   May we not only believe in our hearts, but may we practice in our lives your truth.

ALL   Mold us into well-formed disciples.

GIVE THANKS AND SING

LEADER	O come, let us sing to the Lord. Let us come before His presence with thanksgiving.
ALL	Let us sing to the Lord and bless His name.
LEADER	Make a joyful noise to the Lord with psalms of praise, for the Lord is good.
ALL	Let us sing praises to the Lord.
LEADER	It is a good thing to give thanks to the Lord; for He satisfies the longing soul, and fills the hungry soul with goodness.
ALL	We will open our lips and show forth Thy praises.
LEADER	With grateful hearts we lift our voice in thanksgiving. We remember your loving kindness and tender mercies.
ALL	We praise you for every good and perfect gift.
LEADER	For the life you have given us, for aspiration and hope, for truth, and faith.
ALL	With glad service we will praise thee, O God.
LEADER	For beauty of nature, for day and night, for springtime and fall, for seedtime and harvest.
ALL	We praise thee, O God, for all the bounty of the earth.
LEADER	For the joy of living, the blessings of home and friends, for the support of love and understanding.
ALL	All praise and thanks to God the Father, and to the Son, and to the Holy Spirit.

Scripture Selections: Psa. 95:1,2; Psa. 107:8

GIVE US YOUR HOLY SPIRIT

LEADER

Make us one, Lord, in our desire
To worship and praise you.

RESPONSE

Give us your Holy Spirit.

LEADER

Make us one, Lord, in our awareness
Of your presence and your power.

RESPONSE

Give us your Holy Spirit.

LEADER

Make us one, Lord, in our task
Of spreading the gospel in highways and byways

RESPONSE

Give us your Holy Spirit.

LEADER

Make us one, Lord, in faithfully caring,
For the sick, the poor, the hurting. the needy

RESPONSE

Give us your Holy Spirit.

LEADER

Make us one, Lord, in capturing your Spirit
And patterning our lives after your truth.

RESPONSE

Give us your Holy Spirit.

GOD'S GREATNESS

LEADER   THINK OF GOD'S GREATNESS!
"Great is the Lord and greatly to be praised. His greatness is unsearchable."

HE IS GREAT IN POWER.
"Thou hast made the heaven and the earth by thy great power...there is nothing too hard for thee."

ALL   HE IS GREAT IN MERCY
"The Lord is gracious, and full of compassion...and of great mercy."

LEADER   HE IS GREAT IN SALVATION
"How shall we escape if we neglect so great salvation?"

ALL   HE IS GREAT IN GOODNESS
"How great is Thy goodness, which thou hast laid up for them that fear thee."

Scripture Selections: Psa. 31:19; Psa. 145:3,8; Jer. 32:17; Heb. 2:3

HALLOWED MOMENTS

LEADER	There are wants my heart is telling
RESPONSE	While the Spirit passes by,
LEADER	And with hope my soul is swelling
RESPONSE	While the Spirit passes by.
LEADER	O what prospects now I see, What a life my life must be If Thy seal is placed on me,
RESPONSE	While the Spirit passes by!
LEADER	Here I stand, myself disdaining,
RESPONSE	While the Spirit passes by;
LEADER	Stand in faith, Thy mercy claiming,
RESPONSE	While the Spirit passes by.
LEADER	Let Thy power my soul refine, Let Thy grace my will incline, Take my all and make it Thine,
RESPONSE	While the Spirit passes by.

Salvation Army Song Book #460

KING OF GLORY

LEADER	Who is He in yonder stall, At whose feet the shepherds fall?
RESPONSE	'Tis the Lord! O wondrous story, 'Tis the Lord! The King of Glory.
LEADER	Who is He in deep distress, Fasting in the wilderness?
RESPONSE	'Tis the Lord! O wondrous story, 'Tis the Lord, the King of Glory.
LEADER	Who is He to whom they bring All the sick and sorrowing?
RESPONSE	'Tis the Lord! O wondrous story, 'Tis the Lord, the King of Glory.
LEADER	Who is He on yonder tree, Dies in grief and agony?
RESPONSE	'Tis the Lord! O wondrous story 'Tis the Lord, the King of Glory.
LEADER	Who is He who from the grave Comes to succour, help and save?
RESPONSE	'Tis the Lord! O wondrous story, 'Tis the Lord, the King of Glory.
LEADER	Who is He who from His throne, Rules through all the worlds alone.
RESPONSE	'Tis the Lord! O wondrous story, 'Tis the Lord, the King of Glory, At His feet we humbly bow, Crown Him, Crown Him Lord of all!

Salvation Army Song Book #104

LET GOD BE BLESSED

LEADER   "It is a good thing to give thanks unto the Lord, and to sing praises unto thy name, O most high."

ALL   LET GOD BE BLESSED IN OUR PRAISE.

LEADER   "The effectual, fervent prayer of a righteous man availeth much."

ALL   LET GOD BE BLESSED IN OUR PRAYERS.

LEADER   "I will hear what God, the Lord will speak"

ALL   LET GOD BE BLESSED IN OUR HEARING.

LEADER   "For in God we live, and move; and have our being."

ALL   LET GOD BE BLESSED IN OUR LIVING.

Scripture Selections: Psa. 92:1; Jas. 5:16; Psa. 85:8; Acts 17:28

LIMITLESS LOVE

LEADER   Love divine, from Jesus flowing,
Living waters rich and free,
Wondrous love without a limit,
Flowing from eternity;

RESPONSE   Boundless ocean,
I would cast myself on thee.

LEADER   Love surpassing understanding,
Angels would the mystery scan,
Yet so tender that it reaches
To the lowest child of man.

RESPONSE   Let me, Jesus,
Fuller know redemption's plan.

LEADER   Love that pardons past transgression,
Love that cleanses every stain,
Love that fills to overflowing
Yet invites to drink again;

RESPONSE   Precious fountain,
Which to open Christ was slain.

LEADER   From my soul break every fetter,
Thee to know is all my cry;
Saviour, I am Thine for ever,
Thine I'll live and Thine I'll die,

RESPONSE   Only asking
More and more of love's supply.

Salvation Army Song Book #439

LORD, DIRECT ME

If I can teach and lead, serve and encourage, care and visit, and plan and create,

LORD, DIRECT ME

If I can make a visit to the sick, the elderly, the lonely, or welcome the newcomer to my neighborhood,

LORD, DIRECT ME

If I can show concern for the security and well-being of the family next door,

LORD, DIRECT ME

If I can make home a place of love, communication, and mutual helpfulness,

LORD, DIRECT ME

If I can be a part of a prayer team for the salvation of sinners, and the growth of the Corps,

LORD, DIRECT ME

If I can help to lead my community to be loyal to our nation's highest ideals of freedom and justice,

LORD, DIRECT ME

If I can live by my needs, and not my wants, so that others will not be denied Christ's Gospel

LORD, DIRECT ME

If I can be exemplary, honest, and trustworthy in our world today,

LORD, DIRECT ME

If I can work for peace and friendship to impede division and violence in our society,

LORD, DIRECT ME.

If I can show the spirit of Christ as I walk through the doors of opportunity that open to me,

LORD, DIRECT ME

LORD, I COME TO THEE

LEADER	With my sin and with my sorrow, With my dread of each tomorrow,
ALL	Lord, I come to Thee
LEADER	With my doubts and with my fears With the faults of bygone years, With my agony and tears
ALL	Lord, I come to Thee
LEADER	With my heart's desire and longing, With sad memories o'er me thronging,
ALL	Lord, I come to Thee
LEADER	Save and cleanse and purify, Make me fit to live or die, In Thy mercy hear my cry
ALL	O Lord, I come I come to Thee.

From the song by Erik Leidzen

MAGNIFY GOD

LEADER	Come let us walk in the light of the Lord, and He will teach us of His ways.
ALL	Let God be magnified.
LEADER	The Lord is gracious and merciful, slow to anger, and abounding in steadfast love.
ALL	Let God be magnified.
LEADER	Enter into His gates with thanksgiving and into His courts with praise.
ALL	Let God be magnified.
LEADER	Sing unto the Lord, talk ye of all His wondrous works.
ALL	Let God be magnified.

Scripture Selections: Isa. 2:5,3; Psa. 145:8; Psa. 100:4; Psa. 105:2

OUR PRAYER

Grant that we may endure hardness as a good soldier of Jesus Christ.

HEAR OUR PRAYER, O GOD

Remove from us all fear, all cowardice, all uncertainty, and give unto us that perfect love which casteth out fear.

HEAR OUR PRAYER, O GOD

Strengthened by Thy spirit, may we strive to follow in the steps of those great heroes of the past who counted not their own lives dear unto them.

HEAR OUR PRAYER, O GOD

Grant unto us the high gift of courage that we may follow daily the example of the Master.

HEAR OUR PRAYER, O GOD

PRAISE HIS NAME

LEADER   God that made the world and all things therein; He, being Lord of heaven and earth, dwells not in temples made with hands.

RESPONSE   God's name be praised.

LEADER   Neither is He served by men's hands, as though He needs anything, seeing He himself gives to all life, and breath, and all things.

RESPONSE   God's name be praised.

LEADER   He is not far from each one of us; for in Him we live, and move, and have our being.

RESPONSE   God's name be praised.

LEADER   He appointed the moon for a season; the sun knows His going down.

RESPONSE   God's name be praised.

LEADER   O Lord, my God, you are very great; you are clothed with honor and majesty: who covers yourself with light as a garment.

RESPONSE   God's name be praised.

LEADER   Who laid the foundations of the earth. You cover it with the deep as with a garment: the waters stood above the mountains. You have set a bound that they may not pass over; that they turn not again to cover the earth.

RESPONSE   God's name be praised.

LEADER   O Lord, how manifold are your works! In wisdom have you made them all; the earth is full of your riches.

RESPONSE   God's name be praised.

DOXOLOGY   Praise God, from whom all blessings flow;
Praise Him all creatures here below;
Praise Him above, ye heavenly host
Praise Father, Son, and Holy Ghost.

SCRIPTURE SELECTIONS: Acts 17:24,25; Acts 17:27,28; Psa.104:19;

Psa. 104:1; Psa. 104:5,9; Psa. 104:24

SONG OF THANKS

LEADER
Our Father in heaven, from whom cometh every good and perfect gift,

RESPONSE
We thank Thee for all Thy goodness.

LEADER
For Thy Spirit which makes us conscious of our need of Thee

RESPONSE
We give Thee thanks

LEADER
For a vision of our own powers and capabilities

RESPONSE
We give Thee thanks

LEADER
For the glow of health, the capacity to labor, and the privilege of serving others.

RESPONSE
We give Thee thanks

LEADER
For a proper sense of values, a Christian attitude toward money and other possessions

RESPONSE
We give Thee thanks.

LEADER
Help us to choose the best at all times and put aside those things that are low and mean.

RESPONSE
To make our life a song of thanks.

SAVE SOME STONES

For that noble throng of saints of all ages and all lands who have stood steadfastly for the right against the wrong,

WE PRAISE THEE, O GOD.

For the heritage which these great servants of Thine have passed on to us,

WE PRAISE THEE, O GOD.

For the example of those who were willing to suffer that Thy truth may be preserved.

WE PRAISE THEE, O GOD.

For the courage of those who were indifferent to public opinion

WE PRAISE THEE, O GOD.

GRANT THAT WE MAY ENDURE HARDNESS AS A GOOD SOLDIER OF JESUS CHRIST.

Hear our prayer, O God.

STRENGTHENED BY THY SPIRIT, MAY WE STRIVE TO FOLLOW IN THE STEPS OF THOSE GREAT HEROES OF THE PAST IN OUR SALVATION ARMY WHO COUNTED NOT THEIR LIVES DEAR UNTO THEMSELVES.

Hear our prayer, O God.

GRANT US THE WISDOM TO PRESERVE OUR HISTORY AND OUR TRADITIONS FOR FUTURE GENERATIONS AND FOR THE HONOR AND GLORY OF OUR GOD.

"Let these stones be for a memorial."

Scripture: Joshua 4:7

The Responsive Reading

THE RESPONSIVE READING

The responsive reading is a familiar form of worship expression, and is used effectively and importantly to enrich the worship service.

While it is given recognition particularly for special occasions, the responsive reading can add variety as well as involvement in any worship service.

There are many arrangements available; however, with thought and research a responsive reading can also be created for any theme. The responsive reading does not necessarily take the place of the scripture reading. In most services they are an enrichment selection on the program.

The responsive reading may be scripture only, or scriptural based, but it also could be the treatment of a concept in Christian growth.

Responsive readings wisely chosen will create a mood in worship and help preserve unity in the service. Oral expression by the congregation in a worship service not only provides spiritual stimulation, but also it gives an individual sense in communicating the truth to be shared in the service.

We cannot overestimate the value of the responsive reading in the worship service. Use it often and wisely!

CALVARY LOVE

LEADER | Herein is love, not that we loved God but that He loved us.

RESPONSE | Calvary Love is grand and great.
Indeed, very great, and thoroughly good.

LEADER | God is love and he that dwelleth in love dwelleth in God, and God in him.

RESPONSE | Calvary Love is born of God, and Calvary Love lives in God who is in charge of everything.
He loves us so much.
He calls us His children.

LEADER | For God so loved the world that He gave His only begotten Son that whosoever believeth in Him should not perish but have everlasting life.

RESPONSE | Calvary Love is noble!
It motivates one to do great things.
It stirs one to do something else too--
always long for a pure, more perfect
and transparent life style.

LEADER | Beloved, let us love one another. If God so loved us, we ought also to love one another.

RESPONSE | Calvary Love makes everything that is heavy, light.
Calvary Love shoulders burdens effortlessly.
Calvary Love makes everything that is bitter, sweet.

LEADER | Love suffereth long and is kind. Love envieth not, love vaunteth not itself, is not puffed up, doth not behave itself unseemly.

Love seeketh not her own, is not easily provoked, thinketh no evil, rejoiceth not in iniquity, but rejoiceth in the truth

RESPONSE | Calvary Love is not touchy and grumpy.
It refuses to insist on its own way.
It refuses to be resentful, to feel injury or insult.

LEADER | And now abideth faith, hope and love, these three, but the greatest of these is love.

RESPONSE | Nothing is sweeter than Calvary Love,
more courageous than love,
higher than love,
richer than love.
To sum it all up, nothing is better in heaven and earth than Calvary Love!

LEADER | Love's faith is unfaltering,
Love's hope is never broken,
Love's patience never fails.
Beloved, let us love with Calvary Love.

Responses adapted from Thomas a Kempis, Of the Imitation of Christ, Book 3, Chapter 5
Scripture: I John 4:10; I John 4:16; John 3:16; I John 4:7,11

A CHILD SPEAKS

CHILD 1   I love life!   There's so much to. see, to find, to keep, to give, to be. I need your help.

CHILD 2   Be firm with me and help me feel secure.

CHILD 3   Be honest with me, and don't frighten me into telling untruths.

CHILD 4   Be patient with me, but please don't nag for then I don't listen.

CHILD 1   Talk to me quietly and kindly; please don't shout, and especially when I am with my friends.

CHILD 2   Answer my questions so I won't stop asking. I need information.

CHILD 3   Give me what I need to be comfortable and happy, but not everything I want.

CHILD 4   Teach me to keep a promise, by not breaking promises you make to me.

CHILD 1   Support me when sometimes I must suffer the consequences of my disobedience, or wrong doing.

CHILD 2   Reassure me when my big fears seem small and trivial to you.

CHILD 3   Challenge me to form good habits by correcting my bad habits early in life.

CHILD 4   Instruct me in the ways of God, goodness, and righteousness, so that I may serve God all the days of my life.

DIVINE PARTNERSHIP

LEADER   God calls us to Divine Partnership with Him!

RESPONSE   "Fight the good fight of faith, lay hold on eternal life, whereunto thou art also called, and hast professed a good profession before many witnesses."

LEADER   Entire consecration is necessary!

RESPONSE   "No man that warreth entangleth himself with the affairs of this life; that he may please Him who hath chosen him to be a soldier."

LEADER   Beware of invisible foes!

RESPONSE   "For we wrestle not against flesh and blood, but against principalities, against powers, against the rulers of the darkness of this world, against spiritual wickedness in high places."

LEADER   God will provide the armor!

RESPONSE   "Put on the whole armor of God, that ye may be able to stand against the wiles of the devil."

LEADER   And the spiritual weapons, too!

RESPONSE   "For the weapons of our warfare are not carnal, but mighty through God to the pulling down of strongholds."

LEADER   Beware of the enemy of the soul!

RESPONSE   "Be sober, be vigilant; because your adversary, the devil, as a roaring lion, walketh about, seeking whom he may devour."

LEADER   Divine protection is promised!

RESPONSE   "Be strong and of a good courage, fear not, nor be afraid of them: for the Lord thy God, He it is that doth go with thee; He will not fail thee; nor forsake thee."

LEADER   A word of advice!

RESPONSE   "... be strong in the Lord and in the power of His might."

LEADER   Prepare for a l-o-n-g conflict!

RESPONSE   "These things I have spoken unto you, that in me ye might have peace. In the world ye shall have tribulation, but be of good cheer, I have overcome the world."

LEADER   Ultimate victory is promised!

RESPONSE   "Who shall separate us from the love of Christ? Shall tribulation, or distress, or persecution, or famine, or nakedness, or peril, or sword? Nay, in all these things we are more than conquerors through Him that loved us."

Scripture Selections: 1 Tim. 6:12; 2 Tim. 2:4; Eph. 6:12; Eph. 6:13; 2 Cor. 10:4; 1 Pet. 5:8; Duet. 31:6; Eph. 6:10; John 16:33; Rom. 8:35,37

ENDURING MERCY

LEADER   O that men would praise the Lord for His goodness, and for His wonderful works to the children of men.

RESPONSE   For His mercy endureth forever.

LEADER   He satisfieth the longing soul, and filleth the hungry soul with goodness.

RESPONSE   For His mercy endureth forever.

LEADER   I will take the cup of salvation, and call upon the name of the Lord.

RESPONSE   For His mercy endureth forever.

LEADER   I will say of the Lord, He is my refuge and my fortress: my God, in Him will I trust.

RESPONSE   For His mercy endureth forever.

LEADER   The Lord is my rock, and my fortress, my deliverer, my God, my strength.

RESPONSE   For His mercy endureth forever.

LEADER   Teach me Thy way O Lord; I will walk in Thy truth: unite my heart to fear Thy name.

RESPONSE   For His mercy endureth forever.

LEADER   For the Lord God is a sun and shield: the Lord will give grace and glory: no good thing will He withhold from them that walk uprightly.

RESPONSE   For His mercy endureth forever.

LEADER   I will go in the strength of the Lord God; I will make mention of Thy righteousness.

RESPONSE   For His mercy endureth forever.

Scripture Selections: Psa. 107:21; Psa. 107:9; Psa. 116:13; Psa. 91:2; Psa. 86:1; Psa. 84:11; Psa. 71:16; Psa. 118:1

FOLDED WINGS

LEADER	I will not hurry through this day; I will take time to think and pray.*
ALL	MY SOUL, WAIT THOU ONLY UPON GOD; FOR MY EXPECTATION IS FROM HIM.
LEADER	I will wait and walk with God, remembering ofttimes God walks slowly.
ALL	WAIT ON THE LORD; BE OF GOOD COURAGE; HE SHALL STRENGTHEN THINE HEART. WAIT, I SAY, ON THE LORD.
LEADER	I will wait before God until I feel saturated with His presence; then I will go forth to my next duty with the conscious freshness and vigor of Christ.
ALL	THEY THAT WAIT UPON THE LORD SHALL RENEW THEIR STRENGTH; THEY SHALL MOUNT UP WITH WINGS AS EAGLES; THEY SHALL RUN AND NOT BE WEARY; THEY SHALL WALK AND NOT FAINT.
LEADER	I will wait upon God in confidence, knowing He provides "resting" places as well as "working" places.
ALL	REST IN THE LORD, AND WAIT PATIENTLY FOR HIM; WAIT ON THE LORD, AND KEEP HIS WAY.

* - Ralph Spaulding Cushman; Hilltop Verses and Prayers; Abingdon-Cokesbury Press; New York, Page 73

Scripture: Psa. 62:5; Psa. 27:14; Isa. 40:31; Psa. 37:7, 34

GIVING THANKS ALWAYS

LEADER   O give thanks unto the Lord, for He is good: for His mercy endureth forever.

RESPONSE   O give thanks unto the Lord, call upon His name: make known His deeds among the people.

LEADER   O give thanks unto the Lord of Lords, to Him who alone doeth great wonders.

RESPONSE   O give thanks unto the Lord, for His merciful kindness is great toward us.

LEADER   O give thanks unto the Lord, at the remembrance of His holiness.

RESPONSE   O give thanks unto the Lord; sing unto Him, talk ye of all His wondrous works.

LEADER   It is a good thing to give thanks unto the Lord, and to sing praises unto Thy name, O most High.

RESPONSE   O Lord, our God, we will give thanks unto Thee forever.

Scripture Selections: Psa. 107:1; Psa. 105:1; Psa. 136:4; Psa. 117:2; Psa. 30:4; Psa. 92:1; Psa. 30:12

HOMEMAKER'S BE -- ATTITUDE

LEADER   Happy is the woman whose daily tasks are a labor of love.

ALL   For her happy heart and willing hands makes her labor a service to God.

LEADER   Happy is the woman who sings while she works.

ALL   For singing lightens every load and music strengthens hearts courageous; even the dullest chore glows if she sings while she works.

LEADER   Happy is the woman who knows that cleanliness and godliness walk hand in hand.

ALL   For scouring and scrubbing can express her faith and dusting and sweeping can chase away doubts and fears or even the cobwebs of confusion.

LEADER   Happy is the woman who has an open door to welcome both strangers and friends.

ALL   For love and gracious hospitality enriches family life, and ennobles the mind and speaks of the love of God.

LEADER   Happy is the woman who says "I love you" to children and husband knowing how to touch with a hug or a loving pat.

ALL   For understanding, patience, kindness, and self-esteem are born of love.

LEADER   Happy is the woman who has given freedom to the winged bird of laughter.

ALL   For her buoyant, radiant spirit like the sunshine brightens every corner of her home.

LEADER   Happy is the woman whose home is God-centered and Christ related.

ALL   For she will preserve that which is sacred; the word of God, prayer, and the spiritual disciplines of truth.

IT'S MARCHING TIME

LEADER   Ye have dwelt long enough in this mount:
Turn you, and take your journey
Into the plain, in the hills, and in the vale;
And in the south, and by the sea side.

ALL   Behold, the Lord thy God
Hath set the land before thee:
Go up and possess it.
Fear not, neither be discouraged.

LEADER   The Lord your God which goeth before you
He shall fight for you.
I will show you by what way ye should go.
I have begun to give; begin to possess.

ALL   Blessed shalt thou be when thou comest in,
Blessed shalt thou be when thou goest out,
The Lord shall open unto thee His good treasure.
But thou shalt not go aside from any of His words.

LEADER   I command thee this day to love the Lord thy God,
To walk in His ways, and to keep His commandments,
Then the Lord thy God shall bless thee,
In the land whither thou goest to possess it.

ALL   Be strong and of a good courage,
Fear not, nor be afraid of them;
For the Lord thy God doth go with thee,
He will not fail thee, nor forsake thee.

LEADER   The eternal God is thy refuge,
And underneath are the everlasting arms.

ALL   The beloved of the Lord shall dwell in safety,
And as thy day, so shall thy strength be.

Gleaned from the book of Deuteronomy

References in Deuteronomy: 1:6,7; 1:21; 1:30,31,33; 28:12.4; 5:32,33; 10:12,13;
15:4; 31:6; 33:27; 33:12,25

LIFT UP YOUR HEART

LEADER   Let us lift up our hearts unto God. Unto Thee, O Lord, do I lift up my soul. And the Lord was with Jehoshaphat, and his heart was lifted up in the ways of the Lord.

RESPONSE   When men are cast down, then Thou shalt say, there is a lifting up.

LEADER   Humble yourselves in the sight of the Lord and He shall lift you up.

RESPONSE   The Lord lifteth up the meek.

LEADER   Save Thy people, and bless Thine inheritance, feed them also, and lift them up forever.

RESPONSE   I will extol Thee, O Lord, For Thou hast lifted me up. Thou, O Lord, art a shield for me, My glory, and the lifter up of my head.

Scripture Selections: Lam. 3:41; Psa. 25:1; 2 Chr. 17:6; Job 22:29; James 4:10; Psa. 147:6; Psa. 28:9; Psa. 30:1; Psa. 3:3

LOOK UP

LEADER	Lift up your heads, O ye gates; and be ye lifted up, ye everlasting doors; and the King of glory shall come in.
RESPONSE	Who is this King of glory? The Lord strong and mighty, the Lord mighty in battle.
LEADER	Lift up your heads, O ye gates; even lift them up, ye everlasting doors; and the King of glory shall come in.
RESPONSE	Who is this King of glory? The Lord of hosts, He is the King of glory.
LEADER	Lift up your hearts.
RESPONSE	We lift them up to the Lord.
LEADER	O Lord, open our eyes.
RESPONSE	That we may behold wondrous things out of Thy law.
LEADER	O Lord, open our lips.
RESPONSE	And our mouth shall show forth Thy praise.
LEADER	Praise ye the Lord.
RESPONSE	The Lord's name be praised.
LEADER	From the rising of the sun to the going down of the same, the Lord's name is to be praised.
ALL	O that men would praise the Lord for His goodness, and for His wonderful works to the children of men.

Scripture Selections: Psa. 24:7,8,10; Psa. 119:18; Psa. 51:15; Psa. 113:3; Psa. 107:8

PEACE OF GOD

LEADER   Peace I give unto you...not as the world giveth, give I unto you.

ALL   The effect of the blessing of peace is quietness forever. But there is no real peace around us.

LEADER   Let not your heart be troubled, neither let it be afraid. Ye believe in God, believe also in me.

ALL   But where is peace, when there is no end to war? No end to quarrels. No end to worry. No end to fear and injustice.

LEADER   Great peace have they who love thy law.

ALL   It's easy to read it and to say it, but those who "love thy law" are hurting by war, by greed, by violence, and the lust for power.

LEADER   The Lord will lift up His countenance upon thee, and give thee peace. Acquaint now thyself with Him, and be at peace.

ALL   We would know the ways of peace, and we would seek for peace, but where can peace be found?

LEADER   Depart from evil, and do good; seek peace, and pursue it. For being justified by faith, we have peace with God through our Lord Jesus Christ.

ALL   Then there is a condition to peace. Peace is not the ending of conflict, the absence of violence, or hostility.

LEADER   Put on therefore, mercy, kindness, longsuffering, forbearing one another, forgiving one another; and let the peace of God rule in your hearts.

ALL   As we accept God's idea of peace, we come to know that He will keep us in perfect peace if our mind is stayed upon Him.

LEADER   These things have I spoken unto you, that in me ye might have peace. In the world ye shall have tribulation: but be of good cheer, I have overcome the world.

ALL   We would be the instruments of thy peace; a peace that comes from knowing God and an inner, individual peace of faith and trust.

Scripture: John 14:27; John 14:1; Psalm 119:165; Numbers 6:26; Job 22:21; Psalm 34:14; Romans 5:1; Colossians 3:12,15; John 16:33

A QUALITY OF GLADNESS

LEADER   This is the day that the Lord hath made; we will rejoice and be glad in it.

RESPONSE   I have set the Lord always before me; therefore, my heart is glad. Heart, body and soul are filled with joy. (TLB)

LEADER   I will be glad and rejoice in Thee; I will shout for joy and be glad.

RESPONSE   My meditation of Him shall be sweet, I will be glad in the Lord.

LEADER   My heart is overflowing with a beautiful thought! You love what is good and hate what is wrong. Therefore, God, your God, has given you more gladness than anyone else.

RESPONSE   Thy words were found and they sustain me. They are food to my hungry soul. They are the joy of my heart. (TLB)

LEADER   I will greatly rejoice in the Lord, my soul shall be joyful in my God. He hath clothed me with the garments of salvation. He hath covered me with the robe of righteousness.

RESPONSE   Be glad and rejoice; for the Lord will do great things.

LEADER   Serve the Lord with gladness; with joy shall you draw water out of the wells of salvation.

RESPONSE   O Lord, I will praise you with all my heart, and tell everyone about the marvelous things you do. I will be glad, yes filled with joy because of you.

LEADER   And the ransomed of the Lord shall come with songs and everlasting joy. They shall obtain joy and gladness, and sorrow and sighing shall flee away.

RESPONSE   Rejoice in the Lord alway, and again I say rejoice; Rejoice evermore!

Scripture Selections: Psa. 118:24; Psa. 16:8; Psa. 32:11; Psa. 104:34; Jer. 15:16; Isa. 61:10; Psa. 32:11; Psa. 100:2; Isa. 12:4; Psa. 9:1,2; Isa. 35:10; Phil. 4:4; 1 Thess. 5:16

SANCTUARY

LEADER	When life weighs us down, we need a place where we can draw near to God's heart.
ALL	"Come with me by yourselves to a quiet place, and get some rest."
LEADER	In quietness and seclusion, in retreat, we find new meaning for life.
ALL	"My soul finds rest in God alone; my salvation comes from him." "Wait for the Lord: be strong and take heart, and wait for the Lord." "In quietness and trust is your strength."
LEADER	We must never take flight *from* reality, but we must take flight *to* reality in God, our refuge.
ALL	"God is our refuge and strength, an ever-present help in trouble." "Be still, and know that I am God." "I waited patiently for the Lord, he turned to me and heard my cry. He put a new song in my mouth, a hymn of praise to our God."
LEADER	Sooner or later that which is weak in us, cries for us to lay our burden on Someone who is stronger.
ALL	"Come to Me all ye who are weary and burdened, and I will give you rest." "I pray that out of His glorious riches, God may strengthen you with power through his Spirit in your inner being."
LEADER	If we draw near God's heart we will find sanctuary. Sanctuary that brings strength; sanctuary which is release from hurt and sorrow; sanctuary opening the channel of renewal; sanctuary lifting us on wings of love and support.
ALL	"Those who wait on the Lord will renew their strength. They will soar on wings like eagles; they will run and not grow weary, they will walk and not be faint."

Scripture taken from NIV: Mark 6:31; Psa. 62:5; Psa. 27:14; Isa. 30:15; Psa. 46:10; Psa. 40:1,3; Matt. 11:28; Eph. 3:16; Isa. 40:31

222

SHARING OUR FAITH

LEADER To share our faith we must know Christ in the power of His resurrection and make Him known in His power of love and forgiveness.

RESPONSE WE WILL DECLARE OUR FAITH "THAT AS MANY AS RECEIVE HIM TO THEM WILL HE GIVE THE POWER TO BECOME THE SONS OF GOD"

LEADER To share our faith we must be loyal to Christ and His cause.

RESPONSE AS WE REACH OUT IN SERVICE WITH CHRIST, WE WILL STRIVE TO BE MORE LOYAL TO HIM.

LEADER To share our faith we must practice the law of love.

RESPONSE WE WILL TRY TO LOVE GOD WITH ALL OUR HEARTS, SOULS AND MINDS AND TO BE MORE MINDFUL OF OUR NEIGHBORS.

LEADER To share our faith we must have the spirit of brotherhood in our hearts.

RESPONSE WE WILL TRY TO REMEMBER THAT GOD CREATED OF ONE BLOOD ALL NATIONS OF THE EARTH AND WE WILL TRY TO BE KIND AND SYMPATHETIC WITH ALL WHOM OUR LIVES TOUCH; REGARDLESS OF RACE, OR LANGUAGE, OR COLOR.

LEADER To share our faith, we must be willing to seek new paths of service in the name of Christ.

RESPONSE WE WILL ASK GOD TO OPEN OUR EYES TO THE NEEDS OF THE WORLD AND TO GIVE US FAITH THAT WE CAN HAVE A PART IN THE BRINGING IN OF HIS KINGDOM.

LEADER To share our faith we must talk to the Lord about unbelievers and then talk to unbelievers about the Lord.

RESPONSE WE WILL COMMIT OURSELVES TO PRAYER FOR THE UNSAVED, TO WITNESSING, AND TO SOUL WINNING.

Scripture: John 1:12

TIME MANAGEMENT

LEADER Today is here - each hour with exactly sixty minutes in it - no more, no less.

RESPONSE But as for me I trust in Thee, O Lord: I say, "Thou art my God." "My times are in Thy hand."

LEADER Time is so elusive, so slippery; sometimes it passes with the speed of lightning, and sometimes it drags on inch by inch, and then again it crawls like a snail. Truly time is ticking away.

RESPONSE I will bless the Lord at all times: His praise shall continually be in my mouth.

LEADER Today do not waste time, because the minutes wasted yesterday are lost forever.

RESPONSE Ye observe days,and months and years. Walk in wisdom; walk circumspectly, not as fools, but as wise, redeeming the time.

LEADER Today I will refuse to procrastinate; to put off doing the things that should be done. I will not allow putting off until tomorrow to steal my time, my incentives, my motivation.

RESPONSE Boast not thyself of tomorrow for thou knowest not what a day may bring forth.

LEADER Today I will take time to be thoughtful, kind and tender. I will give a touch of gentleness, a word of assurance, and of tender-caring for those who are hurting.

RESPONSE So teach us to number our days that we may apply our hearts to wisdom. As apostles of Christ we were gentle among you. We loved you so much that we were delighted to share with you not only the gospel of God but our lives as well, because you had become so dear to us.

LEADER Today I refuse to spend time worrying about what might happen, or being anxious, pressured, or troubled.

RESPONSE God is our refuge and strength, a very present help in trouble. Let us therefore come boldly unto the throne of grace...and find grace to help in time of need.

LEADER Today I am determined to manage my time aright by trusting since He has appointed a time for everything.

RESPONSE Trust in God at all times. What time I am afraid, I will trust in God. To everything there is a season, and a time to every purpose under the heaven: God hath made everything beautiful in His time.

Scripture Selections: Psa. 31:15; Psa. 34:1; Gal. 4:10; Eph. 5:11,16; Psa. 27:1; Psa. 90:12; 1 Thess. 2:7,8; Psa. 46:1; Heb. 4:16; Psa. 62:8; Psa. 56:3; Eccl. 3:1,11

TWO CHALLENGES

LEADER The ageless call of God to "Come!" is just as clear today as it ever was! *Come* for personal cleansing.

ALL "Come now, and let us reason together, saith the Lord: though your sins be as scarlet, they shall be as white as snow; though they be red like crimson, they shall be as wool."

LEADER *Come* for a satisfying portion!

ALL "Ho, every one that thirsteth, come ye to the waters, and he that hath no money, come ye, buy and eat; yea, come, buy wine and milk without money and without price."

LEADER *Come* to a set-apart life!

ALL "Wherefore come out from among them, and be ye separate, saith the Lord and touch not the unclean thing; and I will receive you, and will be a Father unto you, and ye shall be my sons and my daughters, saith the Lord Almighty."

LEADER The invitation to "Come!" is usually followed by the challenge to "Go!" *Go* at God's call!

ALL "Also I heard the voice of the Lord, saying, Whom shall I send, and who will go for us? Then said I, Here am I; send me."

LEADER *Go* as God's ambassador!

ALL "Ye have not chosen me, but I have chosen you, and ordained you, that ye should go and bring forth fruit, and that your fruit should remain..."

LEADER *Go* for a specific purpose!

ALL "Go ye into all the world and preach the gospel to every creature."

I'll go in the strength of the Lord,
  In paths He has marked for my feet;
I'll follow the light of His word,
  Nor shrink from the dangers I meet.
His presence my steps shall attend,
  His fulness my wants shall supply;
On Him, till my journey shall end,
  My unwavering faith shall rely.

(Edward Turney)

Scripture Selections: Isa. 1:18; Isa. 55:1; 2 Cor. 6:17; Isa. 6:8;
John 15:16; Mark 16:15

WAITING UPON THE LORD

LEADER   Call unto Me, and I will answer thee and show thee great and mighty things which thou knowest not.

RESPONSE   I will call upon the Lord Who is worthy to be praised...

LEADER   ...when thou prayest, enter into thy closet; and when thou hast shut thy door, pray to thy Father which is in secret; and thy Father which seeth in secret shall reward thee openly.

RESPONSE   Teach me Thy way, O Lord; I will walk in Thy truth: Unite my heart to fear Thy Name...for Thou art my rock and my fortress; therefore, for Thy Name's sake, lead me and guide me.

LEADER   I will instruct thee and teach thee in the way which thou shalt go: I will guide thee with Mine eye.

RESPONSE   Rest in the Lord, and wait patiently for Him...In quietness and confidence shall be your strength.

LEADER   Thou wilt keep him in perfect peace whose mind is stayed on Thee: because he trusteth in Thee. Trust ye in the Lord forever: for in the Lord Jehovah is everlasting strength.

RESPONSE   If ye abide in Me, and My words abide in you, ye shall ask what ye will, and it shall be done unto you...If ye shall ask anything in My Name, I will do it.

LEADER   What various hindrances we meet
In coming to the Mercy Seat!
Yet who that knows the worth of prayer
But wishes to be often there.

RESPONSE   Let us therefore come boldly unto the throne of grace that we may obtain mercy, and find grace to help in time of need.

LEADER   The effectual fervent prayer of a righteous man availeth much.
Thou art coming to a King,
Large petitions with thee bring,
For His grace and power are such
None can ever ask too much.

ALL   THEY THAT WAIT UPON THE LORD SHALL RENEW THEIR STRENGTH: THEY SHALL MOUNT UP WITH WINGS AS EAGLES: THEY SHALL RUN, AND NOT BE WEARY, AND THEY SHALL WALK, AND NOT FAINT. Isa. 40:31

Scripture: Jer. 33:3; Psalm 18:3; Matt. 6:6; Psa. 86:11; Psa. 31:3; Psa. 32:8; Psa. 37:7; Isa. 30:15; Isa. 26:3,4; John 15:7; John 14:14; Heb. 4:16; Ja. 5:16; Isa. 40:31

WINGS OF PEACE

LEADER   Let not your heart be troubled
Let the peace of God rule in your hearts
Follow things that make for peace.

RESPONSE   The peace of God is not always the easy, natural peace of a level road; His peace comes also when we climb the steep with a heavy load.

LEADER   My peace I leave with you,
My peace I give unto you,
Not as the world giveth, give I unto you.

RESPONSE   Peace is not having everything your own way,
Peace is not a calm, sunshiny day.

LEADER   Thou wilt keep him in perfect peace whose mind is stayed on Thee.

RESPONSE   Anxious thoughts, unrest, fears, and discontent may disturb you,
But a quiet, calm, patient spirit will give you peace anew.

LEADER   The peace of God which passeth all understanding will guard your hearts and your thoughts in Christ Jesus.

Scripture Selections: John 14:1; Col. 3:15; Rom. 14:19; Isa. 26:4;

ACCEPTANCE

LEADER   I am the true Vine and my Father is the Gardener. He lops off every branch that doesn't produce.

RESPONSE   And He prunes those branches that bear fruit for ever larger crops.

LEADER   He has already tended you, by pruning you back for greater strength and usefulness.

RESPONSE   We can rejoice when we run into problems and trials for we know that they are good for us: they help us to learn to be patient.

LEADER   Let God train you, for He is doing what any loving father does for his children.

RESPONSE   Don't be bewildered or surprised when you go through fiery trials ahead, for this is no strange unusual thing.

LEADER   Be really glad because these trials will make you partners with Christ in His suffering, and afterward you will have the wonderful joy of sharing.

RESPONSE   God will tenderly comfort you when you undergo these same trials. He will give you strength to endure.

LEADER   Shall we receive only pleasant things from the hand of God and never anything unpleasant?

RESPONSE   It is the Lord's will...let Him do what He thinks best.

LEADER   No trial (suffering) is enjoyable. While it is happening it hurts. But afterward we can see the result, a quiet growth in grace and character.

RESPONSE   So take a new grip with your tired hands, stand firm on your shaky legs.

LEADER   When you go through deep waters of trouble, I will be with you. When you go through rivers of difficulty, you will not drown.

RESPONSE   When I am afraid, I will put my confidence in you. Yes, I will trust the promises of God. This one thing I know: God is for me.

Scripture Selections (from the Living Bible): John 15:1; Rom. 5:3; Heb. 12:7; 1 Peter 4:12; 2 Cor. 1:7; Job 2:10; 2 Cor. 10:11; Jas. 4:18; Heb. 12:11,12; Isa. 43:2; Psa. 56:3

ADVENTURE

LEADER   O Lord, I know it is not within the power of man to map his life and plan his course.

RESPONSE   This great God is our God forever, and ever. He will be our guide until we die.

LEADER   The steps of a good man are directed by the Lord. He delights in each step they take.

RESPONSE   The words of God are a flashlight to light the path ahead of me, and keep me from stumbling.

LEADER   I will instruct you says the Lord, and guide you along the best pathway for your life; I will advise you and watch your progress.

RESPONSE   Don't be afraid, for the Lord will go before you, and will be with you; He will not fail nor forsake you.

LEADER   Show me the path where I should go, O Lord; point out the right road for me to walk.

RESPONSE   You love me! You are holding my right hand, O God: You will keep on guiding me all my life with your wisdom and counsel.

LEADER   If you aren't going with us, don't let us move a step from this place.

RESPONSE   The Lord will work out His plans for my life. And when we obey Him, every path He guides us in is fragrant with His lovingkindness and His truth.

ALL   I know the plans I have for you, says the Lord. They are plans for good, and not evil, to give you a future and a hope.

Scripture Selections (from the Living Bible):
Jer. 10:23; Psa. 48:14; Psa. 37:23; Psa.119:105;
Psa. 32:8; Deut. 31:8; Isa. 25:4; Psa. 73:23; Ex. 33:15;
Psa. 138:8; Jer. 29:11

ALL MY WAYS

LEADER   O Lord, You have examined my heart and know everything about me. You know when I sit or when I stand.

ALL   Lord, I am so habit bound, so earth bound, so work bound. My day moves from children to school, then work at home, home to shopping, home to music lessons, home to the dentist, and home to church.

LEADER   You always understand and know my every thought.

ALL   Trivial tasks control my thoughts. The housework! The meals! The bills! P.T.A.! The laundry! The monotony! The annoyances! The disappointments! The hurts!

LEADER   You chart the path ahead of me and tell me where to stop and rest. Every moment you know where I am.

ALL   I think of all my ways with my family, with my friends, and my neighbors, with those I meet casually in stores or on the bus, with those in authority, or with people who need my love and kindness and sometimes I fail to give it.

LEADER   Lord, you know what I am going to say before I even say it.

ALL   You know my haughty, quick temper, Lord. You know my words that hurt, my gossipy conversation, my foolish boasting, my sometimes critical sharp tongue, when I should speak with love and understanding.

LEADER   Lord, you both precede and follow me, and place your hand of blessing on my head.

ALL   I have felt your hand upon me at the kitchen sink, at the stove, and the dinner table. I have felt your blessing at the telephone and my desk, and often at the beauty parlor.

LEADER   Lord search me and know my heart. Test me and my thoughts. Point out anything that makes you sad, and lead me along the path of everlasting life.

ALL   Then shall I go forth as a true representative of the Lord of love. I shall go forth knowing that you are thinking about me constantly! I shall go forth with joy and a sense of your presence.

Scripture Selection (from the Living Bible) Psalm 139

BEATITUDES FOR LEADERS

BLESSED IS THE LEADER WHO HAS NOT SOUGHT POSITION, OR AN EGO TRIP, BUT WHO SERVES WILLINGLY AND FOR THE LOVE OF GOD.

True greatness is measured by selfless love. Love does not demand its own way.

BLESSED IS THE LEADER WHO KNOWS WHERE HE WANTS TO GO, WHY HE IS GOING THERE, AND HOW TO ACCOMPLISH HIS PURPOSE.

The love you give in your service is the love you keep. Love is very patient and kind; is never haughty or rude.

BLESSED IS THE LEADER WHO KNOWS HOW TO LEAD, BUT IS NOT COMMANDING, PUSHY, OF OVERBEARING.

Love opens doors of opportunity quietly. Love is not boastful or proud. It is not irritable or touchy.

BLESSED IS THE LEADER WHO WALKS CLOSELY BESIDE THOSE HE LEADS, AND ENJOYS THEIR SUPPORT WHILE HE COMMANDS THEIR RESPECT.

Love is like rain and sunshine bringing warmth and growth. Love is never envious or jealous; is not arrogant or conceited.

BLESSED IS THE LEADER WHO IS NOT EASILY DISCOURAGED, AND DOES NOT MAKE EXCUSES WHEN DISCOURAGING SITUATIONS ARISE.

Love enfolds discouragement in a robe of positive achievement. Love is loyal no matter what the cost. Love always believes and expects the best.

BLESSED IS THE LEADER WHO ASSUMES THE TASK OF TRAINING LEADERS AS HE LEADS.

Love always gives more love when it is needed. Love overlooks faults, is never glad when others go wrong, and knows no end to trust.

BLESSED IS THE LEADER WHO ALWAYS SEEKS THE BEST FOR HIS PEOPLE AND HIS MINISTRY.

Love always brings big returns; it cannot be wasted. Love knows no limits to its faith; and hopes under all circumstances.

BLESSED IS THE LEADER WHO CONSIDERS LEADERSHIP A CHALLENGE, AND AN OPPORTUNITY, AND AN AVENUE OF FULFILLMENT.

If we do not love, we do not live. Love never faileth, love goes on forever.

1 Cor. 13 (TLB)

CAPTURE STRENGTH

LEADER   The Lord is my light and my salvation, who shall I fear? The Lord is the strength of my life, of whom shall I be afraid?

RESPONSE   Be strong! Be courageous! Do not be afraid of them. For the Lord your God will be with you.

LEADER   He will neither fail you, nor forsake you. Don't be afraid, for the Lord will go before you and will be with you.

RESPONSE   God has said, "I will never, never fail you nor forsake you." That is why we can say without any doubt or fear, "The Lord is my helper and I am not afraid of anything that mere man can do to me.

LEADER   God hath said, "I myself will go with you and give you success."

RESPONSE   Yes, be bold, and strong! Banish fears and doubt! For remember the Lord, your God, is with you wherever you go.

LEADER   Lead on with courage and strength, O God.

RESPONSE   For though our bodies are dying, our inner strength in the Lord is growing every day.

LEADER   God gives power to the tired and worn out, and strength to the weak.

RESPONSE   They that wait upon the Lord shall renew their strength.

LEADER   They shall mount up with wings as eagles; they shall walk and not faint.

RESPONSE   May the Lord be with you and prosper you. Be strong and courageous, fearless and enthusiastic.

Scripture Selections (from the Living Bible): Psa. 27:1; Duet. 31:7,8;
Heb. 13:5,6; Ex.33:14; Joshua 1:9; 2 Cor. 4:16;
Isa. 40:29,31; 1 Chr. 22:11,13

DISCIPLESHIP

LEADER
: Anyone who wants to follow me must put aside his own desires and conveniences and carry his cross with him every day and keep close to me.

RESPONSE
: No one can become my disciple unless he first sits down and counts his blessings, and then renounces them all for me.

LEADER
: To win the contest you must deny yourselves many things that would keep you from doing your best.

RESPONSE
: I run straight to the goal with purpose in every step.

LEADER
: I am still not all I should be, but I am bringing all my energies to bear on this one thing.

  Forgetting the past and looking forward to what lies ahead, I strain to reach the end of the race, and receive the prize for which God is calling us.

RESPONSE
: It is good for a man to be under discipline.

LEADER
: Cheerfully submit to God's training so that you can begin really to live.

RESPONSE
: God's correction is always right and for our best good, that we may share His holiness.

LEADER
: I know the plans I have for you, says the Lord. They are plans for good and not for evil, to give you a future and a hope.

RESPONSE
: Let us run with patience the particular race that God has set before us. Keep your eyes on Jesus, our leader and instructor.

Scripture Selections: Luke 9:23; Rom. 13:12; Phil. 3:13; Lam. 3:27; Heb. 12:9; Jer. 29:11; Heb. 12:1 (LB)

FITTING THE MOLD

LEADER   Follow God's example in everything you do just as a much loved child imitates his Father.

ALL   Be full of love for others, following the example of Christ who loved you and gave himself to God as a sacrifice to take away your sins.

LEADER   Talk with each other much about the Lord, quoting psalms and hymns and singing sacred songs, making music in your hearts to the Lord.

ALL   Is there any such thing as Christians cheering each other up? Do you love me enough to want to help me? Does it mean anything to you that we are brothers in the Lord?

LEADER   Then make me truly happy by loving each other and agreeing wholeheartedly with each other, working together with one heart and mind and purpose.

ALL   Since you have been chosen by God who has given you this new kind of life and because of his deep love and concern for you, you should practice tenderhearted mercy and kindness to others.

LEADER   Dear friends, let us practice loving each other, for love comes from God and those who are loving and kind show that they are getting to know Him better.

ALL   But if a person isn't loving and kind, it shows that he doesn't know God, for God is love.

LEADER   Since God loved us so much, we surely ought to love each other. When we love each other, God lives in us and his love within us grows even stronger.

ALL   Loving God means doing what he tells us to do. And now we tell all the world that God sent His Son to be their Saviour.

Scripture Selections (from the Living Bible): Eph. 5:1, 2, 19; Phil. 2:1,2; Col. 3:12; 1 John 4:7, 8, 9; 1 John 5:3

A FLASH OF INSIGHT

LEADER   I want men everywhere to pray with holy hands lifted up to God, free from sin, anger, and resentment.

RESPONSE   When you are praying, first forgive anyone you are holding a grudge against, so that your Father in Heaven will forgive you your sins too.

LEADER   Don't let the sun go down with you still angry -- get over it quickly; for when you are angry you give a mighty foot hold to the Devil.

RESPONSE   Remember the Lord forgave you, so you must forgive others.

LEADER   Be gentle and ready to forgive; never hold grudges.

RESPONSE   If a brother sins against you, go to him privately and confront him with his fault. If he listens and confesses it, you have won back a brother.

LEADER   I am Jehovah, the merciful, and gracious God - slow to anger and rich in steadfast love and truth.

RESPONSE   Follow God's example in everything you do just as a much loved child imitates his father.

LEADER   Since you have been chosen by God who has given you this new kind of life, and because of His deep love and concern for you, you should practice tenderhearted mercy and kindness to others.

RESPONSE   When the Holy Spirit controls our lives He will produce this kind of fruit in us: love, joy, peace, patience, kindness, goodness, faithfulness, gentleness, and self-control.

Scripture Selections (from the Living Bible): 1 Tim. 2:8; Mark 11:25,26; Eph. 4:26; Col. 3:13; Matt. 18:15; Ex. 34:6,7; Gal. 5:22,23

A GLAD HEART

LEADER   All living things shall thank you, Lord, and your people will bless you.

RESPONSE   I bless the holy Name of God with all my heart. I will praise the Lord no matter what happens.

LEADER   Praise the Lord! How good it is to sing His praises! How delightful and how right.

RESPONSE   With all my heart I will praise you, I will give glory to your Name forever.

LEADER   It is good to say thank you to the Lord

RESPONSE   Every morning tell Him, "Thank you for your kindness", and every evening rejoice in all His faithfulness.

LEADER   Always be full of joy in the Lord. I say it again, "Rejoice!"

RESPONSE   I will praise you with great joy. You have let me experience the joys of life, and the exquisite pleasures of your own eternal presence.

LEADER   Oh, that men would praise the Lord for His lovingkindness, and for all of His wonderful deeds.

RESPONSE   Think about all you can praise God for and be glad about.

Scripture Selections: Psa. 145:10; Psa. 103:1; Psa. 34:1; Psa. 147:1; Psa. 86:10; 1 Thess. 3:3; Psa. 63:5; Psa. 16:11; Psa. 107:8; Phil. 4:8

HANG IN THERE

LEADER   The steps of a good man are directed by the Lord. He delights in each step they take. If they fall it isn't fatal, for the Lord holds them with His hands.

RESPONSE I am standing here depressed and gloomy. My eyes are ever looking to the Lord for help.

LEADER   Wait for the Lord to handle the matter. Rest in the Lord (hang in there) wait patiently for Him to act.

RESPONSE It is good both to hope and wait quietly for the salvation of the Lord.

LEADER   Troubles are a part of God's plan for us Christians. Here on earth you will have many trials and sorrows; but cheer up, for I have overcome the world.

RESPONSE In my distress, I screamed to the Lord for His help and He heard me; my cry reached His ears.

LEADER   He reached down and drew me out of my great trials. He rescued me from deep waters.

RESPONSE Don't worry about anything, instead pray about everything. Tell God your needs and don't forget to thank Him for all His answers.

LEADER   I will answer them before they even call to me. While they are still talking to me about their needs, I will go ahead and answer their prayers.

RESPONSE I will praise the Lord no matter what happens. I will constantly speak of all His kindness to me.

LEADER   Have faith in God! With God everything is possible.

RESPONSE I will be your God through all your life time. I made you and I will care for you. I will carry you along, and be your Savior.

Scripture Selections (from the Living Bible): Psa. 37:23; Psa. 42:6; Prov.25:15; Prov. 20:22; Psa. 37:7; Lam. 3:26; 1 Thess. 3:3; John 16:33; Psa. 18:6,16; Phil. 4:6; Isa. 65:24; Psa. 34:1; Mark 11:22; Matt. 19:26; Isa. 46:4

237

HELP ME, LORD

LEADER   How long will you forget me Lord? How long will you look the other way when I am in need?

RESPONSE   I will not forget to help you. I've blotted out your sins; they are gone like morning mist at noon.

LEADER   Some may say, "The Lord deserted us; He has forgotten us." Never! Can a mother forget her little child and not have love for her own son? Yet even if that should be, I will not forget you.

RESPONSE   These trials are only to test your faith, to see whether or not it is strong and pure.

LEADER   God is our refuge and strength, a tested help in times of trouble.

RESPONSE   After you have suffered a little while, our God, who is full of kindness through Christ, will give you His eternal glory.

LEADER   He personally will come to pick you up, and set you firmly in place, and make you stronger than ever.

RESPONSE   All who fear God and trust in Him are blessed beyond expression.

LEADER   Such a man will not be overthrown by circumstances.

RESPONSE   He does not fear bad news, nor live in dread of what may happen. He is settled in his mind that God will take care of him.

LEADER   So be truly glad! There is wonderful joy ahead, even though the going is rough for a while.

RESPONSE   Here on earth you will have many trials and sorrows, but cheer up, for I have overcome the world. I am holding you by your right hand. Don't be afraid, I am here to help you! I am with you, that is all you need!

Scripture Selections (from the Living Bible): Psa. 13:1; Isa. 44:21; Isa. 49:14; 1 Peter 1:7; Psa. 46:1; 1 Pet. 5:11; Psa. 112:1; 1 Peter 1:6; John 16:23; Isa. 41:10

HIS VERY OWN

LEADER   You are God's own personal possession. You belong to Christ, and Christ is God's.

RESPONSE   Long ago, even before He made the world, God chose us to be His very own, through what Christ would do for us.

LEADER   Your own body does not belong to you. For God has bought you with a great price.

RESPONSE   So use every part of your body to give glory back to God, because He owns it.

LEADER   How can we be sure that we belong to Him?

RESPONSE   By looking within ourselves, are we really trying to do what He wants us to?

LEADER   See how very much our Heavenly Father loves us, for He allows us to be called His children.

RESPONSE   He has put His brand upon us - His mark of ownership - and given us His Holy Spirit in our hearts as a guarantee that we belong to Him.

LEADER   "They shall be mine," says the Lord of Hosts, "in that day when I make up my jewels."

RESPONSE   My soul claims the Lord as my inheritance; therefore, I will hope in Him.

Scripture Selections (from the Living Bible): Deut. 32:9; 1 Cor. 3:23; Eph. 1:4; 1 Cor. 6:19; 1 Jn. 2:3; Rom. 8:17; 2 Cor. 1:22; Mal. 3:17; Lam. 3:24

LANGUAGE OF HEAVEN

LEADER   Whatever you do or say, let it be as a representative of the Lord Jesus.

RESPONSE   Remember what Christ taught and let His words enrich your lives and make you wise.

LEADER   Let your conversation be gracious as well as sensible, for then you will have the right answer for everyone.

RESPONSE   A good man's speech reveals the rich treasures within him.

LEADER   A man's heart determines his speech. Whatever is in the heart overflows into speech.

RESPONSE   Don't ever forget that it is best to listen much, speak little, and not become angry.

LEADER   Don't talk so much. You keep putting your foot in your mouth. Be sensible and turn off the flow.

RESPONSE   If any one can control his tongue, it proves that he has perfect control over himself in every other way.

LEADER   Help me, Lord, to keep my mouth shut and my lips sealed.

RESPONSE   Gentle words cause life and health.

Scripture Selections (from the Living Bible): Col. 3:17,16; Col. 4:6; Matt. 12:35,34;
Luke 6:45; Jas. 1:19; Prov. 10:19;
Jas. 3:2; Psa. 141:3; Prov. 15:4

THE SECRET

LEADER   The God of Israel gives strength and mighty power to His people. Blessed be God!

RESPONSE   The eyes of the Lord search back and forth across the whole earth, looking for people whose hearts are perfect toward Him, so that He can show His great power in helping them.

LEADER   God is your strong fortress. Your strength must come from God's mighty power within you. Your power and success comes from God.

RESPONSE   I am with you - that is all you need. My power shows up best in weak people.

LEADER   I am glad to be a living demonstration of Christ's power, instead of showing off my own power and abilities. The less I have - the more I depend on Him.

RESPONSE   He gives power to the tired and worn out, and strength to the weak.

LEADER   I can do everything God asks me to do with the help of Christ who gives me the strength and the power.

RESPONSE   Much is required from those to whom much is given. Who is adequate for such a task as this?

LEADER   Fear not, for I am with you. Be not dismayed, I am your God. I will strengthen you. I will help you. I will uphold you with my victorious right hand.

RESPONSE   The Holy Spirit displays God's power through each of us as a means of helping the entire church.

LEADER   God has given each of you some special abilities; be sure to use them to help others.

RESPONSE   May our strength match the length of our days.

Scripture Selections (from the Living Bible): Psa. 68:35; 2 Chr. 16:9; Eph. 6:10; Isa. 40:29; 2 Cor. 12:9; Phil. 4:13; Isa. 41:13; 1 Cor. 12:7; Deut. 33:25

SOMETHING IS HAPPENING

LEADER   The Lord God says, I am ready to hear...and to grant them their requests. Let them but ask.

RESPONSE   Keep praying until the answer comes. Pray all the time and ask God for anything in line with the Holy Spirit's wishes.

LEADER   The reason you don't have what you want is that you don't ask for it. Ask, and you will be given what you ask for. For everyone who asks, receives.

RESPONSE   Don't be weary in prayer; keep at it; watch for God's answers and remember to be thankful when they come.

LEADER   And we are sure of this, that He will listen to us whenever we ask Him for anything in line with His will.

RESPONSE   And if we really know He is listening when we talk to Him and make our requests, then we can be sure that He will answer us.

LEADER   Don't worry about anything; instead pray about everything; tell God your needs and thank Him for His answers.

RESPONSE   The eyes of the Lord are intently watching all who live good lives and He gives attention when they cry to Him. Yes, the Lord hears a good man when he calls to Him for help.

LEADER   If you want to know what God wants you to do, ask Him, and He will gladly tell you, for He is always ready to give a bountiful supply of wisdom to all who ask Him.

RESPONSE   Present your petitions over my signature. And I won't need to ask the Father to grant you these requests, for the Father Himself loves you dearly because you love me.

Scripture Selections (from the Living Bible): Ezk. 36:37,38; Luke 18:1; Eph.6:18; Jas. 4:2; Matt. 7:7; Col. 4:2; 1 Jn. 5:14; Phil. 4:6; Psa. 34:15; James. 1:5; John 16:26,29

DIVINE WHISPERINGS

LEADER   Take time to be holy, speak oft with Thy Lord

RESPONSE   He that dwelleth in the secret place of the most High shall abide
(men)   under the shadow of the Almighty.

RESPONSE   Abide in Him always, and feed on His word.
(women)

ALL   If ye abide in Me, and My words abide in you, ye shall ask what ye
will, and it shall be done unto you.

LEADER   Take time to be holy, the world rushes on.

RESPONSE   And when Jesus had sent the multitudes away, He went up into a
(men)   mountain apart to pray, and when the evening was come, He was
there alone.

RESPONSE   And Jesus said, unto the disciples, "Come ye yourselves
(women)   apart...and rest awhile for there are many coming and going."

LEADER   Spend much time in secret, with Jesus alone.

ALL   When you pray enter into your closet, and when you have shut the
door, pray to your Father which is in secret; and your Father, which
sees in secret shall reward you openly.

LEADER   Take time to be holy, let Him be your guide.

RESPONSE   The Lord shall guide thee continually and thou shalt be like a
(men)   watered garden, and like a spring of water, whose waters fail not.

RESPONSE   In joy or in sorrow, still follow thy Lord,
(women)   And looking to Jesus, still trust in His word.

ALL   Blessed is the man, whose delight is in the law of the Lord, and in
His law does He meditate day and night.

LEADER   Take time to be holy, be calm in thy soul

RESPONSE   In thy presence is fullness of joy, and at thy right hand are
(men)   pleasures forever more.

RESPONSE   By looking to Jesus like Him thou shalt be
(women)   Thy friends in thy conduct His likeness shall see.

ALL   Be not conformed to this world: but be transformed by the
renewing of your mind, that you may prove what is that good and
acceptable and perfect will of God.

From the Salvation Army Song Book #458
Scripture: Psa. 91:1; John 15:7; Matt. 14:23; Mark 6:31;
Matt. 6:6; Isa. 58:11; Psa. 1:2; Psa. 16:11; Rom. 12:2

ENABLED

LEADER	I'll go in the strength of the Lord.
RESPONSE	The Lord is my strength and song, and He is become my salvation; He is my God.
LEADER	I'll go in the strength of the Lord, In paths He has marked for my feet.
RESPONSE	Teach me your way, oh, Lord, and lead me in a plain path. Your shoes shall be iron and brass; and as your day so shall your strength be.
LEADER	His presence my steps shall attend; His fullness my wants shall supply; On Him, 'til my journey shall end, my unwavering faith shall rely.
RESPONSE	You will show me the path of life; in your presence is fullness of joy. At your right hand there are pleasures for evermore.
LEADER	I'll go in the strength of the Lord to work He appoints me to do His wisdom and power my sufficiency prove.
RESPONSE	Trust in the Lord forever, for in the Lord Jehovah is everlasting strength. Take hold of His strength. Go from strength to strength.
LEADER	I'll go in the strength of the Lord, to conflicts which faith will require.
RESPONSE	Be strengthened with might by His Spirit in the inner man, that Christ may dwell in your heart by faith; and being fruitful in every good work, strengthened with all might according to His glorious power.
LEADER	His grace as my shield and reward, my courage and zeal shall inspire, With His sword of truth in my hand, to suffer and triumph I'll go.
RESPONSE	My grace is sufficient for thee for my strength is made perfect in weakness. The Lord stood with me and strengthened me.
ALL	I can do all things through Christ which strengthens me.

From the Salvation Army Song Book #734
Scripture: Ex. 15:2; Psa. 27;11; Deut. 33:25; Psa. 16:11; Isa. 26:4;
Isa. 27:5; Psa. 84:7; Eph. 3:16; Col. 1:10;
2 Cor. 12:9; 2 Tim. 4:17; Phil. 4:13

THE MIGHTY GOD

LEADER	Praise to the Lord, the Almighty, the King of creation; Praise Him in glad adoration.
ALL	Behold Lord, thou hast made the heaven and earth by thy great power and thy stretched out arm, and there is nothing too hard for thee.
LEADER	Praise to the Lord! Ponder anew what the Almighty can do. Gladly for aye, we adore Him.
ALL	The mighty God the Lord of hosts is His name. Great in counsel, and mighty in works.
LEADER	A mighty fortress is our God, A bulwark never failing; Lord Saboth is His name, from age to age the same.
ALL	Oh, how great is thy goodness which thou hast laid up for them that fear thee, for them which trust in thee.
LEADER	O worship the King, all glorious above; And gratefully sing His power and His love.
ALL	Great is the Lord and greatly to be praised; And His greatness is unsearchable.
LEADER	Our shield and defender, the ancient of days; Pavilioned in splendor and girded in praise.
ALL	O Lord, all men shall speak of thy might, and I will declare thy greatness.
LEADER	O tell of His might, O sing of His grace; Whose robe is the light; Whose canopy is space.
ALL	O Lord how great are thy works, and thy thoughts are very deep.
LEADER	Strong in the Lord of Hosts, and in His mighty power; Who in the strength of Jesus trusts, is more than conqueror.
ALL	Thine, O Lord, is the greatness, and the power, and the glory and the victory, and the majesty.
LEADER	I'll go in the strength of the Lord; to work He appoints me to do. I'll go in the strength of the Lord; to conflicts which faith will require.
ALL	Through God we shall do valiantly. Traveling in the greatness of His strength.

From the Salvation Army Song Book #19, 1, 16, 695

Scripture: Jer. 32:17,19; Psa. 31:19; Psa. 145:3,6; Psa. 92:5; I Chr. 29:11; Psa 60:12; Isa. 63:1

OUR REFUGE

(This reading is most effective when a line of the Hymn, "Jesus, Lover of my Soul" is sung as a Solo, and the response will be given by an individual, a Corps Cadet Brigade, a speaking quartet, or the congregation.)

JESUS, LOVER OF MY SOUL

"Having loved His own that were in the world, He loved them unto the end"

LET ME TO THY BOSOM FLY:

"There was at the table reclining on Jesus' bosom one of his disciples"

WHILE THE NEARER WATERS ROLL,

"I am come into deep waters, where the floods overflow me."

WHILE THE TEMPEST STILL IS HIGH:

"I would haste me to a shelter from the stormy wind and tempest."

HIDE ME, O MY SAVIOUR, HIDE,

In the day of trouble He will keep me secretly in his pavilion; in the covert of his tabernacle will He hide me."

TILL THE STORM OF LIFE BE PAST:

"Trust in the Lord forever, for in the Lord, is everlasting strength."

SAFE INTO THE HAVEN GUIDE:

"Then are they glad because they are quiet; so he bringeth them into their desired haven."

O RECEIVE MY SOUL AT LAST.

"And they stoned Stephen, calling upon the Lord, and saying, Lord Jesus, receive my spirit."

OTHER REFUGE HAVE I NONE:

"God is our refuge and strength, a very present help in trouble."

HANGS MY HELPLESS SOUL ON THEE:

"The Lord will not suffer the soul of the righteous to famish"

LEAVE, AH! LEAVE ME NOT ALONE,

"Himself hath said, I will in no wise fail thee, neither will I in any wise forsake thee."

STILL SUPPORT AND COMFORT ME

"I will give thanks unto thee, O Lord, for thou comfortest me."

ALL MY TRUST ON THEE IS STAYED,

"Salvation will He appoint for walls and bulwarks."

ALL MY HELP FROM THEE I BRING:

"Thou wilt keep him in perfect peace whose mind is stayed on thee, because he trusteth in Thee."

COVER MY DEFENSELESS HEAD

"O Lord, thou hast covered my head in the day of battle."

WITH THE SHADOW OF THY WING.

"In the shadow of thy wings will I take refuge."

PLENTEOUS GRACE WITH THEE IS FOUND,

"My grace is sufficient for thee, for My strength is made perfect in weakness."

GRACE TO COVER ALL MY SIN

"Where sin abounded, grace did abound more exceedingly"

LET THE HEALING STREAMS ABOUND:

"Everything shall live whither the river cometh."

MAKE AND KEEP ME PURE WITHIN

"Create in me a clean heart, O God; and renew a right spirit within me."

THOU OF LIFE THE FOUNTAIN ART,

"In Him was life, and the life was the light of men."

FREELY LET ME TAKE OF THEE:

"He that is athirst, let him take the water of life freely."

SPRING THOU UP WITHIN MY HEART,

"The water that I shall give him shall become in him a well of water springing up unto eternal life."

RISE TO ALL ETERNITY.

"Whosoever drinketh of the water that I shall give him shall never thirst, ...and out of him shall flow rivers of living water.

From the Salvation Army Song Book #737

Scripture Selections: John 13:1; John 13:23; Psa. 69:2; Psa. 55:8; Psa. 27:5; Isa. 26:4; Psa. 107:30; Acts 7:59; Psa 46:1; Prov. 10:3; Isa. 41:10; 2 Cor. 1:4; Prov. 3:3; Isa. 26:5; Psa. 140:7; Psa. 57:1; 2 Cor. 12:9; Rom 5:20; Ez. 47:9; Psa. 51:10; John 1:4; Rev. 22:17; John 4:14; John 7:38

PRAISE BREAK

LEADER	The Lord is my light and my salvation; whom shall I fear? The Lord is the strength of my life.
RESPONSE	Living in the fountain, walking in the light. Now and ever trusting Jesus and His might.
LEADER	I will bless the Lord at all times. His praise shall continually be in my mouth. How precious are thy thoughts unto me, O God.
RESPONSE	Always realizing Jesus and His smile To be ever with me, in me all the while.
LEADER	O give thanks unto the Lord: sing unto him; talk of His wondrous works; glory in His holy name; let the heart of them rejoice that seek the Lord.
RESPONSE	Having for my portion Jesus and His joy Joy which none can hinder, nothing can alloy.
LEADER	I will praise Thee, O Lord, among the people for through God we shall do valiantly.
RESPONSE	Living and believing, saved from every fear, Working and receiving heavenly wages here.
LEADER	O sing unto the Lord a new song, for He hath done marvelous things; His right hand and His holy arm has given Him the victory. For the Lord is great and greatly to be praised. Psa. 98:1 Psa. 96:4
RESPONSE	Fighting for His glory, standing by His cross, Whether it be profit, whether it be loss.
LEADER	Yea, though I walk through the valley of the shadow of death I will fear no evil...surely goodness and mercy shall follow me all the days of my life; and I shall dwell in the house of the Lord forever.
RESPONSE	By and by He'll call me; lay thy weapon down, Ended is thy warfare, come and take thy crown.

From the Salvation Army Song Book #352

Scripture: Psa. 27:1; Psa 34:1; Psa. 139:17; Psa. 105:1,2,3; Psa 108:3,13;

Psa. 98:1; Psa. 96:4; Psa. 23:4,6

PRAISE AND HONOR

LEADER   Ye servants of God, your Master proclaim,
And publish abroad His wonderful name;

RESPONSE   The Spirit of the Lord God is upon me; because He hath anointed me to preach good tidings to the meek; He has sent me to bind up the broken hearted, to proclaim liberty to the captives, and to proclaim the acceptable year of the Lord.

LEADER   The name all-victorious of Jesus extol;
His kingdom is glorious and rules over all.

RESPONSE   His name shall be called Wonderful, Counselor, the Mighty God, the Everlasting Father, the Prince of Peace. Of the increase of His government and peace there shall be no end.

LEADER   God ruleth on high, almighty to save;
And still He is nigh, His presence we have.

RESPONSE   God has given Him a name which is above every name; that at the name of Jesus every knee should bow and every tongue confess that Jesus Christ is Lord, to the glory of God the Father.

LEADER   The great congregation His triumphs shall sing,
Ascribing salvation to Jesus our King.

RESPONSE   Now thanks be unto God, which always causes us to triumph in Christ.
For this is the victory that overcomes the world, even our faith.

LEADER   Then let us adore and give Him His right,
All glory and power, all wisdom and might.

RESPONSE   And Christ was made flesh and dwelt among us, and we beheld His glory; the glory as of the only begotten of the Father, full of grace and truth.
For thine is the kingdom and the power, and the glory forever.

LEADER   All honor and blessing, with angels above,
And thanks never-ceasing and infinite love!

RESPONSE   O give thanks unto the Lord; sing unto Him, talk of all His wondrous works. Glory in His holy name, let the heart of them rejoice that seek the Lord.

From the Salvation Army Song Book #24

*Scripture: Isa. 61:1; Isa. 9:6; Phil. 2:9,10,11; 2Cor. 2:14; I Jn. 5:4;
Jn. 1:14; Matt. 6:13; Psa. 105:1,2,3*

QUIET REFLECTION

ALL   The Lord is my Shepherd, I shall not want

LEADER   The King of love my Shepherd is,
Whose goodness faileth never;
I nothing lack if I am His
And He is mine for ever.

ALL   He makes me to lie down in green pastures; He leads me beside still waters

LEADER   Where streams of living water flow
My ransomed soul He leadeth
And where the verdant pastures grow
With food celestial feedeth.

ALL   He restores my soul; He leads me in paths of righteousness for His name's sake.

LEADER   Perverse and foolish oft I strayed,
But yet in love He sought me,
And on His shoulder gently laid
And home rejoicing brought me.

ALL   Yea though I walk through the valley of the shadow of death I will fear no evil for he is with me.

LEADER   In death's dark vale I fear no ill
With Thee, dear Lord, beside me:
Thy rod and staff my comfort still,
Thy cross before to guide me.

ALL   He prepares a table before me in the presence of my enemies;
He anoints my head with oil; my cup runs over.

LEADER   And so through all the length of days
Thy goodness faileth never;
Good Shepherd, may I sing Thy praise
Within Thy house for ever.

ALL   Surely goodness and mercy shall follow me all the days of my life; and I shall dwell in the house of the Lord forever.

From the Salvation Army Song Book #53

Scripture Selection: Psalm 23

READY RESPONSE

LEADER	Lord, I make a full surrender; All I have I yield to Thee
MEN	Yield yourselves unto the Lord, and serve the Lord your God.
LEADER	Whosoever forsaketh not all that he hath, he cannot be my disciple.
WOMEN	For Thy love, so great and tender, Asks the gift of me.
ALL	Lord, I bring my whole affection, Claim it, take it for Thine own.
LEADER	If any man will come after me, let him deny himself and take up his cross and follow me.
ALL	Safely kept by Thy protection, Fixed on Thee alone.
LEADER	Lord, my will I here present Thee Gladly, now no longer mine;
MEN	But what things were gain to me, those I counted loss for Christ. Yea, doubtless, I count all things but loss for the excellency of the knowledge of Christ Jesus my Lord.
WOMEN	Let no evil thing prevent me Blending it with Thine.
ALL	Lord my life I lay before Thee; Hear this hour the sacred vow.
LEADER	I am crucified with Christ, nevertheless I live; yet not I, but Christ liveth in me; and the life which I now live I live by the faith of the Son of God who loved me and gave himself for me.
ALL	All Thine own I now restore Thee, Thine forever now.
LEADER	Blessed Spirit, Thou hast brought me Thus my all to Thee to give;
WOMEN	For the blood of Christ has bought me, And by faith I live.
ALL	Show Thyself O God of power, My unchanging, loving Friend;
LEADER	In the day when I cried you answered me, and strengthened me with strength in my soul. That I might walk worthy of the Lord; strengthened with all might according to His glorious power.
ALL	Keep me till, in death's glad hour, Faith in sight shall end.

From the Salvation Army Song Book #504

*Scripture Selections: 2 Chr. 30:8; Luke 14:33; Matt. 16:24;
Phil. 3:7,8; Gal. 2:20; Col. 1:10,11*

SECRET OF HIS PRESENCE

(Sing Chorus) *"In the secret of Thy presence,*
In the hiding of Thy power,
Let me love Thee, let me serve Thee,
Every consecrated hour."

LEADER In the secret of Thy presence,
Where the pure in heart may dwell,
Are the springs of sacred service
And a power that none can tell.

RESPONSE There my love must bring its offering,
There my heart must yield its praise,
And the Lord will come, revealing
All the secrets of His ways.

LEADER More than all my lips may utter,
More than all I do or bring,

RESPONSE Is the depth of my devotion
To my Saviour, Lord and King.

LEADER Nothing less will keep me tender;
Nothing less will keep me true;

RESPONSE Nothing less will keep the fragrance
And the bloom on all I do!

(Sing Chorus) *"In the secret of Thy presence,*
In the hiding of Thy power,
Let me love Thee, let me serve Thee,
Every consecrated hour."

LEADER Blessed Lord, to see Thee truly,
Then to tell as I have seen,
This shall rule my life supremely,
This shall be the sacred gleam.

RESPONSE Sealed again is all the sealing,
Pledged again my willing heart,
First to know Thee, then to serve Thee,
Then to see Thee as Thou art.

ALL In Thy presence is fullness of joy; at Thy right hand there are
pleasures for evermore. *Psa. 16:11*

From the Salvation Army Song Book #591

WALKING WITH GOD

LEADER   Walk in love as Christ also hath loved you. We walk by faith and
not by sight. How wonderful it is to walk with God
Along the road that holy men have trod;

RESPONSE   How wonderful it is to hear Him say:
Fear not, have faith, 'tis I who lead the way!

LEADER   In everything by prayer and supplication with thanksgiving let your
requests be made known unto God.
How wonderful it is to talk with God
When cares sweep o'er my spirit like a flood;

RESPONSE   How wonderful it is to hear His voice,
For when He speaks the desert lands rejoice!

LEADER   O praise the Lord, praise Him all ye people.
How wonderful it is to praise my God
Who comforts and protects me with His rod;

RESPONSE   How wonderful to praise Him every hour,
My heart attuned to sing His wondrous power!

LEADER   The disciples were all filled with the Holy Ghost, and they spake the
word of God with boldness.
How wonderful it is to fight for God,
And point poor sinners to the precious Blood;

RESPONSE   How wonderful it is to wield His sword
'Gainst sin, the enemy of Christ, my Lord!

LEADER   Now we see through a glass darkly, but then face to face.
How wonderful 'twill be to live with God
When I have crossed death's deep and swelling tide.

RESPONSE   How wonderful to see Him face to face
When I have fought the fight and won the race.

From the Salvation Army Song Book #583

Scripture Selections: Eph. 5:2; 2 Cor. 5:7; Phil. 4:6;
Psa. 117; Acts 4:31, 1 Cor. 13:12

WORTHY VESSELS

LEADER   O Lord, thou art our Father; we are the clay, and thou the potter; and we all are the work of thy hand.

RESPONSE   Have thine own way, Lord, have thine own way;
Thou art the potter; I am the clay;
Mould me and make me after thy will,
While I am waiting yielded and still.

LEADER   O God, thine hands have made me, and fashioned me together.
Thou hast made me as the clay.

RESPONSE   Have thine own way Lord, have thine own way;
Search me and try me Master today.

LEADER   And the vessel that the potter made of clay was marred...so he made it again another vessel as seemed good for the potter to make it.

RESPONSE   Have thine own way, Lord, have thine own way
Wounded and weary, help me I pray.

LEADER   Then the word of the Lord came to Jeremiah saying, "Behold as the clay is in the potter's hand, so are ye in my hand"

RESPONSE   Have thine own way, Lord, have thine own way;
Hold o'er my being absolute sway.

LEADER   Who art thou, O man, that thy repliest against God? Shall the thing formed say to him that formed it, "Why has thou made me thus?"

RESPONSE   Have thine own way, Lord, have thine own way,
Fill with thy spirit till all may see
Christ only, always, living in me.

LEADER   Hath not the potter power over the clay, of the same lump to make one vessel unto honor, and another unto dishonor. If a man therefore purge himself, he shall be a vessel unto honor, sanctified, and meet for the Master's use, and prepared unto every good work.

RESPONSE   But we have this treasure in earthen vessels, that the excellency of the power may be of God and not of us.

From the Salvation Army Song Book #487

Scripture: Isa. 64:8; Job 10:9; Jer. 18:4,6; Rom. 9:20,21; 2 Tim. 2:21; 2 Cor. 4:7

CHRISTIAN FAMILY THERAPY

LEADER   What a treasure is a happy, joyous, glad, laughing family

RESPONSE   Thou hast put gladness in our hearts. We will be glad and rejoice in Thee.

LEADER   Laughter is as holy, and hallowed as prayer. Certainly it should be one of our favorite sounds in the home.

RESPONSE   Be glad in the Lord and rejoice ye righteous: and shout for joy all ye that are upright in heart. Let all the joys of the godly well up in praise to the Lord, for it is right to praise Him. And they sang praises with gladness, and bowed their heads and worshipped.

LEADER   How pathetic is the home where Christians are somber and always squelch a laugh. A home that somehow has the look of an old basset hound.

RESPONSE   But let the righteous be glad; let them rejoice before God: yea let them exceedingly rejoice.

LEADER   Impatience is blocked when Johnny accidentally spills his milk and mother smiles; a smile that triggers the laughter of acceptance by the rest of the family.

RESPONSE   Satisfy us in our earliest youth with Thy lovingkindness, giving us constant joy to the end of our days. Anxious hearts are very heavy, but a word of gladness and encouragement does wonders. (TLB)

LEADER   One of the most joyous hours of the day should be around the family table. Experiences related, silly incidents reported, and laughter shared. Sometimes shared loudly, sometimes quietly, sometimes hilariously. Always enjoyable laughter!

RESPONSE   And the disciples continuing daily in one accord in the temple, and breaking bread from house to house, did eat their food with gladness and singleness of heart.

LEADER   Mary snickered when we started family prayers and soon all the kids were snickering. Dad stopped praying and laughed quietly, saying, "I'll bet the angels are giggling too." Then we really prayed!

RESPONSE   Thou wilt show me the path of life: in Thy presence is fullness of joy; at thy right hand there are pleasures evermore.

LEADER   Jesus rebuked the religious stuffed shirt Pharisees. Surely Jesus enjoyed a laugh or two with His disciples. He hinted at it in the Beatitudes, and when He spoke to His disciples.

RESPONSE   Rejoice and be exceeding glad for great is your reward in heaven.

These things have I spoken unto you, that my joy might remain in you, and that your joy might be full.

Scripture Selections: Psa. 4:7; Psa. 32:11; Psa. 68:3; Psa. 147:1 (TLB); Psa. 90:14 (TLB); Acts 2:46; Psa. 16:11; Matt. 5:12; John 15:11

HEARTFELT THANKSGIVING

LEADER   Though I offer my Thanksgiving in November but forget that each day merits my thanks, I am at heart ungrateful.

RESPONSE   And though I praise Thanksgiving as a noble tradition and desire it should be observed by all, but by my life express no devotion to God or thoughtfulness to others, I am not really grateful.

LEADER   And though I have a great family feast and share a bit with the needy, but my heart is dutiful or smug, I am still ungrateful.

RESPONSE   Heartfelt Thanksgiving doth magnify the Lord, is never an occasion for pride or idle boasting. Is never selfish nor unmindful of the needs of others; never wearies of service.

LEADER   Heartfelt Thanksgiving is not fretful, but always glad,

- lightens our burdens,
- deepens our joys,
- sustains our faith,
- heals our sorrows.

RESPONSE   Heartfelt Thanksgiving never fails,
But whether there be possessions they shall fail,
But whether there be privileges they shall cease,
But whether there be freedom it may vanish away;
But Thanksgiving of the Heart always triumphs.

LEADER   For what earthly goods denied, Heartfelt Thanksgiving bestowed in spiritual happiness. What life made seem futile, Heartfelt Thanksgiving made purposeful. What circumstances made insurmountable, Heartfelt Thanksgiving gave conquering power.

RESPONSE   And now abides -
Thanksgiving of the Mind,
Thanksgiving of the Purse,
Thanksgiving of the Heart,
But the greatest of these is Thanksgiving of the Heart.

LINKED IN LOVE

(Mother's Day or Father's Day)

LEADER Love is kind...never jealous...never haughty or selfish... Love does not demand its own way.

RESPONSE Love is big enough to share...to give...to release...to cultivate...to understand...to enjoy.

LEADER Let love be your greatest aim. All the special gifts and powers from God will some day come to an end, but love goes on forever.

RESPONSE Love looks beneath the surface and sees an untapped reservoir of ability. Both members of a couple free each other to discover and develop their own capacities.

LEADER If you love someone you will believe in him and always expect the best.

RESPONSE I love you--
Not only for what you have made of yourself
But for what you are making of me.

LEADER Let us not love in word, neither in tongue; but in deed and truth. Let us really love and show it by our actions.

RESPONSE I love you--
For passing over all the foolish, weak things
That you can't help dimly seeing
And bringing into the light all the beautiful.

LEADER If you love someone you will be loyal no matter what the cost.

RESPONSE I love you--
Not only for what you are
But for what
I am when I am with you.

LEADER If you love someone you will always stand your ground in defending him or her.

RESPONSE I love you--
Because you are helping me to make
Out of the lumber of my life
A Temple
Out of the work of every day
A Song.

From Roy Croft's, Best Loved Poems of American People, (Garden City Publishing Co., Garden City, New York, 1936, p. 25)

Scripture: I Cor. 13 (LB); I John 3

THE PEOPLE GIVE THANKS

LEADER   O give thanks unto the Lord, for He is good: for His mercy endureth forever.

RESPONSE   Thanks be unto God for His unspeakable gift.

LEADER   O give thanks unto the Lord, call upon His name, make known His deeds among men.

RESPONSE   Thanks be to God which always causeth us to triumph in Christ.

LEADER   O give thanks unto the name of the Lord.

RESPONSE   Thanks be to God which giveth us the victory through our Lord Jesus Christ.

LEADER   O give thanks unto the Lord, at the remembrance of His holiness.

RESPONSE   Thanks be to God which put the same earnest care into the heart of you.

ALL   So we thy people will give Thee thanks forever

Scripture Selections: Psa. 107:1; 2 Cor. 9:15; Psa. 105:1; 1 Cor. 8:16; Psa. 122:4; 1 Cor. 15:57; Psa. 30:4; 2 Cor. 8:16; Psa. 70:13

THANKS BE TO GOD

LEADER   Let us come before His presence with thanksgiving; joy and glad-
          ness shall be found therein; thanksgiving, and the voice of melody:

RESPONSE Thanks be to God for His unspeakable gift.

LEADER   Enter into His gates with thanksgiving and into His courts with
          praise.

RESPONSE Thanks be to God which giveth us the victory through our Lord
          Jesus Christ.

RESPONSE Thanks be to God for your loving deeds and your strong faith.

LEADER   In everything give thanks for this is the will of God in Christ Jesus
          concerning you.

RESPONSE Thanks be to God which always causeth us to triumph in Christ.

LEADER   I thank Christ Jesus my Lord, who hath enabled me, for that He
          counted me faithful putting me into the ministry.

RESPONSE Thanks be to God the glorious Father of our Lord Jesus Christ; who
          gave you wisdom to see clearly, and really understand who Christ is
          and all He has done for us.

LEADER   For all things are for your sakes, that the abundant grace might
          through the thanksgiving of many redound to the glory of God.

RESPONSE Thanks be to God and the Father of our Lord Jesus Christ for we
          have heard how much you trust in the Lord and how much you
          love His people.

LEADER   Therefore, will I give thanks unto Thee, O Lord, and sing praises to
          Thy name.

RESPONSE Thanks be to God which put the same earnest care into the heart of
          you.

LEADER   What thanks can we render to God for the joy and delight you have
          given us in our praying for you?

RESPONSE Thanks be to God that you yourselves became an example to all the
          other Christians and that the work of the Lord has spread out from
          you to others everywhere, even far beyond your boundaries.

*Scripture Selections: Isa. 51:3; Psa. 100:4; 2 Cor. 9:15; 1 Thess. l:2;
1 Thess. 5:18; 2 Cor. 2:14; 1 Tim. 1:12; Eph. 1:15,16 (TLB); 2 Cor. 4:15;
Col. 1:3,4 (TLB); Psa. 18:49; 2 Cor. 8:16; 1 Thess. 3:9 (TLB); 1 Thess. 1:7,8, (TLB)*

UNTO US A CHILD IS BORN

LEADER   For unto us a Child is born; unto us a Son is given; and the government shall be upon his shoulder.

ALL   These will be His royal titles: "Wonderful", "Counselor," "The Mighty God", "The Everlasting Father," The Prince of Peace".

LEADER   His ever-expanding, peaceful government will never end. He shall rule with perfect fairness and justice from the throne of his father David.

ALL   He will bring true justice and peace to all the nations of the world. This is going to happen because the Lord of heaven's armies has dedicated himself to do it!

LEADER   That night some shepherds were in the fields outside the village, guarding their flocks of sheep. Suddenly an angel appeared among them and the landscape shone bright with the glory of the Lord.

ALL   They were badly frightened, but the angel reassured them.

LEADER   "Don't be afraid!" he said. "I bring you the most joyful news ever announced, and it is for everyone! The Savior, yes, the Messiah, the Lord has been born tonight in Bethlehem.

ALL   "How will you recognize Him? You will find a baby wrapped in a blanket, lying in a manger!"

LEADER   Suddenly, the angel was joined by a vast host of others - the armies of heaven - praising God.

ALL   "Glory to God in the highest heaven," they sang, "and peace on earth for all those who are of good-will."

LEADER   When this great army of angels had returned again to heaven, the shepherds said to each other, "Come on! Let's go to Bethlehem! Let's see this wonderful thing that has happened, which the Lord has told us about."

ALL   They ran to the village and found their way to Mary and Joseph. And there was the baby, lying in the manger.

LEADER   The shepherds told everyone what had happened and what the angel had said to them about this child. And all who heard the shepherd's story expressed astonishment, but Mary quietly treasured these things in her heart and often thought about them.

ALL   Then the shepherds went back again to their fields and flocks, praising God for the visit of the angels, and because they had seen the child, just as the angel had told them.

Scripture (from the Living Bible): Isa. 9:6,7; Luke 2:8-20

WELL DONE!

(In appreciation of Army Bands and Songsters)

LEADER   Music is a wondrous, timeless link with God. We are grateful for the gift of music and its ministry to our spirits.

RESPONSE   Praise ye the Lord!
Praise God in His Sanctuary
Make a joyful noise unto the Lord
Praise Him in the congregation of His saints.

LEADER   Music enriches our worship and opens a door for the Holy Spirit to walk in and touch us.

RESPONSE   Talk with each other about the Lord,
Quoting psalms and hymns
Offering praise with voices and instruments
Making music in your hearts to the Lord.

LEADER   We express our appreciation to the Bandmaster, the Band Locals, and to the Band members for your faithfulness in attendance, and for your leadership in congregational singing.

RESPONSE   Praise the Lord!
Praise Him with the sound of the trumpet
Praise Him with the timbrel
Praise Him upon the loud cymbals,
Praise Him upon the high sounding cymbals.

LEADER   We thank the Lord also for the hallowed, sacred, moving moments of worship during a band selection; and the joyous, exciting, exhilarating moments of a march.

RESPONSE   Serve the Lord with gladness
From the rising of the sun
To the going down of the same,
The Lord's name be praised!

LEADER   The anthems, the songs, the hymns of our Songster Brigade lift our souls to enjoy a deepened sense of worship.

RESPONSE   Sing unto the Lord
Bless His name
For He hath done marvelous things
How good it is to sing His praises.
How delightful and how right.

LEADER   We are grateful for the sincerity, the empathy, and spiritual meaning that comes to us through the singing of the Songsters.

RESPONSE   Break forth into singing
             Let them praise the name of the Lord with singing
             Sing forth the honor of His name
             O sing unto the Lord a new song
             Rejoice and sing praise.

LEADER   For your interest in music, your joy of participation, your desire to
             improve, and your love of The Salvation Army; we thank our Band
             and Songsters.

RESPONSE   We will praise Thee, O Lord
             With our whole heart.
             We will worship in Thy holy temple,
             We will praise Thy name
             For Thy loving kindness and Thy truth;
             We will make music in the ways of the Lord;
             For great is the glory of the Lord.

Scripture Selections: Psa. 150 & 100; Eph. 5 (TLB); Psa. 150; Psa. 100; Psa. 113;
Psa. 98; Psa. 147; Psa. 66; Isa 14:7; Psa. 96; Psa. 138

THE WORD

(Bible Sunday)

The world is full of lesser words, but there is only one WORD, Jesus Christ:

"For His name is called THE WORD OF GOD."

HE IS THE WORD OF CREATION

"In the beginning was the Word, and the Word was with God, and the Word was God. The same was in the beginning with God. All things were made by him; and without him was not anything made that was made. In him was life; and the life was the light of men."

HE IS THE WORD OF PERSONIFICATION

"And the Word was made flesh, and dwelt among us (became a human being and lived among us-Phillips) and we beheld his glory, the glory as of the only begotten of the Father, full of grace and truth."

OURS IS THE WORD OF RECONCILIATION

"God was in Christ, reconciling the world unto himself and hath committed unto us the word of reconciliation, and hath given to us the ministry of reconciliation."

OURS IS THE WORD OF COMMUNICATION

"Study to show thyself approved unto God, a workman that needeth not to be ashamed, rightly dividing the word of truth."

"Open thou mine eyes, that I may behold wondrous things out of thy word."

"For the entrance of thy words giveth light; it giveth understanding unto the simple."

"I will not forget thy word...for thy word is pure, therefore thy servant loveth it."

OURS IS THE WORD OF DEMONSTRATION

"Knowing that whoso keepeth thy word, in him, verily, is the love of God perfected."

"And I rejoice in thy word."

MAY THIS BLESSING BE UPON US ALL

May the triune God enrich your life and living today and all future days-- "for there are three that bear record in heaven, the Father, the Word, and the Holy Ghost;"

by Mrs. Myra Olley

Scripture Selections: Rev. 19:3; John 1:1-4; John 1:14; 2 Cor. 5:18,19; 2 Tim. 2:15; Psa. 119:18,130,16,140,162; Psa. 130; Psa. 16; Psa. 140; Psa. 162 1 John 5:7

Youth Group Devotions

FAITH

READ: Selected verses from Hebrews 11.

> Faith is not merely praying
> Upon your knees at night.
> Faith is not merely straying
> Through darkness to the light.
>
> Faith is not merely waiting
> For glory that may be;
> Faith is not merely hating
> The sinful ecstasy.
>
> Faith is the brave endeavor,
> The splendid enterprise,
> The strength to serve whatever
> Conditions may arise.
>
> (Kiser)

TEXT TO MEMORIZE: "Be not faithless, but believing." John 20:27.

FOR DISCUSSION:

Why is faith so important in a Christian's life?

How do we get faith? What are some things that destroy it? Does school aid or hinder Christian faith?

Do you believe if you have faith enough, mountains will be moved?

PRAY: For a faith that cannot be destroyed, a faith that will help you to lead others to Christ. Pray that every camper may get into the SPIRIT of Camp from this very first day.

SING: My faith looks up to Thee
Thou Lamb of Calvary, Saviour Divine.
Now hear me while I pray,
Take all my guilt away,
Oh, let me from this day be wholly Thine.

Lord, increase my faith,
Lord, increase my understanding.
I would endeavor to be more like Thee,
Day by day.

Trust and obey,
For there's no other way,
To be happy in Jesus,
But to trust and obey.

GRATITUDE

READ: Luke 17:11-16

O God, we thank Thee for everything.

For the glory and beauty and wonder of the world;

For the glory of springtime, the tints of the flowers, and their fragrance;

For the glory of the summer flowers, the roses, cardinals, and red-winged blackbirds;

For the glory of the autumn, the scarlet and crimson and gold of the forest;

For the glory of winter, the pure snow on the shrub and trees.

We thank Thee that Thou hast placed us here to use Thy gifts for the good of all.

TEXT TO MEMORIZE: "In everything give thanks: for this is the will of God in Christ Jesus concerning you." 1 Thess.5:18.

FOR DISCUSSION:

For what should we be thankful?

Do you always remember to say "thank you" for gifts given to you and when someone does something for you?

For what should we say "thank you" to God?

How can we show our gratitude toward others? Toward God?

Can you think of some times when Jesus said "thank you"? What do we mean by "saying grace"?

PRAY:

For a thankful heart, always. That God will help us to say "thank you" to those who are kind to us.

Express in prayer your own thanks to God for what He has given you, and done for you.

SING: Thank you, Lord, for saving my soul
Thank you, Lord, for making me whole;
Thank you, Lord, for giving to me
Thy great salvation, so rich and free.

Praise Him with melody,
    Praise Him with song,
Tell of His holiness
    All the day long.
Give Him all majesty
    Earth can afford.
Praise Him with melody,
       Praise ye the Lord!

LOVE

READ: John 3:16; Matthew 5:44; Matthew 22:35-40

> Saviour, teach me day by day
> Love's sweet lesson to obey;
> Sweeter lesson cannot be.
> Loving Him who first loved me.
>
> How shall I my life employ?
> Love will be my only joy;
> Ever new that joy will be,
> Loving Him who first loved me.
>
> So will I rejoice to show
> All the love I feel and owe;
> Ever serving, ever free,
> Loving Him who first loved me.
>
> (Jane E. Leeson)

TEXT TO MEMORIZE: "Thou shalt love the Lord thy God with all thy heart, and with all thy soul, and with all thy strength, and with all thy mind; and thy neighbor as thyself." Luke 10:27.

FOR DISCUSSION:

Think of those whom you love - your family, your friends. Why do you love them?

Is there anyone whom you do not love? Why?

Have you any enemies? What does Jesus say about loving our enemies?

Try this day to show love for someone who doesn't seem to be loved by anyone else.

PRAY: For your loved ones - for your enemies. Pray for those in enemy countries who want to be Christians and cannot, because the rulers of their countries will not allow it. Pray that you may be able to show love and understanding toward all those with whom you come in contact this day - and every day.

SING: God's love is wonderful! (repeat)
Wonderful that He should give His son to die for me.
God's love is wonderful!

Love lifted me.
When no one but Christ could help,
Love lifted me.

PRAYER

READ: Psalm 51

> What various hindrances we meet
> In coming to the Mercy Seat!
> Yet who that knows the worth of prayer
> But wishes to be often there!
>
> Prayer makes the darkest cloud withdraw.
> Prayer climbs the ladder Jacob saw,
> Gives exercise to faith and love,
> Brings every blessing from above.
>
> Restraining prayer, we cease to fight;
> Prayer makes the soldier's armor bright;
> And Satan trembles when he sees
> The weakest saint upon his knees.
>
> (William Cowper)

TEXT TO MEMORIZE: Jesus said, "And whatsoever ye shall ask in my name, that will I do, that the Father may be glorified in the Son." John 14:13.

FOR DISCUSSION:

What is prayer? Do we all need to pray?

When should we pray?

Does God always answer prayer?

Where, and how, did Jesus pray? How does He teach us to pray?

Why is Corps Cadets a good place to learn to pray?

Have you ever helped someone else to pray?

Can you pray aloud in public, or only silently?

PRAY: For your family, your friends, the other girls in the class, for someone who needs your special prayer, for yourself, and then, the Lord's Prayer.

SING: Teach me how to love Thee   Whisper a prayer in the morning,
Teach me how to pray.   Whisper a prayer at noon,
Teach ms how to serve Thee   Whisper a prayer in the evening,
Better day by day.   To keep your heart in tune.

> God answers prayer in the morning.
>   Etc.
> Prayer changes things in the morning.
>   Etc.

SERVICE

READODE: Romans 12.

My Creed

This is my creed: to close my eyes
To little faults of those around me;
To strive to be found as each day dies
Some better than the morning found me;
To ask for no unearned applause,
To cross no river until I reach it,
To see the merit of the cause
Before I follow those who preach it.

This is my creed: to try to shun
The sloughs in which the foolish wallow;
To lead where I may be the one
Whom weaker men may choose to follow.
TO KEEP MY STANDARD ALWAYS HIGH,
TO FIND MY TASK AND ALWAYS DO IT;
THIS IS MY CREED - I WISH THAT I
COULD LEARN TO SHAPE MY ACTION TO IT.

(Kiser)

TEXT TO MEMORIZE: "For whosoever will save his life shall lose it; but whosoever will lose his life for my sake, the same shall saves it." Luke 9:24

FOR DISCUSSION: How can I best be of service to others?

How can I serve God best?

What opportunities are there in my Corps for service to God, and others? Do I always take these opportunities?

What can I do when I go home to serve both God and my fellow men more?

PRAY: That God will use your life in the best way possible to serve others.

That you may seek and find the work which God has for you to do - then when you go home, continue to walk steadfastly in the way which the Master has laid out for you.

For courage to accept every challenge to service that may come to you.

SING: I'll follow Thee, of life the Giver,
I'll follow Thee, suffering Redeemer,
I'll follow Thee, deny Thee never.
By Thy grace, I'll follow Thee.

271

WHAT GOD WANTS

READER: Mark 10:17-27

> Oh, young and fearless Prophet of ancient Galilee
> Thy life is still a summons to serve humanity
> To make our thoughts and actions,
> Less prone to please the crowd.
> To stand with humble courage for truth,
> With hearts uncowed.
>
> (S. Ralph Harlow)

TEXT TO MEMORIZE: "If any man will come after me, let him deny himself, take up his cross, and follow Me." Matt. 16:24.

FOR DISCUSSION:

> What do we mean by doing God's will?
> Who? What? When? Where? is doing God's will?
> What does God's word say that Jesus wants from us?
> God wants us to praise Him.   (Psa. 105:1,2)
> God wants us to know the Bible.   (2 Tim. 2:15)
> God wants us to pray.   (1 Thess.5:17)
> God wants us to give thanks.   (1 Thess. 5:18)
> God wants us to give to Him.   (Mal. 3:10)
> God wants us to work for Him.   (   )
> Can you find other verses?   (   )

PRAY: That we will be willing to listen and obey God's voice when He speaks. That we will be willing to be and do what God wants, and not what we want.

SING: "What a Friend"

READ:
> Youth, oh youth, can I reach you
> Can I speak and make you hear?
> Can I open your eyes to see me
> Can My presence draw you near?
> Is there a prophet among you
> One with a heart to see and know?
> I will flash my secrets to him
> He shall watch my glory grow.
>
> (Anonymous)

WORSHIP

READ: 1 Chronicles 16:23-29

> O, come, let us worship and bow down,
> Let us kneel before the Lord, our Maker;
> For He is our God,
> And we are the people of His pasture and the
>   sheep of His hand.
>
> Worship the Lord in the beauty of holiness,
> Bow down before Him, His glory proclaim;
> Gold of obedience, and incense of lowliness
> Kneel and adore Him - the Lord is His name.
>
> Truth in its beauty, and love in its tenderness,
> These are the offerings we lay on His shrine;
> These, tho' we bring them in trembling and fearfulness,
> He will accept in the Name all divine.
>
>   (Sherwin)

FOR DISCUSSION:

Where can we worship God?

How should we act when we are worshipping God?

How should we enter God's house?

Is a Salvation Army building the house of God?

What is reverence?

When you are worshipping, do you like to be disturbed by whispering, laughing, loud talking, or other noises?

TEXT TO MEMORIZE: "Bless the Lord, O my soul: and all that is within me, bless His holy name." Ps. 103:1.

PRAY: That you may learn how to worship God, and that you may not be a disturber when others also are trying to worship. Pray for closer companionship with God and a better understanding of Him through worship.

SING: Draw me nearer, nearer,
Nearer, blessed Lord,
To the Cross where Thou hast died.
Draw me nearer, nearer,
Nearer, blessed Lord,
To Thy precious bleeding side.

In the secret of Thy presence,
In the hiding of Thy power,
I will love Thee,
I will serve Thee,
Every consecrated hour.

Part IV

The Worship Center

Worship Centers
General

FUNCTION AND USE

PURPOSE

A worship center is a focal or interest center for inspiration or interpretation. It should both enrich and enhance the worship service as well as create an atmosphere of worship. While it may use the symbols of The Salvation Army, the church and our faith, it must be more than symbolic.

PREPARATION

The table for the worship center may be of varying size or shape, depending on the theme and the materials used in developing it. Some suggestions for developing worship centers may be:

1. Select a theme or one idea to develop.

2. Interpret a verse or a passage of Scripture.

3. Relate the worship center to the theme or to a season.

4. Carefully select colors for both meaning and harmony of blend.

   The following are a few color symbols that might be helpful:
   White - purity, holiness, clarity
   Black - evil, sin, night, despair
   Brown - earth, warmth, or barren and unfruitfulness
   Red - love, valor, or danger
   Yellow - light, wisdom, or treachery
   Blue - loyalty, truth, faith
   Green - life, hope, fruitfulness, or envy and jealousy
   Purple - royalty, kingship, government

5. It is a good idea that the basic cloth have a contrasting color in a soft material or ribbon, that can be draped in a flowing manner to tie together parts of the worship center.

6. Articles or materials used should not lie flat; use easels or boxes covered with contrasting material or ribbons to give varying levels.

7. Create varying heights.

8. The Bible or a scroll should be given a special place.

9. A candle may or may not be used.

10. Strive for balance. Remember each object you use has pulling power.

11. Give consideration to perspective with respect to background and foreground. You are in a sense painting a picture.

12. Check for eye level of worshipers and also view your worship center from the seating angle of the worshipers.

13. Simplicity is always power. Don't put too much in your worship center. It must not have a crowded or overloaded look.

PRESENTATION

The worship center may be a completed unit. It may be used for participation in the Call to Worship, in a Testimony Service, or a Responsive Reading. It may be built as the participants develop the worship center, or as the leader develops the theme. Always make the worship center relevant, and seek the guidance of the Holy Spirit as you prepare and build it.

The interpretation of a worship center is very necessary to effectiveness. This is especially important when the technique is unfamiliar. After they have been used several times, the worship center will be meaningful with little interpretation as the worshiper will identify and find personal meanings. A worship center will create atmosphere but also attitudes. Be sure it speaks.

NOTE:

File folders make excellent easels. See the drawing below.

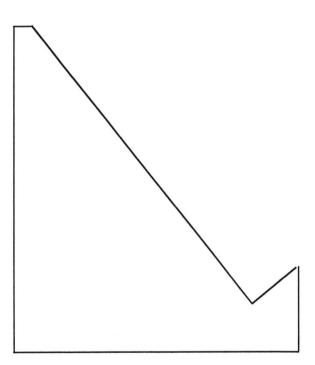

280

BASKETS OF PROMISE

PURPOSE — An adventure with baskets and promises to stimulate an awareness of the truth and power of God's promises that are available to us.

MATERIALS — As this would be an appropriate worship center for fall, a brown cloth with a gold contrast would be effective. Choose eight (8) baskets of varying sizes and shapes. One basket should be without a handle to make a frame for the Bible to rest in as well as being the Bible stand. The items for each basket should be ready to be used in the worship center. The labels on each basket should be large enough to be read by the audience.

ARRANGEMENTS — The basket framed Bible would be placed in the center of the table, and the other baskets arranged attractively around it. Risers made from books, and draped with the soft gold material could provide varying levels on which to place the baskets.

PROCEDURE — The items to be placed in each basket are listed in the presentation. Some scripture will be suggested and some items are open for the leader's interpretation and creativity. These can be arranged in the order as suggested or only the baskets desired by the leader can be used.

PRESENTATION — Our baskets of promise each have a message to tell, and though our basket conversation will be homey, the significant promises will reveal great truths.

1. THE MARKET BASKET

Grandma had a market basket. Today we have a shopping cart. We can shop in God's store of promise:

Bag of Joy	(Isa. 12:3)
Box of Laughter	(Prov. 17:22)
Loaf of Courage	(Duet. 31:6)
Jar of Honey	(Prov. 16:24)
Can of Strength	(Psa. 71:16)

2. MAY BASKET

The basket should be filled with artificial flowers labeled, or flowers from construction paper with the centers labeled.

"Say it with flowers". It could be one of the following or one of your own choosing; - "I love you" or "Have a nice day". It could be a word like thoughtfulness, praise, or generosity. You could use scripture or short phrases from your favorite poems.

3. WASTE BASKET

Use a small desk waste basket. A waste basket is a convenient and functional basket. We need them in every room...etc. It is also absolutely essential to have a waste basket in the room of our thoughts, attitudes, emotions, words, etc. Then we could discard our criticism, resentments, gossip, anxieties, and fears. (Have index cards marked with these, and drop them in the waste basket as they are mentioned.)

4. EGG BASKET

City slickers don't know much about the egg basket. We are more familiar with dainty blue, pink, yellow shining egg cartons, but the farmer's wife goes for the gathering of the eggs with her basket. The egg basket is the basket of faith.

5. WASH BASKET

Although the washer and dryer have outmoded the washboard and the clothes line, we still have the lowly wash basket. Perhaps there is something in the wash basket for us. A box of All for cleansing (Psa. 51:2) A box of Bounce for freshness and renewal (Psa. 51:10)

6. FRUIT BASKET

The fruit basket is a delightful basket of summer fruit. You could refer to Galatians 6:22 or you could use John 15.

Other baskets could be used in similar manner such as the Picnic basket, Bushel basket, and the Cookie basket.

A BASKET OF FRUITFUL SERVICE

PURPOSE:

An important work of God, the Holy Spirit, is to produce Christian graces or the fruit of the Spirit. In fact, Biblical writers place a greater stress on the moral and ethical results of the Holy Spirit indwelling than on any other aspect of the work of the Holy Spirit.

Solid Christian character is truly the work of the Holy Spirit.

Paul outlines the fruit of the Spirit in Gal. 5:22.

All nine are moral virtues and pertain to our attitudes and our character.

Note in this passage the word fruit is in the singular. It is never suggested that the Christian exhibit only "SOME" of the fruit of the Spirit. We are to manifest ALL the fruit of the Spirit. We don't say "Today I'll work on love, tomorrow I'll try to produce joy, later I'll concentrate on gentleness. When the Holy Spirit dwells in us, HE produces ALL the fruit of the Spirit - a full complement of spiritual graces.

We never by hard work or diligent effort produce the fruit of the Spirit. The fruit of the Spirit is not your fruit or my fruit or the fruit of the Church or The Salvation Army. It is the SPIRIT'S fruit.

PROCEDURE:

Let us listen to words of Jesus in John 15, as suggested by the leader.

READER 1   John 15:1,2

READER 2   John 15:8

Paul in Romans further explains the fruitful quality of living.

READER 3   Romans 6:22

Fruit unto holiness suggests three things: First, the life that we live RESEMBLES God.

READER 4   Matthew 12:33

READER 5   Matthew 21:19

Second, the fruit of the Spirit is a REPRODUCTION of God's nature. Man does not manufacture fruit on a tree. God does. We do not live the Christian life by our own effort.

READER 6   John 15:4,5

Third, it REACHES after God. As the tree grows, it grows upward, so we grow in the Spirit reaching after God.

READER 7   Mark 4:31,32

CONCLUDE READING TOGETHER Psalm 1:1-3

A BASKET OF FRUITFUL SERVICE

MATERIALS

Basket with some fruit in it

Oil Lamp

Bible on Stand

We must never let our work basket be empty.

ARRANGEMENT

We will place our fruit in the Basket of Service as suggested by Gal. 5:22 and also relate the graces of the fruit of the Spirit to the Love Chapter 1 Cor. 13.

ADD A PIECE OF FRUIT FOR EACH GRACE

1. Love is never lost. If not reciprocated it will flow back and soften and purify the heart of the giver. "Love seeketh not her own."

2. Joy is our wings. We can do nothing well without joy. "Love rejoiceth not in iniquity but rejoiceth in the truth."

3. Peace is the evening star of the soul. "Love hopeth all things, endureth all things."

4. Longsuffering is tenderness of feeling. "Love suffereth long and is kind."

5. Gentleness. True gentleness is love in society. "It is not easily provoked - love vaunteth not itself."

6. Goodness. In nothing do men so nearly approach God as in doing good to men. "Love thinketh no evil, doth not behave itself unseemly."

7. Faith is the eye that sees God, and the hand that clings to Him. "Love beareth all things, believeth all things."

8. Meekness. The meek are not those that are never angry, but those who feeling anger control it. "Love envieth not, is not puffed up."

9. Temperance is reason's girdle - the strength of the soul is self control. "Love doth not behave itself unseemly."

CHRIST IS THE ANSWER

PURPOSE
To help us to see we must not look around us for answers or solutions to our problems, or the problems of the world for Christ is the answer.

MATERIALS
A dark blue cloth, a large white 4" candle in a brass holder with a floral candle ring. The open Bible should be lying flat on the table with a gold Bible marker. A picture of Eugene Burnand's painting "Go and Teach".

ARRANGEMENT
The picture should be large enough so details can be seen, when placed on the easel. Candle to right side of the picture and the Bible in front of it.

PROCEDURE
Call to Worship

<u>What Christ is to Us</u>

The Shield from every dart;
The Balm for every smart;
The Sharer of each load;
Companion on the road.

The Door into the fold;
The Anchor that will hold;
The Shepherd of the sheep;
The Guardian of my sleep.

The Friend with whom I talk;
The Way by which I walk;
The Light to show the way;
The Strength for every day.

The Source of my delight;
The Song to cheer the night;
The Thought that fills my mind;
The Best of All to find - is Jesus.

(Anonymous)

CHORUS   "Christ is the Answer"

INTERPRETATION OF THE PAINTING

Eugene Burnand, the Swiss painter has depicted a great challenge in his picture "Go and Teach". Burnand is trying to interpret correctly the relationship between Christ and his disciple. Garbed in the Eastern dress, Christ is standing with his left arm around the young man's shoulder - the disciple. Christ's head is slightly bent toward the young man, and a great red cloak covers both persons. The eyes of Christ are raised and he looks beyond to the horizon. The disciple's face is intent, his brow is knitted, he focuses his eyes upon some distant object. He sees a specific goal; a task; something he must work at; a job to tackle. It is something grand and something compelling! The right hand of Christ is extended outward in a

285

suggestive manner. So real is the picture one can almost hear Jesus say, "Follow Me." I go to the shores of Galilee, to the troubled soul, to the wounded life, and teach righteousness. I go to Capernaum, to teach truthfulness. "Follow Me," I go to Nazareth to teach gentleness and kindness. I go to Jerusalem to teach unselfishness. "Follow Me," says a great personality standing over a lesser one and by life and word transmitting power to go and teach.

SCRIPTURE *(To be read by 6 different persons)*

Christ is the answer for He has	Authority (Matt. 28:18)
Christ is the answer for He knows our	Needs (Phil. 4:19)
Christ is the answer for He is our	Saviour (Luke 19:10)
Christ is the answer for He is the	Way (John 14:6)
Christ is the answer for He is	Eternal (Rev. 22:13)
Christ is the answer for He offers	Rest (Matt. 11:28)

CHORUS "Follow, follow, I will follow Jesus"

FAIREST LORD JESUS

PURPOSE:	To lead the worshippers to a greater awareness of the beauty of Jesus as revealed in nature.
MATERIALS:	Globe, spring flowers, yellow candle, cross, picture of Jesus. The hymn "Fairest Lord Jesus."
ARRANGEMENTS:	The worship table should have a green or yellow cloth with only a Bible on an easel in the center of the table. Leader reads the scripture and places the objects on the worship center as the verses of "Fairest Lord Jesus" are being sung. With each verse the leader places the objects designated in the desired position on the worship table.
PROCEDURE:	Leader introduces the worship center by alluding to the purpose and suggested remarks as to how music and poetry has enriched our worship experiences. The Crusader hymn, "Fairest Lord Jesus" has been arranged by Richard Willis and has added its own dimension to our faith. The piano could play softly in the background during the remarks and the leader would continue by quoting the first verse of scripture with the response following. The conclusion could be an invitation for the audience to unite in singing "Praise God from whom all blessings flow." The poem suggested could be used responsively, or read by the leader.

PRESENTATION:

Leader	"One thing have I desired of the Lord, that will I seek after; that I may behold the beauty of the Lord. (Psa. 27:4)
Response	Fairest Lord Jesus, *(Globe)* Ruler of all nature, O Thou of God and man the Son, Thee will I cherish, Thee will I honor, Thou, my soul's Glory, Joy, and Crown.
Leader	"He is altogether lovely" (Song of Solomon 5:16)
Response	Fair are the meadows, *(Spring Flowers)* Fairer still the woodlands, Robed in the blooming garb of spring: Jesus is fairer, Jesus is purer, Who makes the woeful heart to sing.
Leader	"The Lord will arise upon thee, and His glory shall be seen upon thee." (Isa. 60:2)

Response	Fair is the sunshine, *(Candle)* Fairer still the moonlight, And all the twinkling starry host: Jesus shines brighter, Jesus shines purer, Than all the angels heaven can boast.
Leader	"And nations shall come to thy light, and kings to the brightness of thy rising." (Isa. 60:3)
Response	Beautiful Saviour; *(Cross)* Lord of all nations; Son of God and Son of man. Glory and honor, Praise, adoration, Now and evermore be thine.
Leader	"O Lord, how excellent is thy name in all the earth." (Psa. 8:1)
Response	All fairest beauty, *(Picture of Jesus)* Heavenly and earthly, Wondrously, Jesus, is found in thee: None can be nearer, Fairer or dearer, Than thou, my Saviour, art to me.
Song	"Praise God, from whom all blessings flow"
Poem	How many of us ever stop to think Of music as a wondrous, magic link With God, taking sometimes the place of prayer, When words have failed us, 'neath the weight of care, Music that knows no race, or country, or creed, But gives to each according to his need.

(Anonymous)

FULFILLMENT

PURPOSE:
The dedication of skills in Corps service will only be used of God in the measure that there is a consecration of the person, the self. This worship center should involve the Local Officers.

MATERIALS:
The Holiness Table or the altar could be used. Bible, Cornet or music used by the Songsters. Brief Case and Several Programs.

ARRANGEMENT:
The above items are brought to the Holiness Table or altar and placed there by four representative locals as each one in turn listens to the remarks of the leader.

PROCEDURE:
The representatives sense by the remarks of the leader that the gift alone is not acceptable so he leaves his gift and returns to his place.

The fifth representative comes to the altar or Holiness Table with no gift but singing:

"Take my life and let it be
Consecrated Lord to Thee
Take myself and I will be
Ever only all for Thee."

The representative kneels at the altar empty handed in consecration of self.

Remarks are made by the leader and the invitation to other representatives to come and kneel by their gift. They respond. Representative number 5 rises and leaves. Then each one in turn takes their gift and leaves. The leader interrupts each one as they are returning to their place with an adaptation of Oxenham's Great Hearts, "Where are you going?"

The representatives then respond with the answer given them when they were asked to participate.

PRESENTATION:
FULFILLMENT

To be what we are, and to become what we are capable of becoming in Christ Jesus and within the framework of His will is the only end of living.

Life is not success, achievement, getting ahead or getting to the top. The most satisfying, glorious, exciting, concept of life is fulfillment. This concept is expressed by our Lord when he said, "I am come to fulfill."

Fulfillment is being in the right place; God's place at the right time. It is being able and willing to do what needs to be done, and what God wants done at the moment. It is standing quietly

289

in place, ready to function when God's opportunity comes. Fulfillment is being a channel. Fulfillment is always our availability more than our ability.

As Local Officers you have been fulfilling His will in many ways. There have been tools you have used to assist you in fulfilling His will.

Many and varied are the tools involving your skills in the Corps. Perhaps you could bring to the altar something significant that has enabled you in your sense of fulfillment.

(Representative #1 responds immediately bringing a Bible.)

LEADER: Yes, to Sunday School teachers a knowledge of the Word is important. Understanding it too, "for it is profitable for instruction, reproof, correction, that the man of God may be thoroughly furnished unto all good works." But this is not enough. God wants more! We need skilled teachers in our Corps who know the Word, but teaching can be just "words."

(Representative leaves Bible and returns to place)

(Representative #2 responds bringing a cornet.)

LEADER: Bands and Songsters and music can enrich our worship, create a worshipful atmosphere, bring us readily into God's presence, open doors of praise, involve youth as well as adults in the Corps program, but it alone is sounding brass or tinkling cymbal. No, much more is needed.

(Representative leaves the cornet and returns to place)

(Representative #3 responds bringing a briefcase to the altar.)

LEADER: The Salvation Army needs administrators of Corps functions and Corps business with integrity, loyalty with high principles of excellence, correctness, promptness, and of business acuity. The Corps Sergeant Major, the Corps Secretary, the Corps Treasurer are all men and women of leadership and ability in these areas, but involvement with an attache case, or executive know-how is not enough. No, these alone are weighed in the balance and found wanting.

(Representative leaves briefcase and returns to place)

(Representative #4 responds bringing a number of Corps programs.)

LEADER: Programs! Programs! Programing demands a big slice of our time, thought and energy. And rightfully so. Good programing creates interest, stimulates involvement, enhances, invigorates, revives, inspires, and in fact embellishes any activity. Yes, we need good, thoughtful, God-inspired programing, but programs alone have a big minus. A program needs a spirit, a life to clothe it, a program needs more -- much more. *(Representative leaves programs and returns to place)*

Background music "Take my Life"

(Representative #5 comes singing "Take my Life" and kneels at the altar.)

LEADER: Oh God, what offering shall I give?
Take my love, my Lord I pour
At thy feet its treasure store
Take myself and I will be
Ever only all for Thee.

Then the glory of God shall be displayed in teaching music, administration, programing, and our sole business will be to honor and praise God. Come kneel by your offering, touch it, and give yourself with it. *(Representatives come and kneel and take their offering leaving in turn.)*

The worship center presentation could close at this point if desired, or you could follow the instructions given in the procedure with Oxenham's poem as follows:

LEADER: Where are you going, Salvationist teacher? (S.S. Teacher or C.C. Counselor)

(Representative replies as he leaves the altar:)

To lift today above the past
To make tomorrow sure and fast
To nail God's colors to the mast.

LEADER: Then God go with you, Salvationist teacher.

LEADER: Where are you going, Salvationist musician? (Bandsman or Songster)

(Representative replies as he leaves the altar:)

To fight a fight with all my might
For truth and justice God and right
To grace all life with His fair light.

LEADER: Then God go with you, Salvationist musician.

LEADER: Where are you going, Salvationist administrator? (C.S.M, Corps Sec. or Corps Treasurer)

(Representative replies as he leaves the altar:)

To break down old dividing lines
To carry out my Lord's designs
To build again His broken shrines.

LEADER: Then God go with you, Salvationist Administrator.

LEADER:	Where are you going, Salvationist program builder? (Gd. Leader or H. L. Secretary)
	(Representative replies as he leaves the altar:)
	To set all burdened peoples free To win for all God's liberty To establish His sweet sovereignty.
LEADER:	Then God go with you, Salvationist program builder.
LEADER:	Where are you going, consecrated Local Officer?
	(Representative stands and leaves altar.)
	To seek through faith a greater height To adventure on in the night To lead men upward to the Light
	Then God go with you Local Officer.
	Benediction as in Romans 8:4

A HOLY WALK

Psalm 24

PURPOSE:	To enrich the Word of God as the participants make their contribution to the worship center.
MATERIALS and ARRANGEMENT	The worship table has a green cloth with a white ribbon down the center. Each participant brings his contribution and places it reverently at a given place in the worship center and then reads the assigned scripture.
PROCEDURE:	
LEADER:	Read Psalm 24:1,2 "The earth is the Lord's, and the fulness thereof; the world, and they that dwell therein. For he hath founded it upon the seas, and established it upon the floods."
READER:	*(Bringing a globe to the worship center)* "Through faith we understand that the worlds were framed by the word of God." (Hebrews 11:3) "All things were made by Him, and without Him was nothing made that was made." (John 1:3)
LEADER:	Read Psalm 24:3a "Who shall ascend into the hill of the Lord?"
READER:	*(Bringing a Bible to the worship table.)* "Thy word have I hid in my heart, that I might not sin against thee." (Psalms 119:11)
LEADER:	Read Psalm 24:3b "Who shall stand in His holy place? He that hath clean hands." (Psalm 24:4)
READER:	*(Bringing praying hands to the worship center)* "The Lord rewarded me according to my righteousness: according to the cleanness of my hands hath he recompensed me." (Psalm 18:20)
LEADER:	Read Psalm 24:3b and verse 4b "Who shall stand in His holy place? He that hath a pure heart, who hath not lifted up his soul unto vanity or sworn deceitfully."
READER:	*(Bringing a large gold or white heart to worship table)* "Now the end of the commandment is charity out of a pure heart, and of a good conscience, and of faith unfeigned." (1 Timothy 1:5) "Blessed are the pure in heart for they shall see God." (Matthew 5:8)
LEADER:	Read Psalm 24:5,6 "He shall receive the blessing from the Lord, and righteousness from the God of his salvation. This is the generation of them that seek him that seek thy face, O Jacob."
READER:	*(Bringing a candle and placing it near Bible)* "The entrance of thy words giveth light; it giveth understanding unto the simple." (Psalm 119:130)

LEADER:	Read Psalm 24:7 "Lift up your heads, O ye gates; and be ye lifted up, ye everlasting doors; and the King of glory shall come in.
READER:	Read Psalm 24:8a "Who is this King of Glory?"
LEADER:	Read Psalm 24:8b "The Lord strong and mighty, the Lord mighty in battle."
READER:	Read Psalm 24:10a. "Who is this King of Glory?
LEADER: and READER	Read Psalm 24:10b "The Lord of hosts, He is the King of Glory."

A SCRIPTURE HARVEST

PURPOSE	To thank God for all His love and grace.
MATERIALS	Brown worship cloth with soft orange material or ribbon. A large horn of plenty. Four large baskets filled with fruit. Four girls in peasant costumes. Open Bible on stand with gold marker ribbon. Orange candle in brass candlestick.
ARRANGEMENT	Empty horn of plenty, candlesticks, unlit candle and open Bible on the table. Girls in peasant costumes come down aisle with baskets of fruit on their arms singing

"Come ye thankful people come."

PROCEDURE	The leader quotes the verse Psalm 92:1 "It is a good thing to give thanks unto the Lord" and lights the candle.

He invites the congregation to join in singing:

(Tune "Old Hundred")

Thank God for all His love and grace
Thank God for this, His holy place
Thank God for patient, loving care
Thank God and all His goodness share.

The girls in peasant costumes fill the baskets as they speak their lines.

PRESENTATION	1. And God said, 'Let the earth bring forth herbs yielding seed, and the fruit tree yielding fruit after his kind'; and it was so.
	2. And the Lord spake unto Moses, saying, "The fifteenth day of the seventh month shall be the feast of the tabernacles."
	3. When ye have gathered in the fruit of the land, ye shall keep a feast unto the Lord seven days."
	4. And thou shalt not appear before the Lord empty; every man shall give as he is able according to the blessing of the Lord.

Lev. 23:34,35,39;-Duet. 16:16,17

The leader will then lead the congregation in the following responsive reading.

LEADER	O give thanks unto the Lord, for He is good: for His mercy endureth forever. (Psa. 107:1)
ALL	Thanks be unto God for His unspeakable gift. (2 Cor. 9:15)
LEADER	O give thanks unto the Lord, call upon His name, make known His deeds among men. (Psa. 105:1)
ALL	Thanks be to God which always causeth us to triumph in Christ. (2 Cor. 2:14)

LEADER	O give thanks unto the name of the Lord. (Psa. 122:4)
ALL	Thanks be to God which giveth us the victory through our Lord Jesus Christ. (1 Cor. 11:57)
LEADER	O give thanks unto the Lord, at the remembrance of His Holiness. (Psa. 30:4)
ALL	Thanks be to God which put the same earnest care into the heart of you. (2 Cor. 8:16)
LEADER	In everything give thanks for this is the will of God in Christ Jesus concerning you. (1 Thess. 5:18)
ALL	So we thy people will give thee thanks forever. (Psa. 79:13)

STOP AND GO

PURPOSE
: To show that the Christian walk is ever a new, unfolding, challenging, and exciting experience.

ARRANGEMENT
: Have a red cloth on the table. Use yellow and green ribbons to join the poster traffic signs together. Have the following poster signs in readiness: walk, stop, yield, crossroad, speed limit, curve, school crossing, etc.

PROCEDURE
: The poster traffic signs will be added to worship center by the leader. They should be placed on easels, that have been previously arranged on the table. You may want to add other traffic signs to the ones that have been suggested and prepare your own comments.

PRESENTATION
: Sing or quote the following choruses:

"Travel Along in the Sunshine"
"Keep in Step"
"I Walk with the King"

Using each poster traffic sign make a few remarks similar to those suggested:

WALK in truth...   (John 14:6)

YIELD your will...   (Phil. 2:5)

CROSSROAD seek God's direction... (Psa. 32:8)

SPEED LIMIT not too fast, not too slow...
stay with Jesus   (Gen. 6:9)

SCHOOL CROSSING walk in love... (Eph. 5:2)

CURVE walk circumspectly...   (Eph. 5:15)

STOP AND GO   (John 12:35)

    WAIT you've got a yellow light

    STOP the light is red

Hear what God the Lord has said
The Stop Sign is His word,
The invitation you often heard
It's the traffic sign today,
Jesus says, "I am the way"

The light is Green
Go! Go!
Stop trying like mad
To do what others do
Whether it is good or bad.

Just go - leave it all
Get away - go with God
You've heard His call

CHORUS
: "O Man of Galilee"

TAKE TIME TO BE HOLY

PURPOSE
To emphasize the importance of using our time wisely. The worship center could be used without comments, featuring the song and the scripture. It would adapt easily for a birthday, senior citizen or Home League meeting.

MATERIALS
A yellow cloth reminding us of the days of our lives: the brightness, the joy, the laughter, the day time of life. Bright green contrasting material or ribbon for the everlasting quality of time: yesterday, today, and tomorrow. Candlestick and dark green candle. A Bible and Bible stand, easel for pictures, a clock, praying hands, a branch, a sitting monk, a standing monk (either ceramic or wood carving), flowers in vase, picture of Jesus.

ARRANGEMENT
The candlestick and candle, the Bible stand and the easel for picture will be on the table. The other objects will be added as the song progresses.

PROCEDURE
Soloist will sing the words that are underlined, and the leader recites the Scripture and places the object on the Worship table. The objects should be easily accessible, but not obvious to the audience.

PRESENTATION
There are three kinds of time. There is clock time; the way we measure our seconds, our minutes, our hours, our days and our years. A birthday is your own personal mark in time, between the past and the future, yesterday, today, and tomorrow.

Then there is nature's time; the succession of the seasons - spring, summer, autumn, and winter. We have these seasons in our lives too. There is the springtime of life when we dream dreams and shape our plans and our hopes. The world seems fresh and new. The summer of life is the season of maturing. It is a time when we think, we work, we grow. The doors of opportunity swing ajar and we walk through. We set new goals and we view new horizons.

The autumn is a time of harvesting. All the joys and fruits of our labors. As we watch new things come into being, we gather up all the wealth of our living. There's the pleasure of simple things, precious friendships, a rosebush we planted, a word, a smile, or thought.

The season of contentment comes with the winter of life. At this time we look at the sweetness of the past, memories, happy experiences, moments of laughter and love which we have embraced. We may not be free from cares and sighs, but we let the petals of past blossoms fall into the stream of time, and allow the treasures of the present to add beauty to the memories of the past.

Then there is God's time. There are many references in the Bible with respect to God's time, but Paul in writing to the Ephesians counsels us to "Walk circumspectly, redeeming the time." (Eph. 5:16) A poet has simply explained it in verse which has been set to music in "Take time to be Holy."

Verse 1

Solo	Take time to be holy *(Place clock)*
Scripture	"I will call upon the Lord, evening and morning and at noon will I pray." (Psa. 55:17)
Solo	Speak oft with thy Lord *(Praying hands)*
Scripture	"Men ought always to pray." (Luke 18:1) "Continue instant in prayer." (Rom. 12:12)
Solo	Abide in Him always *(Branch)*
Scripture	"Abide in me, and I in you. As the branch cannot bear fruit of itself, except it abide in the vine, no more can ye, except ye abide in me." (John 15:4)
Solo	And feed on His word *(Bible)*
Scripture	"In His law shalt thou meditate day and night." "Thy word have I hid in my heart" (Joshua 1:8)
Solo	Make friends of God's children (Psa. 119:11)
	Help those who are weak Forgetting in nothing His blessing to seek.

Verse 2

Solo	Take time to be holy Let Him be thy guide *(Light candle)*
Scripture	"Thy Word is a lamp unto my feet and a light unto my path." (Psa. 119:105)
Solo	And run not before Him, whatever betide... *(Sitting monk)*
Scripture	"Wait on the Lord and be of good courage." (Psa. 27:14)
Solo	In joy or in sorrow, still follow the Lord And looking to Jesus, still trust in His Word *(Standing monk with Bible)*
Scripture	"Christ suffered for us leaving us an example that we should follow in His steps." (1 Peter 2:2)

Verse 3

Solo	<u>Take time to be holy, the world rushes on</u> *(Flowers)*
Scripture	"Be ye holy in all manner of conversation" (1 Peter 1:15)
Solo	<u>Spend much time in secret, with Jesus alone</u> *(Praying hands)*
Scripture	"Pray without ceasing. In everything with prayer and supplication, let your requests be made known unto God... (Phil. 4:6; 1 Thess. 5:17)
Solo	<u>By looking to Jesus, like Him thou shalt be</u> <u>Thy friends in thy conduct, His likeness shall</u> <u>see.</u> *(Picture of Jesus)*
Scripture	"Let your life (light) so shine before men that they may see your good works and glorify your father which is in heaven." (Matt. 5:16)

TODAY IS WONDROUS

Psalm 24

PURPOSE
: To bring an awareness of God's blessing of majesty and beauty in the autumn season.

MATERIALS
: A burnt orange cloth with contrasting shades of brown, or the reverse. In fact any colors could be used that pick up the varying shades of the leaves. You will need autumn leaves, a globe (lighted if possible) praying hands, a heart, a cross, a Bible, easels, and a candlestick and a yellow candle.

ARRANGEMENT
: Candlestick and candle on the table, also the Bible easel, and the easel for the heart cut-out and hands. If not using an easel for the heart and the hands, be sure that they can be seen.

PROCEDURE
: The leader will recite Psalm 24 or have it read while the objects are placed on the Worship Center table. Comments can be made with respect to the fall season, its beauty, its meaning, as a season of reverence and reflection. Sing first verse of "Fairest Lord Jesus"

PRESENTATION
: Psalm 24

"The earth is the Lord's and the fullness thereof"
(Let the autumn leaves fall and scatter on the table.)

"The world and they that dwell therein. For He hath founded it upon the seas and established it upon the floods"
(Place the globe on the table.)

"Who shall ascend into the hill of the Lord? or who shall stand in his holy place. He that hath clean hands"
(Place the hands on the easel.)

And a pure heart, who hath not lifted up his soul unto vanity or sworn deceitfully" *(Place heart)*

"He shall receive the blessing of the Lord" *(Place Bible)* "And righteousness from the God of His salvation" *(Place cross)*

"This is the generation of them that seek Thee, that seek thy face O Jacob." *(Light candle)*

"Lift up your heads, O ye gates; and be ye lifted up ye everlasting doors, and the King of Glory shall come in."

(Sing verse of "Fairest Lord Jesus" and if desired you can use the following scripture as the afterglow of God's presence with us.)

The warm, russet brown afterglow of patience. Heb. 10:36

The soft green permeating afterglow of truth and understanding. Prov. 3:3,4

The delicate, rich, clear afterglow of tact. Gal. 6:10

The brilliant red afterglow of cheerfulness and good humor. Prov. 17:22

The deep abiding, dark purple tint of tolerance. Matt.7:1

The good hearty, flaming scarlet afterglow of confidence. Isa. 30:15

TREASURES

PURPOSE

A time to reflect on the great gifts God has given us, which are the treasures of His grace. It also incorporates the idea that it is our turn to give the treasures of our heart and our love.

MATERIALS

Light blue cloth with a soft darker blue or dark blue wide ribbon.

A treasure chest with open lid and perhaps a gold chain spilling over the side. A clock, praying hands or cut-out hands from a visual aid, a sheet of music, a purse or money, a heart, a candle, and a jewel box with the lid closed. Between the treasure chest and the jewel box an open Bible. In the jewel box a rose pin, a cross necklace, a butterfly pin, a mustard seed necklace, and a string of pearls.

ARRANGEMENT

Someone who has been appointed brings an object to be put in the Treasure Chest representative of the treasures we bring to God. These may all be placed so that they can be seen, extending from the treasure chest, or placed near it.

The leader will also refer to the gifts we receive from God, and the participants assigned gifts we receive from God will come and take from the jewel box his gift and arrange it on worship table near the jewel box.

PROCEDURE

The hymn "Take my Life" will be sung as a solo or by the Songsters as the representative brings his gift. Verse 1 would be the gift of the clock; verse 2 - hands; verse 3 - music; verse 4 - purse or money; verse 5 - heart. The leader will light the candle and refer to the Bible. A verse of scripture will be read by each participant who takes a gift from the jewel box.

PRESENTATION

Call to Worship

Treasures on earth - what do they matter?
Storm and swift wind so soon will scatter;
Treasures of Heaven - these we can see
Paving the road to Eternity.

Song: Last verse of "Take my Life"

Poem: **TREASURE CHEST**

Make for yourselves a treasure box,
But not for gems and gold-
Fill it with things more rare and fine,
As full as it will hold.

Into it place your kindly thoughts,
Your love, your tenderness,
Your joys, your charity, your hopes,
Your faith that God will bless.

And then when dark days come along
And your bright prospects mar,
Open the treasure box and see
How very rich you are!

LEADER We all have treasures- glowing, glittering, exquisite gifts, some very simple, but all gifts of service we can bring to God. Let us fill our treasure chest with our gifts to God.

Song: "Take my Life"

(As verse 1 is sung, the participant brings clock and places it near treasure chest.)

PARTICIPANT I would give my time to God.

(On verse 2 the participant brings hands and places them near the treasure chest.)

PARTICIPANT I gladly give my service to God.

(During verse 3 the participant brings a sheet of music.)

PARTICIPANT All my talents, whatever they may be, I give freely to God.

(During verse 4 the participant brings purse or money.)

PARTICIPANT I would never be a miser with God's gift of money. I would give it to Him to spread joy and happiness everywhere.

(During verse 5 participant brings a heart and places it in the treasure chest.)

PARTICIPANT Love is the treasure of my heart, and I never want to hoard it. Let me be a spendthrift in giving all my love.

LEADER *(Lighting the candle)*

Every day will I bless Thee, and I will praise Thy name forever. (Psa. 145:2)

(Takes the open Bible in hand.)

"The Lord will open to thee His good treasure." (Duet. 28:12)

(Replaces the Bible.)

God has given us many treasures. They cannot be bought with silver or gold. They are the gift of God and we seek them from His hand. These great and priceless treasures, the Lord will open unto us *(open lid of jewel box)*. Let us find out what He is waiting to give us.

PARTICIPANT *(Comes and takes out the rose pin)*

The rose pin speaks of the love of God. "Herein is love, not that we loved God, but that He loved us."(1 John 4:10)

304

PARTICIPANT   *(Taking the cross necklace from jewel box)*

"The cross speaks of the salvation of God. "For by grace are ye saved through faith, and that not of yourselves; it is the gift of God." (Eph. 2:8)

PARTICIPANT   *(Taking the string of pearls)*

Pearls speak of The Pearl of Great Price, Jesus himself. "I am come that they might have life, and that they might have it more abundantly." (John 10:10)

PARTICIPANT   *(Taking out the mustard seed necklace)*

The mustard seed speaks of faith the majestic working gift of God. "Without faith it is impossible to please Him, for He that cometh to God must believe that He is and that He is a rewarder of them that diligently seek Him." (Heb. 11:6)

PARTICIPANT   *(Takes out the butterfly pin)*

The butterfly finds life as it emerges from the darkness of the cocoon. "The gift of God is eternal life through Jesus Christ our Lord." (Romans 6:23)

TREASURES OF DARKNESS

"I will give thee the treasures of darkness, and hidden
riches of secret places." (Isaiah 45:3)

There are treasures in the darkness
    Gold and silver cannot buy,
In deep hidden secret places
    We may find a good supply.
God controls this box of treasures,
    He has always kept the key,
We may have them for the asking,
    They are free for you and me.

Faith is one uplifting treasure,
    When the darkest clouds appear,
Hope another shining jewel,
    Like the stars when skies are clear,
Courage stands in steadfast beauty,
    With firm hand to guide us through,
Patience waits God's own good pleasure,
    Works in us His will to do.

These are treasures of the darkness,
    And we need their guiding light,
Till we reach that heavenly harbor,
    Yonder where there is no night.
These are riches that are hidden
    In the secret place of prayer,
Take them, hold them fast forever,
    They will lighten every care.

Irena Arnold

(Mrs. Commissioner William C. Arnold)

THE WORD OF GOD

PURPOSE
: The Bible as described by the writers of this sacred book.

MATERIALS
: Dark blue cloth with contrasting pale blue ribbon or soft chiffon.

Easels, Bible stand, box with draped material to raise the Bible in the background.

ARRANGEMENT

Bible	-	Center back
Lamp	-	Right side
Monks	-	Ceramics or sometimes of carved wood
Sword	-	Either a cut-out or a real one
Seed	-	Near front and raised
Bread	-	On cutting board to left
Hammer	-	Center front (this can be a small one)

PROCEDURE
: Several methods can be used:

The worship center could be completed and the leader quote the scripture references.

It could be used as a Call to Worship and the participants would bring the symbols to the worship table and quote the scripture.

It might be used similarly in the testimony meeting.

It could be a part of the program with the leader making remarks as suggested and building the worship center.

With additional research and comments, it could be used for a Bible Study.

PRESENTATION
: The Bible is for today! In these uncertain times the unchanging Word of God can provide confidence and security, as well as comfort, guidance, and strength.

We believe the Bible is the Word of God and locked within this vault of truth is all that man needs to live an abundant, satisfying, useful, happy, life.

Not only is the Bible the Word of God, but it is a set of rules, a map, a chart, a guide so that we don't go wrong and mess up our lives.

But the glory that gilds the sacred page of this living Word is the never-failing promises to all who read and believe. Promises of strength when our pathway is rough and the way is long. Promises of grace when troubles and trials cloud our day. Promises of comfort when the storms of sorrow and sadness threaten to overwhelm us.

At the annual National Prayer Breakfast in February of 1983 President Reagan urged the nation to read the Bible because "inside its pages lie all the answers to all the problems man has ever known. Let us resolve to read, learn, and try to heed, the greatest message ever written."

So the writers of the Bible have described God's word in many ways. Let us take a prayerful look at this precious old book to find the tokens of love that will lighten and brighten our way.

God's instructions concerning His word as found in Joshua 1:8. *(Place the Bible)*

Thou shalt meditate therein day and night *(Place monks)*
God's word gives direction
(Lamp to be placed as scripture is given.)
Psa. 119:105
Psa. 119:130

God's word a source of life
(Place the packet of seeds.)
Luke 8:11
Mark 4:14

God's word is protection
(Place the shield and the sword.)
Eph. 6:16,17
Psa. 91:4

God's word is a tool
(Place the hammer.)
Jer. 23:29

God's word is spiritual food
(Place the bread and cutting board.)
Matt. 4:4
Psa. 119:103

The Bible is for today!   2 Tim. 3:16

Lord, if thy written Word
Should need an explanation
Then let thy Word in us
Experience Incarnation

WORLD SERVICES

(This is an adaptation of the service for Local Officers - "Fulfillment")

PURPOSE
To involve all centers of Corps activity in the spirit of World Services giving, specifically Soldiers, Sunday School, Songsters, Home League, Band and League of Mercy.

ARRANGEMENT
World Globe or Unisphere at back of worship table. Seven brass candlesticks and candles.

PROCEDURE
Each representative will come to the worship center as outlined below with a candle and object depicting their area of service. They will place their gift on the table and make a gesture to light a candle. The Leader will interrupt before they light the candle suggesting the world needs more than service. The representative will walk to designated place with unlighted candle as other representatives bring a gift and likewise leave it on the altar and walks to designated place beside the altar.

Finally a representative comes with a gift but makes no attempt to light candle, but kneels and prays. After praying the representative lights the candle.

In turn each representative returns, takes their gift and kneels by the worship table. One by one they all stand, light their candle and start to return to their place in the congregation. The Leader stops them with a question and they each respond with the two lines given them from John Oxenham's poem "Greathearts." (This is an adaptation of the poem.)

The congregation will respond responsively at the conclusion.

PRESENTATION

LEADER:
The spirit of man is the candle of the Lord.
(Lights the center candle.)

The world is darkened by sin, poverty, ignorance, hate, greed, and prejudice. Can the spirit of man bring light to such dense darkness?

Yes, for in Christ is Light and the light is the light of men and the light shineth in the darkness. But God needs the Light of man's spirit - his gift of talent, time, and money. In our Corps are there those who will dedicate themselves to our World Services, and keep bringing light to darkened corners of the earth?

1. SOLDIER (Brings Army cap or hat to altar, places it and would start to light the candle.) (Leader interrupts.)

LEADER Yes, active soldiers are needed, but World Services needs more. Unless we give from an open purse it is empty performance.

309

(Soldier walks with unlit candle to side of the altar.)

2. SUNDAY SCHOOL TEACHER *(Brings Bible and Quarterly-- attempts to light the candle.)*

    LEADER *(interupting)* As a representative of the Sunday School you study God's Word, but knowledge of God's Word without the spirit of material giving will profit so little.

    (Sunday school teacher walks with unlit candle to designated place by altar.)

3. SONGSTER *(Brings the book "Gems for Songsters" attempts to light a candle.)*

    LEADER *(Interrupting)* A sad, discouraged, weary world needs the song of a Songster. A song may soothe heartache, but it needs more. It needs the soul of the singer who gives and gives freely.

    (Songster walks away with unlit candle to designated place.)

4. HOME LEAGUE SECRETARY *(Brings praying hands to the altar and attempts to light candle.)*

    LEADER *(interrupting)* Yes, we have heard that the Family that prays together stays together, and the Home League is to be commended for endorsing this principle, but the world needs a generous spirit to clothe the spirit of prayer.

    (Home League Secretary walks away with unlit candle and stands in designated place by the altar.)

5. BANDSMAN *(Brings instrument places it on altar and attempts to light a candle.)*

    LEADER *(interrupting)* Music! What a fine gift from the Army band, but music as a talent can be only sounding brass or a tinkling cymbal. It alone can never penetrate the darkness. We need more, much more. We need an open, giving heart of love.

    (Bandsman with unlit candle takes designated place by altar.)

6. YOUTH GROUP MEMBER *(Brings tambourine or Guard Sash and attempts to light the candle.)*

    LEADER *(Interrupting)* Oh, yes, we have heard about your "Wake-a-thon". A great idea and so profitable to World Services, but it is not only in giving or doing that there is blessing. You see though we give everything we have to feed the poor, but do not love others it is of no value whatsoever.

    (Youth Group member walks to designated place with unlit candle.)

310

7. <u>LEAGUE OF MERCY SECRETARY</u> *(Brings a basket of fruit, places it on the altar, then kneels and sings)*

> "Take my silver and my gold
> Not a mite would I withhold
> Take myself and I will be
> Ever only all for Thee."

All the representatives listen, then one by one in no particular order they come to worship table and take their gift and kneel. When all are kneeling with a brief moment for prayer, the League of Mercy Secretary stands. She lights her candle and places it in the holder on the worship table. She starts down the aisle with her gift and is questioned by the leader. She answers from her place in the aisle with the response that was given to her.

In turn each representative will do the same. Following are the responses each will give.

LEADER	Where are you going, League of Mercy worker?
RESPONSE	To reach out and touch with love, The sick and sorrowing of every clime To give my heart, my money, my time.
LEADER	Then God go with you, League of Mercy worker.
LEADER	Where are you going, Salvation Army Soldier?
RESPONSE	To set all burdened peoples free To win for all God's liberty By our money His salvation see.
LEADER	Then God go with you, Salvation Army Soldier
LEADER	Where are you going, Sunday School Teacher?
RESPONSE	With the pennies and dimes our Sunday School gives We'll seek through faith a greater height And lead men upward to the Light.
LEADER	Then God go with you, Sunday School Teacher.
LEADER	Where are you going, Salvationist Songster?
RESPONSE	Our gift of song and money Will break down old dividing lines Will carry out love's design And build again God's broken shrines.
LEADER	Then God go with you, Salvationist Songster.
LEADER	Where are you going, Home League Secretary?
RESPONSE	The gift from our treasury Will lift today above the past Will make tomorrow sure and fast Will nail God's colors to the mast.

LEADER	Then God go with you, Home League Secretary.
LEADER	Where are you going, Salvationist Bandsman?
RESPONSE	We'll send our marching dollars, and We'll play with all our might, For truth and justice, God and right To grace all life with His fair light.
LEADER	Then God go with you, Salvationist Bandsman.
LEADER	Where are you going, Youth Group member?
RESPONSE	To reach out to all of youth To speak for Christ, to make them hear With love and our offerings to bring them near.
LEADER	Then God go with you, Youth Group member.
NOTE:	A large brass plate, or an offering plate at the front of the worship table should be ready to receive the offerings that each of the groups above would bring with them. These they would place in the offering as they first come to the worship table.

CONGREGATION RESPONSE: Song #828 "All the World"
(S.B. 1953 Edition)

(This could lead into the World Services offering.)

Worship Centers
Holy Week

INTRODUCTION

The worship centers presented here are for services each day of Holy Week or for a service each week preceding Easter during Lent.

They are similar but not repetitive, and are developed under four (4) themes:

1. Facing Calvary

2. Touched by Jesus

3. They Stood by Him

4. Personalities around the Cross

If you prepare the worship center, have your chapel open early with soft lights in the auditorium, and invite your people to come for personal meditation and prayer; this will make the worship center more meaningful and the service more effective.

You may suggest they spend a few moments at the altar; stand in solitude and absorb the spirit of the worship center, or sit in the pews and read the interpretations of the worship center. Encourage waiting in His presence, and hearing the Holy Spirit speak.

Although you may have the interpretation of the worship center available before the service, it is also important that it be included in the beginning of the service.

FACING CALVARY

<table>
<tr><td>PURPOSE</td><td>We all face Calvary. Time may separate us from those who faced Calvary in the year of our Lord, but as each Worship Center brings to our remembrance someone who faced Calvary, may the meaning, the power, the reality of "Facing Calvary" this Lenten season not elude us. Quietly and simply may we each come close to the cross as we worship "Facing Calvary."</td></tr>
</table>

A TIME OF REMEMBRANCE - THE CENTURION

<table>
<tr><td>MATERIALS
and
ARRANGEMENT</td><td>A large cross of natural wood in the background. Palms on either side. A purple drape on the cross for the kingship of Jesus the Son of God.</td></tr>
</table>

A red cloth on the worship table with a white longer underskirt, and a white ribbon down center of the red cloth. Built up sections (with books) covered with red soft draping material. Small cross on side on built up center section. Open scroll in front of built up section placed on book rack for visibility. Large (4" x 8") red candle in white candle holder with a spring floral candle ring.

Red cord from right arm of cross, running to hook in ceiling directly above the worship center, and on the cord hanging from the hook suspend a small cross.

A stump of tree for the whipping post (a large fireplace log standing on end) with a whip on top of it, a soldier's helmet and tunic nearby. Resting on the stump is a sword and a sponge on a reed.

<table>
<tr><td>INTERPRETATION</td><td>CENTURION</td></tr>
</table>

On this particular Passover, I was stationed in Jerusalem.

I knew there would be trouble. The cause of the tension was Jesus, a Jewish prophet. He claimed to be the promised Messiah as foretold by Isaiah *(scroll)*. He was the lamp of hope *(candles)* for all Israel, their promised King *(cross in the background with purple drape and crown)*.

NARRATOR

For God so loved the world that out of eternity He flung the scarlet cord *(red cord)* and laid on His Son the iniquity of us all. He was wounded for our transgressions; He was bruised for our iniquities; He was oppressed and afflicted yet He opened not His mouth; He was brought as a lamb to the slaughter; for the transgression of my people was He stricken and made His soul an offering for sin *(suspended cross)*.

The chastisement of our peace was upon Him, and with His stripes we are healed. The Lord laid on Him the iniquity of us all, and He became obedient unto death, even the death of the cross. Yes, we remember the scarlet promises that came through the prophets, through Roman authority, and through the cross *(red cord)*.

CENTURION

I am a Centurion *(soldier's helmet)* with soldiers under me. I knew this Jesus had superb courage, for I was on duty in the Judgment Hall. I was one who mocked, spit upon Him, smote Him *(whipping post, soldier's helmet and tunic, and the whip)*. I also am under orders, and by the worst chance in the world, I was in charge of the execution squad. I'm used to seeing men die *(sword)* but this was different. For me, it was not mockery when I ordered that His lips be moistened in death *(sponge on reed)*. I can't understand it, I can't explain it, but somehow I knew that in death He had won. I'm a soldier, I can't pack convictions in nice phrases but as He died, involuntarily I cried out, "Truly this is the Son of God." In a moment He came to my soul and with His stripes I was healed. I was a new soldier under new orders. *(white ribbon)*.

FACING CALVARY

PURPOSE

We all face Calvary. Time may separate us from those who faced Calvary in the year of our Lord, but as each Worship Center brings to our remembrance someone who faced Calvary, may the meaning, the power, the reality of "Facing Calvary" this Lenten season not elude us. Quietly and simply may we each come close to the cross as we worship "Facing Calvary."

A TIME OF PREPARATION - THE LAST SUPPER

MATERIALS
and
ARRANGEMENT

Undraped large cross in the background with a spotlight and a color wheel arranged so as to cast a shadow on the back wall of platform.

A long table with a white cloth. Thirteen votive or altar candles arranged around the table. In the center of the table place the Jewish Menorah. On either side place the chalice with the grapes spilling over the top, and the broken bread in a basket. Have the towel and the basin on a small table to the side of the large table, with the closed Bible. In a conspicuous spot at the front of the large table have the money bag.

INTERPRETATION

John, the beloved disciple, will always speak to us of a closeness and communion born only of a great love. There is a shining golden light of love *(Hanukkah Menorah, symbolic of dedication)* that radiates down through the centuries even though the Last Supper marks the beginning of the end in the book of Christ's life *(the closed Bible)*.

In a small room in a house in Jerusalem, Jesus was surrounded by His disciples *(votive candles marking their places)* and was breaking bread with them. Christ took the bread *(broken bread)*, blessed it, and brake it, and gave it to the disciples. Thus He suggested His voluntary offering of love - Himself. *(The basin and the towel symbolize the servanthood of our Lord, who humbled Himself and took upon Him the form of a servant and became obedient unto death, even the death of the cross)*.

Christ delighted to do the will of God and even gave thanks for the bitter cup *(chalice with the grapes)*. Knowing full well the contents of the cup, He drained it to the bitter dregs. They all drank of it, even Judas who later betrayed his Lord *(the money bag)*.

There is a part of that cup for each of us. Can we give thanks for a distasteful cup we must drink? Do we sometimes murmur or complain about our cup? In love we must take our cup from His pierced hand and trust Him for grace and strength to drink of its bitter contents.

If we are partakers of His sufferings, then we shall be partakers of His glory. 1 Peter 4:13

My life must be Christ's broken bread,
    My love His outpoured wine,
A cup o'erfilled, a table spread
    Beneath His name and sign,
That other souls, refreshed and fed
    May share His life through mine.

(Albert Orsborn)

FACING CALVARY

PURPOSE

We all face Calvary. Time may separate us from those who faced Calvary in the year of our Lord, but as each Worship Center brings to our remembrance someone who faced Calvary, may the meaning, the power, the reality of "Facing Calvary" this Lenten season not elude us. Quietly and simply may we each come close to the cross as we worship "Facing Calvary."

A TIME FOR PENITENCE - PETER

MATERIALS
and
ARRANGEMENTS

A large cross in the background with a rough brown cloth at the bottom of the cross (earth) and on it several rocks of varying sizes. A red drape on the arms of the cross.

A gold cloth on the worship table. A set of Biblical or early 18th century scales (two dishes suspended on arms from a center beam); in one dish have a small globe and in the other balance a small cross. An open Bible with a red ribbon for a book mark. A rooster, and a gold candle in a brass holder.

INTERPRETATION

LEADER

A time for penitence. No soul has ever been more penitent than Peter as he faced Calvary. So our worship center relates to Peter's denial which was the reason for his repentance. As we think of his denial we would ask Peter some questions as part of the interpretation.

PETER

I know not this man.

Now, why did I say that and deny Him? Well, I'll be careful and not do it again (*scales representing the weighing of situations*). She taunted me again, and I had to repeat that lie (*self, world, in balance with the cross*). Now, I really messed it up, swearing to prove my innocence. Was that the cock crowing? (*rooster*) Jesus will never forgive me, and I loved Him so (*cross in the background, red drape*).

JOHN

Peter, we just can't understand what happened to you. You said you would never deny Him. Why did you do it?

PETER

Why? Why? Why? I've asked myself a thousand times.

JOHN

Don't you know why?

PETER

Honestly, I don't. It just happened so quick. I never intended to do it!

JOHN

But you did it three times, and you were there and saw His suffering and shame.

PETER

I know, but I was afraid, then.

320

JOHN	Not you Peter, not you afraid.
PETER	Yes ME!
JOHN	Peter, when Jesus looked at you, it was a look of disappointment. But, oh Peter, it was a look full of compassion, love and understanding. *(Bible)*
LEADER	Peter was saved because he heard a cock crow, and it broke his heart when he remembered Christ's words *(candle of truth)*. The cock crowing said, there is another day *(gold cloth)*. If we listen in the darkness of our denial, we will find the cross, the sunrise of a new day, and our broken, penitent heart will know God's unending mercy *(desolate, lonely cross on rocky Golgotha)*.

It was for me, yes, even me
That Jesus died on Calvary;
My soul to cleanse from all its guilt,
His precious blood my Saviour spilt.

FACING CALVARY

PURPOSE

We all face Calvary. Time may separate us from those who faced Calvary in the year of our Lord, but as each Worship Center brings to our remembrance someone who faced Calvary, may the meaning, the power, the reality of "Facing Calvary" this Lenten season not elude us. Quietly and simply may we each come close to the cross as we worship "Facing Calvary."

MATERIALS
and
ARRANGEMENTS

Large cross in the shadows. Brown material at the base with rocks around base of the cross. Artificial green grass on floor of platform with several rocks interspersed with potted plants and flowers. Ferns and greenery appropriately placed to make the semblance of a garden. To the side of the platform have a large rock; this could be placed on a box covered with light tan material to give the appearance of a mound of dirt. On this, project a picture of Christ kneeling in the garden with hands on rock you have built.

INTERPRETATION

A TIME FOR FREEDOM--THE GARDEN OF GETHSEMANE

LEADER

Let us kneel with the Master in the Garden of Gethsemane and find our way to true freedom. Jesus kneels alone, before facing Calvary and prays as He faces His decision and makes His dedication. Not a decision of resignation, but a decision of acceptance of God's will.

In the garden Jesus gathers strength to meet the naked horror of the cross. The Garden of Gethsemane, located on the Mount of Olives was in all probability the private garden of a friend of the Master. He frequently went there to pray and meditate.

Jesus left eight of the disciples at the entrance to the garden and took three of His closest friends with Him.

Jesus then goes a little farther and faces His crisis alone. As He kneels before a barren rock *(rock and flowers)* with outstretched, yet clasped hands, Jesus prays alone. Jesus repeats the words, "My Father, if it be possible let this cup pass from me. Nevertheless not as I will, but Thy will be done." *(cross)*

Alone in the garden *(garden scene)* our Lord faced His decision. He did not choose the weak way of doing God's will, by just resigning to it. His decision was the acceptance of God's will; --the torture of the cross, the bitter cup of death so that God's purpose might be accomplished.

This acceptance made His decision a great, compelling dedication. Jesus rose from His knees with victory and freedom in His heart. A victory of faith!

Yes, we kneel today, and feel the throb of Christ's heart in the garden. A Christ who makes demands, who asks for decisions, who prays for our dedication.

The acceptance of whatever is His will in our lives, not resignation to it, is the way of victory, freedom, and joy. Accepting His will, we shall walk the path of freedom and faith.

THEY STOOD BY HIM

PURPOSE	Three disciples failed to stand by Him.
	...it could have been such a divine act, but they were so human.
	...it could have been so comforting to know that three disciples were saying, "We are sharing this with you."
	WE CAN STAND BY...
	...it is not too late to understand
	...it is not too late to know His sorrow
	...it is not too late to feel His struggle and dedication.
MATERIALS and ARRANGEMENTS	A large standing cross in back of platform with a purple drape for Christ's kingship. A brown cloth at the base of the cross. Rocks of varying sizes at the foot of the cross. The remainder of the platform made into a garden scene. One large rock at the side of the platform could speak of the rock where Jesus knelt in Gethsemane.
INTERPRETATION	THEY STOOD BY HIM, IN THE GARDEN
LEADER:	In a garden, Jesus gathered strength to meet the naked horror of the Cross. The Garden of Gethsemane, located on the Mount of Olives, was in all probability the private garden of a friend of the Master. He went there frequently to pray and meditate.
	The word "Gethsemane" means an olive press. It was a place where picked olives were piled up and pressure put on them to extract the oil. In this place, according to history and prophecy, Jesus was to tread the wine press alone. (Isaiah 63:3)
	Jesus left eight of the disciples at the entrance of the garden and took three of His closest friends with Him. Jesus then went a little farther and faced His crisis alone. Jesus knelt before a barren rock *(rock at the side)* and with outstretched, yet clasped hands, prayed alone, "My Father, if it be possible, let this cup pass from Me. Nevertheless, not as I will, but Thy will be done."
	(The three disciples listen:)
JAMES	That prayer - it freezes my blood.
JOHN	He says it over and over again. I think I see beads of sweat on His brow.
PETER	It shines in the moonlight on his folded hands.
JOHN	There is so much pain in that prayer.
PETER	I'm afraid!

JAMES	I'm sleepy! If we went to sleep we wouldn't hear the agony.
JOHN	How can I sleep when I hear the throb of my Master's heart.
PETER	But if we sleep we won't hear it.
JAMES	Come on, let's sleep!

And Jesus came and found them asleep. And He went a little farther and fell on His face and prayed saying the same words. (Matthew 26:39) It was this verse of Scripture that inspired the artist Hermann Clementz to paint the well-known picture of CHRIST IN GETHSEMANE. In the gallery where it is shown, the interpretation of the picture includes the following:

"The constant challenge of Christ in Gethsemane to every follower of the lowly Nazarene is to GO A LITTLE FARTHER. Crowd close to Him. Go a little farther in your loyalty...a little farther in Church attendance...a little farther in cooperation...a little farther in helping people..." A little farther in standing by the sorrowing, the suffering, the hurting ones around us, and never fail Him or them.

THEY STOOD BY HIM

PURPOSE

THEY STOOD BY HIM...

What an undying distinction to minister by just "standing by"...

...it isn't a big thing to do, really;

...it doesn't seem to be of any practical significance;

BUT

TO STAND BY HIM...

...it was a sensitive thing to do;

WE STAND BY TODAY...

...Stand by and feel - "For ME...He died";

MATERIALS
and
ARRANGEMENT

A red cloth on the worship table and near the back a cross laid on its side. Bible on stand with a white ribbon over a black ribbon with the edge of the black showing. Two brass candle holders with two tall white candles. Near the table a large fireplace log standing on end, reminding us of the whipping post. Whip, sandals, sword, soldier's tunic and helmet. Stool for helmet, sword, and tunic. Whip and sandals on the whipping post.

INTERPRETATION

HE STOOD BY...AND SHARED IN CROSS BEARING

SIMON OF CYRENE

(Matthew 27:32; Mark 15:21; Luke 23:26)

Would you like to reconstruct with me the scene on the "Way of Sorrows"?

The gates of the Procuratorium opened, and a squad of Roman soldiers *(sword, tunic, and helmet)* under an officer, led Jesus forth. The crown of thorns was still on His head; but His face was hidden, for He was almost bowed to the ground with the weight of the cross *(cross on side)*.

Because of all He had endured during the night, His strength was drained away; and He could not carry His cross any further. He fell under the weight of it. This only brought the lash of the soldiers: *(whip on the post)*.

He gained a measure of strength; and by sheer force of will, rose, lifted His cross, and moved on.

Then His strength gone, He strained forward; but He could not move the cross. Again and again the whip lash *(whip on post)*. The welts from the whip oozed blood for our redemption *(the red cloth)* and the Sinless One *(pure white ribbon)* became sin for us *(black ribbon under the white)*.

Then it was the soldiers could have said, "Go, you fool; carry it for Him." So they removed the cross from the back of Jesus and tied it to Simon's, as the Scripture says *(candle and Bible)*..."and on him they laid the cross."

Cyrene is a district in North Africa under Roman rule; and during the exile, it was colonized by a large number of Jews. Simon is a Jewish name; and according to Acts 6:9 there was a synagogue in Cyrene.

So it was very possible this was not the first time Simon had heard of Jesus. In all probability, he had visited Jerusalem on one of the feast days. He probably heard Jesus and could have witnessed one of His miracles.

Somehow, it would seem he just never forgot the words of Jesus. It is thought he believed, counted himself a follower, and undoubtedly had gone home and told his wife and his sons, Rufus and Alexander about Jesus. (Mark 15:21; Romans 16:13)

The Gospel accounts leave much to our supposition regarding Simon of Cyrene, so if he was compelled to bear the cross as he stood by, it was the compulsion of his heart. With a powerful hand and a firm, mighty grip, he got under the weight of the cross.

If it was thrust upon him, it was because *he stood by* with a heart full of compassion for the Suffering One. It never is inferred that he chafed under the task or bristled by the obligation. NO! He counted it a privilege to share in the cross bearing.

Simon of Cyrene bore
The cross of Jesus - nothing more.
His name is never heard again,
Nor honored by historic pen,
Nor on the pedestals of fame,
His image courts the loud acclaim.

Simon of Cyrene bore
The cross of Jesus - nothing more.

And yet, when all our work is done
And golden beams the western sun
Upon a life of wealth and fame
A thousand echoes ring our name;
Perhaps our hearts will humbly pray:
"Good Master, let my record say
Upon the page Divine, 'He bore
The cross of Jesus' - nothing more!"

(Poem quoted from Dr. Harry Rimmer)

327

THEY STOOD BY HIM

(Luke 23:49)

PURPOSE

THEY STOOD BY HIM...

...it wasn't an easy thing to do, but they stood by to the very end.

TO STAND BY HIM...

...it was a brave man's choice; a choice of faith.

WE CAN STAND BY TODAY...

...stand by and feel the cross on which He bore our sin.

MATERIALS
and
ARRANGEMENT

A large cross in the background with a black silk drape on the arm beams of the cross. In the center of the arm beams a crown of thorns with a piece of red silk filling the center of the crown of thorns. A red cloth on the worship table with a lighted world globe, and a small cross nearby. A red ribbon from the small cross to the globe. A large white candle and an open Bible.

INTERPRETATION

THEY STOOD BY HIM ON GOOD FRIDAY
FRIENDS AT GOLGOTHA

Let us go to Golgotha. Golgotha, the place of skulls, was the hill not far away from the city walls where Rome crucified its condemned. A ruling from the government said that all who suffered death upon this hill should remain hanging upon the cross until the birds had eaten their flesh.

This made Golgotha a word of terror among the Jews. It was near the northeast gate of the city so the Jews could easily avoid it.

To go to Golgotha meant stumbling against bones of corpses scattered there; worming your way through crosses encrusted with blood and half-eaten bodies, shuttling through bodies clearly alive, convulsed and twisted with pain. Death sighs hung in the air, and the stench of death polluted it. Golgotha was sown with human bodies, and the hill was soaked through and through with human suffering.

Golgotha is death! Here Jesus died. The cross was not beautiful; it was rugged, it was cruel, it was death *(black drape).*

"And all the people that came together to that sight, beholding the things which were done, smote their breasts. And all his acquaintance, and the women that followed Him from Galilee, stood afar off, beholding these things." (Luke 23:48,49)

Those who loved Him, knew Him, and followed Him, as they beheld the crown of thorns that pierced His lovely brow, felt their sins make each thorn more pointed and add sharpness to the nails, but they also knew that the prophecy was being fulfilled, "He was wounded for our transgressions, He was bruised for iniquities, and the chastisement of our peace was upon Him; and with His stripes we are healed." (Isa. 53:5)

Think of Golgotha. Look at the cross and see the amazing love of Christ and wonder how He could die for you. It will bring you to your knees and in self-commitment you will want to say:

Love so amazing, so divine
Shall have my soul, my life, my all.

(Isaac Watts)

INDIFFERENCE

When Jesus came to Golgotha, they hanged Him on a tree,
They drove great nails through hands and feet, and made a Calvary;
They crowned Him with a crown of thorns, red were His wounds and deep;
For those were crude and cruel days, and human flesh was cheap.

When Jesus came to Birmingham, they simply passed Him by;
They never hurt a hair of Him, they only let Him die;
For men had grown more tender, and would not give Him pain;
They only just passed down the street; and left Him in the rain.

Still Jesus cried, "Forgive them, for they know not what they do";
And still it rained the wintry rain that drenched Him through and through;
The crowds went home and left the streets
Without a soul to see,
And Jesus crouched against a wall, AND CRIED FOR CALVARY!

(Studdert Kennedy)

THEY STOOD BY HIM

PURPOSE

There is no more supportive ministry than to just "stand by"...

it certainly is not necessary, nor will it change anything...

TO STAND BY HIM...

...it was such a sympathetic and understanding gesture

WE STAND BY HIM TODAY...

...stand by and see - "He loved me and gave Himself for me."

MATERIALS
and
ARRANGEMENT

A blue cloth and gold cord would be most appropriate on the worship table. Scroll with a red ribbon across it; the scroll should be open. A white cross on background of table. In front of cross a small manger. A small white robe draped over the foot of manger. A tall, slender candle in brass holder.

INTERPRETATION

"THEY STOOD BY AND WATCHED HIM DIE"

MARY, THE MOTHER

An ache seems to crash in on our hearts as we read John 19:25 - "...there stood by the cross of Jesus His mother..." Brief words, yet freighted with tragedy as we see "love looking into Heaven through tears." The rulers derided, the soldiers mocked, the crowd taunted and ridiculed; and all saw Him die; but one felt Him die. Mary felt and suffered the physical anguish and pain of Jesus. She knew this was the fulfillment of the earlier prophecy (the Old Testament scroll) "A sword shall pierce thy heart".

The shadow of the cross (white cross with shadow on back wall) fell over Mary's early days of motherhood (blue cloth) when she knew that "the Holy thing" born of her was to be the Saviour of the world (red cord across the scroll).

Scripture does not record she spoke a single word during the agony of Jesus. Perhaps the horror of the crucifixion left her speechless.

No one knew Jesus as intimately and lovingly as did His mother. How her thoughts must have raced through the thirty years before His ministry when He had been her devoted, considerate Son.

The sacred moments when she cradled Him in her arms and angels sang "Joy to the World" (the manger). Where was the joy in this?

The first time His curls were cut, she had saved just two. She remembered the linen tunic she had made for His first visit to the Temple. She recalled walks in the fields among the flowers, teaching Him his verses, instructing Him in the Torah (the scroll). She saw Him standing among the rabbis in the Temple, white and shining in the second tunic she had made for Him.

Even as she remembered, she saw the soldiers casting lots for the last cloak she had made for Him (robe over the manger). A cloak she had made during solitary hours in Nazareth. She could not care for Him in person during those three years of ministry, so she made Him a cloak without seams.

If only she could go to Him now and wipe the blood and sweat from His brow. She looked at the hands she had washed and held, now bruised and bleeding. She did not weep. Her face was set, and her brave heart would bear all.

Mary had called him "Tinoki" my little one and He had called her "Emi" mother. She wanted only one word from Him - "Emi" but he looked at her and said, "Woman, behold thy son." This was the sharpest thrust of the sword in her heart. He broke forever the mother-son relationship, and truly became the Son of God. There was pain, too, in the sensitive heart of Jesus as He renounced earth's dearest ties to become the Saviour of the world. Mary knew that now she was just a believer. She stood quietly by and entered into the fellowship of His suffering and FELT Him die.

THEY STOOD BY HIM

PURPOSE
THEY STOOD BY HIM...

...it will not bring the plaudits or acclaim of the world;

TO STAND BY HIM...

...it was amazingly kind and full of love;

WE CAN STAND BY HIM TODAY...

and be "crucified with Christ" and "live, yet not I, but Christ liveth in me."

MATERIALS

and
ARRANGEMENT

A large white cross in the background of the platform with a white drape on the arm beams of the cross. Easter lilies at the foot of the cross. The cross should be spotlighted. Worship table with a white cloth and an arrangement of Easter lilies. Brass candle holders of varying heights with white candles. An open Bible on a stand.

INTERPRETATION

"THEY STOOD BY ON EASTER"

MARY MAGDALENE ON EASTER MORNING

When I heard they had arrested Jesus, I rushed to Pilate's Hall. The mob was hysterical. They wanted to kill Him. I felt I had to be at his side, but the soldiers wouldn't let me into the Hall.

I heard them laugh at Him and torture Him. Their cruelty was beyond anything I could imagine.

When He came out, He was wearing a crown of thorns they had shoved on His head so hard that the skin was torn and blood trickled down His face. I stayed as close as I could all the way to Calvary, and I saw Him struggle beneath the weight of the cross.

I stood by Mary and John at the foot of the cross and watched Him die. I wanted to run away - it hurt me so, but I couldn't leave. I loved Him! He was so good. How could they do this to Him?

I spent Saturday in prayer, and I was so thankful He loved me and forgave me.

Sometimes I thought I would cry, I missed Him so much. But I didn't cry, for it seemed He was so much a part of me He would never leave me. After sunset, I went to Salome's house with the other women to prepare spices for the anointing of the body of Jesus.

While the sky was still gray, the next morning we walked through the dewy grass to Joseph's garden. The soldiers were gone. The stone was rolled away. The tomb was empty. They had stolen His body! The other women hurried to tell the disciples. All I could do was stand by the tomb and cry.

Then it happened. Someone walked up behind me, and asked me why I was weeping. The gardener, I thought. "Where have you taken Jesus?" "Mary, Mary," He said. I turned around. It was Jesus. He wasn't dead. He was alive!

As long as I live I will hear Him speak my name. He was alive, and I knew it. I had seen Him. "Go tell Peter," He said. I wanted to go and tell everyone. He is alive! I tell you, "He is alive!" He loves you. He cares about you: He is your friend.

THE GLORY WAY

Now that the Christ is risen, *(lilies on the cross)*
Now with the darkness gone, *(circling rays of light)*
The road lies out before us,
Upward, and on and on.

There are His sandal footprints,
There is His form ahead,
Straight and strong and compelling,
The Christ that they left as dead.

Nothing can dim His glory, *(white drape on cross)*
Nothing can stay His feet,
And countless are they who follow
Him down each lane and street.

And I would be one among them,
Along the Glory Way; *(rays of light)*
I would arise and follow
The risen Christ today.

(Grace Noll Crowell)

THEY SHARED HIS CROSS

THE CRITICS AND CRITICISMS

PURPOSE

Bearing shame and scoffing rude
In my place condemned He stood
Sealed my pardon, with His blood,
Hallelujah, what a Saviour--(Philip P. Bliss)

Stronger than the dark, the light
Stronger than the wrong, the right
With faith and hope and love I pray
Dear Christ, help me to stand by You today.

(Anonymous)

MATERIALS
and
ARRANGEMENT

A dark green cloth with a lighter green material for draping
would be appropriate for the worship table. A scroll with a gold
cord comes across the closed Bible. In the background three
crosses. Several votive or altar candles at different heights,
made by covering boxes with the light green material.

INTERPRETATION

The dark green cloth of the worship table and the three crosses
are significant of the words of the poet:

"There is a green hill far away
Without a city wall
Where the dear Lord was crucified
Who died to save us all."

The three crosses set the crucifixion scene, while the scroll
speaks of the priests and prophets who would link prophecy
with fact, as recorded in the Bible today, but to the critics a
closed book. The altar candles, like tongues of fire, depict the
fiery tongue of the critics. The candle by the crosses clearly
indicates that the fiery witness of the disciples of the Lord will
be a more burning authority than the fiery tongue of any critic.
Truth triumphs!

To the end, Lord, let me stand! Keep me true!

THEY SHARED HIS CROSS

MISTAKEN TEARS OF THE WOMAN

PURPOSE

Yet deeper do I ponder,
His cross and sorrow see,
And ever gaze in wonder
Why Jesus dies for me.
And shall I fear to own Him?
Can I my Lord deny?
No! let me love Him, serve Him,
And meet Him by and by.

(William A. Hawley)

MATERIALS
and
ARRANGEMENT

On the worship table use a blue cloth with a gold silk draping material. Large cinnamon or gold candle with a fall flower, candle ring. Picture of Jesus by H. R. Dombek *(Jesus looking heavenward with a tear about to fall from His right eye)*. Chalice with a bunch of grapes falling over the side. Bible on easel with a red ribbon from the picture of Jesus through the gold drape at the base of the picture and falling over the Bible as the book mark. On a raised area covered with the gold draping material, have cut-outs of Bible women standing as if looking at the picture of Jesus.

INTERPRETATION

"Why weepest thou?" "Daughters of Jerusalem weep not for me!" (John 20:13; Luke 23:28)

Jesus envisions the cross on his way to Golgotha and in it He sees the salvation of the world as foretold in the scripture. The scarlet cord through both the Old and the New Testaments. The chalice symbolizes the bitter cup He must drink and the grapes as so aptly described by General Orsborn :

> *"Beyond the brook the winepress stands"*
> *"My love must be His outpoured wine"*

The Bible women cut-outs speak of the daughters of Jerusalem; a group of caring, loving women so very sensitive to the suffering of Jesus. Luke describes them as a "company of women, which bewailed and lamented him." The women cannot hold back the tears.

Then Jesus turns to them and says, "Daughters of Jerusalem, weep not for me, but weep for yourselves, and for your children." (Luke 23:28) And the proof of the moment is this that all tears shall be banished, for Jesus said, "Be of good cheer for I have overcome the world." (John 16:33)

TOUCHED BY JESUS

JUDAS

PURPOSE

Miracle of all miracles -
  He touched me
    Tenderly,
      Lovingly,
        Divine.

Oh, blessed touch -
  Transforming,
    Amazingly kind,
  He touched me in the way;
    I touched Him...
      Felt Him today!

MATERIALS
and
ARRANGEMENT

A brown worship cloth on the table. In the background a cross draped with black net. Altar or votive candles. A money bag and beside it a stack of silver half dollars. Hanging from the side of the table a long piece of rope. In the front of table a closed Bible and beside it an unlighted tall candle. Bread in basket and chalice.

INTERPRETATION

(Matthew 26: 17-30)

JUDAS: I must be heard! Will no one believe me? I must see someone. I must speak to someone. I have betrayed a man who loved me. Do you hear me? I betrayed Him with a kiss *(cross draped with black net)*. He preached goodness and humility *(altar candles)*. He was my friend and broke bread with me. I drank from his cup *(bread and chalice)*.

I sold His love for a bag of silver. Thirty pieces of silver! *(money bag and stack of silver)* For one brief moment, I loved something more than I loved Him.

Woe is me! Betrayer! I lived so close to Him and yet I fell. I have sinned. They have their silver, all 30 pieces of it, but I have my guilt. Oh, God, my guilt *(rope)*

And I thought He would save himself.

OBSERVER:

Judas, if you were so sure of this, that He would save Himself, why didn't you go and ask Him to forgive you? You had time. Why didn't you go to the cross, rather than go and hang yourself?

Judas, why did you close the book of truth, and snuff out the light? *(closed Bible and unlighted candle)*

"He thought of you, He thought of me,
When hanging there in agony;
O wondrous love for you and me,
It broke His heart on Calvary."

(F. Morris)

336

TOUCHED BY JESUS

PILATE

PURPOSE

He touches us when alone, struggling with failure, fears, blunders, and frustrations.

MATERIALS
and
ARRANGEMENT

For the worship table use a royal blue cloth. Entwine a narrow black ribbon around a gold cord. Place the scepter in center of the table, and wrap the cord loosely around the base of the scepter. Let it fall across the center and down over the edge of the table. A white cross is at the back of the table on a raised level covered with a blue net. At the side of the table have a water jug, basin and towel. A small crown resting on the edge of the open Bible with a tall candle beside it would complete the worship table.

INTERPRETATION

(Matthew 27:1,2; 27:11-25)

Pilate was not a base, evil, hateful man. Pilate was a well-intentioned man, but he was a weak, insecure and fearful man. *(the dark cord around the gold cord)*. Pontius Pilate was the Roman procurator of Judea *(the scepter)* and as suggested by the Jews in argument with Pilate, he wanted to be King Caesar's friend *(John 19:12; the royal blue cloth)*.

The wife of Pilate, Claudia, had a dream of the just Jesus *(white cross in the blue net)* and urged Pilate to be honorable and courageous. So the struggle began. Pilate's fear of unpopularity, of losing his office, the fear of loss of social standing, and prosperity, together with ambition and security stand opposed to justice and truth *(the gold cord crossing over the dark)*.

Then the fierce struggle in the mind of Pilate was over. Selfishness had won. Pilate excused his cowardly action by washing his hands *(water jug, basin, towel)*. Though Pilate said he was innocent, his guilt could not be so easily washed away. When he drew his hands out of the basin, they were figuratively washed in blood.

Pilate washed his hands, but the blood guiltiness was on his soul - forever. He had not judged Christ. Christ had judged Pilate.

The Kings of Kings *(the golden crown)*, the Lord of Lords would reign forever and ever.

Pilate's weakness was such a common one. Which shall rule in our life? The law of the spirit *(the Bible)* or the law of the flesh? Shall the light of truth *(candle)* in eternity reveal we did not compromise?

Then it is the brave man chooses
While the coward stands aside
Till the multitudes make virtue
Of the faith they had denied.

(James R. Lowell)

FOOTNOTES

1. Charles Laughton - "Storytelling" (The Atlantic Monthly) No. 6, p. 72

2. "Oral Interpretation" (Boston: Houghton Mifflin Company, 1952) p. 12

3. "The New York Times" (April 2, 1961) Sec. 6, p. 39

4. Charles Reynolds Brown, "The Art of Preaching" (New York: The MacMillan Company) p.204

5. "Vocal and Literary Interpretation of The Bible" (New York: The MacMillan Company. 1903) p.294

6. "Reading Literature Aloud" (New York: Oxford University Press, Inc., 1962) p.10

7. "Elements of Rhetoric" (Boston: James Monroe and Company, 1844) pp. 269 - 270

8. Gerald Kennedy, "His Word Through Preaching" (New York: Harper & Row Publishers, 1947) p. 73

9. "Voice and Speech Handbook" (Englewood Cliffs, N.J., Prentice-Hall, Inc., 1955)

10. "Songs of Hope" (New York: Harper and Brothers Publishers, 1938) p.15

11. "Spiritual Hilltops" (New York: Abingdon Press, 1960) p.106

12. "Best Loved Poems, Recessional" (New York: Garden City Publishing Co., 1936) p.295

13. "Spiritual Hilltops" (New York: Abingdon Press, 1960) p.106

14. "Interpretation of the Printed Page" (Chicago: Row Peterson & Co., 1915) p.247

15. "Leaves of Grass" (Philadelphia: David McKay Company, 1900)

WORSHIP

Part I

THE NATURE OF WORSHIP 5
    Defining Worship 5
    Something Happens when we Worship 6
    The Focus of Worship 6

THE FUNCTION OF WORSHIP 7
    Presentation--What do I Feel? 7
    Communication--What happens to me? 7
    Application--What must I do? 8

THE STRUCTURE OF WORSHIP 10
    Uncover New Approaches 11
    The Call to Worship 12
    The Prayer 12
    The Benediction 12
    Scripture Reading 13
    The Christian Calendar Lectionary 15
    Recover our Salvation Army Heritage 16
    The Expression of Worship 17

THE PRACTICE OF WORSHIP 20
    Personal Worship 20
    Family Worship 21
        What are the ingredients? 21
        How do we start? 21
        Where do we have it? 22
        What do we do? 23
        Who should lead? 24

FAMILY WORSHIP WORKSHOP 24
        Infant 24
        Pre-schooler 25
        Juniors 25
        Teens and Adults 26
        Suggested Devotional Aids 27

CHORAL SPEECH

Part II

INTRODUCTION 35

UNDERSTANDING CHORAL SPEAKING 36
    VALUES 36
    PURPOSE 37

STYLES AND ARRANGEMENTS 39
    Definition 39

METHODS OF ARRANGEMENTS 40
    Unison 40
    Refrain 40
    Antiphonal 41
    Group and Part Speaking 41

INSTRUMENTS OF THE CRAFT 42
    The Speaking Ensemble 42
    Interpretation 42
    The Director 44
        Skills 44
        Selection of Materials 44
        Tone Range 44
        Voice Quality 45
        Exercises 45

TECHNIQUES OF INTERPRETATION 49
    Voice 49
        Pitch 49
        Quality 50
        Volume 50
        Duration 51
    Phrasing 52
    Timing 53
    Pause 54
    Rhythm 55

ORGANIZATION FOR PERFORMANCE 57
    Procedures 57
    Arrangement 57

REHEARSAL 58

    Sharing 59

    Personal Commitment 59

    Good Reading Copy 59

    Marking for Reading 60

    Testing 62

    Briefing 62

    Memorization 62

Part III

SELECTIONS FOR WORSHIP ENRICHMENT

THE CALL TO WORSHIP 72

CHORAL SPEECH SELECTIONS 93

THE LITANY 181

RESPONSIVE READINGS 207

YOUTH GROUP DEVOTIONS 265

WORSHIP CENTERS... 277

Alongside Me 79
Always Praising 81
Approach, The 80
Bless the Lord 80
Chosen 80
Delight of Praising 81
Discovery..88
Enlightenment 82
Free Us 82
Give Us Awareness 87
God's Word and You 82
Great Reverence 85
Honoring Father 83
Holy is His Name 83
House of the Lord 83
Hush! Draw Near..85
Image of God 84
Insistent Sounds 87
In Us 84
Joyful Worship 86
Joy Overflows 85
Let Us Worship 84
Meditation 85
Our Confidence 86
Open Our Hearts..84
Praising Heart, A 87
Praise Him...89
Quest, The...86
Something Happens 81
Song of Love 89
Take Time 80
Unhurried Time...88
What Great Love 89
Praise God (Brief Calls to Worship) 83
From The Salvation Army Song Book 75

CHORAL SPEECH (General)

Abiding in Him 95
Call to Decision 96
Called and Enlisted 100

Carry On 102

Clothed with Strength 103

Contentment 104

Divine Commission 105

Go for Gold 107

God Stepped into the World 109

Go Moses! Go Today! 111

Great Commission, A 115

Happiness is...God with Us 117

Heart of Compassion 119

Holy Stance, A 122

Know the Truth 123

Life's Desire 124

Life Service 125

Living Joyfully 127

Living Water 128

March On! Salvation Soldier 129

Modern Prayer and the Psalms, A 130

Moment to Decide 132

On to Conquer 133

Our World 134

Salvation Army Begins in America, The 136

Search, The 138

Search Ends, The 139

Storm at Sea, The 140

Time is Life 141

Unmerited Mercy 143

Wait on the Lord 144

Weapons of Faith 145

What is a Family? 147

Who Will Go? 149

Witness to the Light 151

Worshiper, The 153

CHORAL SPEECH (Special Occasions)

CHRISTMAS

But He Came 157

Christmas is Over 159

Emmanuel 160

Rejoice! Messiah Comes 162

No Room 164

Why a Star? 166

EASTER

Blessing, The 168
Golgotha 169
Lamb of God, The 171
Our Saviour 172

THANKSGIVING

Heartfelt Thanksgiving 173
Thanksgiving 175
Overflowing Heart, The 177
Praise Him in His Sanctuary 178

THE LITANY

Arranging Tomorrow 184
Awareness 185
Come, my Lord 186
Commited Heart, The 188
Creation 187
Disciples in the Making 189
Give Thanks and Sing 190
Give Us your Holy Spirit 191
God's Greatness 192
Hallowed Moments 193
King of Glory 194
Let God be Blessed 195
Limitless Love 196
Lord, Direct Me 197
Lord, I Come to Thee 198
Magnify God 199
Our Prayer 200
Praise His Name 201
Song of Thanks 202
Save Some Stones 203

RESPONSIVE READINGS (General)

Calvary Love 210
Child Speaks, A 211
Divine Partnership 212
Enduring Mercy 213

Folded Wings 214
Giving Thanks Always 215
Home Maker's Be-Attitude 216
It's Marching Time 217
Lift up Your Heart 218
Look Up 219
Peace of God 220
Quality of Gladness, A 221
Sanctuary 222
Sharing Our Faith 223
Time Management 224
Two Challenges 225
Waiting Upon the Lord 226
Wings of Peace 227

RESPONSIVE READINGS (TLB)

Acceptance 228
Adventure 229
All My Ways 230
Beatitudes for Leaders 231
Capture Strength 232
Discipleship 233
Fitting the Mold 234
Flash of Insight, A 235
Glad Heart, A 236
Hang in There 237
Help Me Lord 238
His Very Own 239
Language of Heaven 240
Secret, The 241
Something is Happening 242

RESPONSIVE READINGS (from the Salvation Army Song Book)

Divine Whisperings 243
Enabled 244
Mighty God, The 245
Our Refuge 246
Praise Break 248
Praise and Honor 249
Quiet Reflections 250
Ready Response 251

Secret of His Presence, The 252

Walking with God 253

Worthy Vessels 254

RESPONSIVE READINGS (Special Occasions)

The Christian Family   (Family Recognition) 255

Heartfelt Thanksgiving   (Thanksgiving) 256

Linked in Love   (Mother's Day - Father's Day) 257

People Give Thanks, The   (Thanksgiving) 258

Thanks be to God   (Thanksgiving) 259

Unto Us a Child is Born   (Christmas) 260

Well Done   (Recognition Band-Songsters) 261

The Word   (Bible Sunday) 263

YOUTH GROUP DEVOTIONS

Faith   267

Gratitude 268

Love   269

Prayer 270

Service 271

What God Wants 272

Worship 273

Part IV

WORSHIP CENTERS (General)

A Basket of Fruitful Service 283

Baskets of Promise 281

Christ is the Answer 285

Fairest Lord Jesus 287

Fulfillment 289

Holy Walk, A 293

Scripture Harvest, A 295

Stop and Go 297

Take Time to be Holy 298

Today is Wondrous 301

Treasures 303

Treasures of Darkness 306

Word of God, The 307

World Services 309

WORSHIP CENTERS (Holy Week)

Facing Calvary
    Centurion, The 316
    Disciples - Last Supper, The 318
    Peter's Remorse 320
    Jesus in Gethsemane 322

They Stood by Him
    Disciples in the Garden 324
    Simon of Cyrene 326
    Friends at Golgotha 328
    Mary, the Mother 330
    Mary Magdalene 332

They Shared His Cross
    The Critics 334
    The Women 335

Touched by Jesus
    Judas 336
    Pilate 337

OLD TESTAMENT

Genesis
1 .... 142, 152
28 .... 83, 144

Exodus
3 .... 101, 114
15 .... 89, 244
33:14,15 229,232
34 235

Leviticus
19, 20 83

Numbers
6:26 220

Deuteronomy
1-31 217
6:5-7 148
11:6 123
31:6 212
31:7 232
31:8 .... 229, 232
32:9 239
33:5 239
33:25 .... 241, 244

Joshua
1:8, 9 154,232
4:7 203

1 Samuel
3:9 .... 86, 106

1 Kings
8:56 84
18:17-39 99

1 Chronicles
16:8 74
16:9, 11 .... 74, 86
22:11, 13 .... 232, 245

2 Chronicles
2:5 99
14:11 99
16:9 241
17:6 218
30:8 251

Nehemiah
8:10, 11 .... 85, 87

Job
2:10 228
10:9 254
22:21 220
22:29 218
24:14 123

Psalms
1:2 243
1:17 253
3:3 218
4:7 255
5:7 85
7:17 87
9:1 .... 74, 221
10 80
13:1 238
16:11 .... 236, 243-4
                        255, 263
16:8 221
18:3 226
18:6, 16 237
18:49 259
22 131
23:4 ...... 104, 248, 250
23:6 248
24:7 ...... 122, 168, 219
24:8 219
24:10 219
25:15 218
27:1 .... 83, 224,
                        232, 248
27:5 247
27:6 73
27:11 244
27:14 .... 144, 154
                        214, 222
28:9 218
30:4 ...... 215, 218, 258
30:12 215
31:3 226
31:15 .... 142, 224
31:19 .... 192, 245
32:8 .... 226, 229
32:11 .... 221, 255
33:3, 4 74
33:12 73
34:1 248

34:14 220
34:15 242
35:9 118
37:7 .... 214, 226
37:23 .... 229, 237
37:34 214
40:1 .... 74, 131, 222
40:3 222
42:6 ...... 128, 131, 237
46:1 .... 86, 224
                        238, 247
46:10 .... 154, 222
48:14 .... 86, 229
50:23 87
51:10 247
51:15 .... 87, 219
55:8 247
56:3 .... 86, 142, 228
57:1 247
60:12 245
62:5 .... 214, 222
62:8 224
63:5 236
66 .... 87, 262
67:3 81
68:3 255
68:35 241
69:2,3 .... 128, 247
70:13 258
71:8, 16 .... 87, 213
73:23 229
84:7 244
84:11 213
85 .... 86, 106
86:1 213
86:10 236
86:11 226
90:12 224
90:14 255
91:1 .... 88, 95, 243
91:2 213
92:1 .... 195, 215
92:2 81
92:5 245
95 .... 86, 190, 195
96:1 .... 86, 131, 262
96:4 .... 87, 248

98 .... 248, 262
100 .... 74, 83, 127,
131, 199, 221,
259, 262
102 131
103:1 ...... 80, 81, 176
177, 236
104: 81, 201, 221
105:1 .... 215, 248,
249, 258
105:2 .. 199, 248, 249
105:3 .... 248, 249
107:1,2 258
107:8 .. 73, 190, 215,
219, 236
107:9 213
107:21 213
107:30 247
108:3, 13 248
112:1 238
113:3 .... 219, 262
116:13 .... 74, 213
117:1 253
117:2 215
118:1 213
118:24 .... 87, 221
119:11 82
119:16, 18 .... 82, 219,
263
119:48 74
119:97, 103 87
119:105 .... 82, 229
119:130 .... 82, 236
119:140, 162 263
119:165 220
122:4 258
125 144
136:4 .... 176, 215
138:8 .... 74, 229, 262
139:17 138, 230, 248
140:7 .... 247, 263
141:3 240
145:2 87
145:3 .... 84, 192, 245
145:8 .... 192, 199
145:10 236
147:1 .. 236, 255, 262

147:6 218
150: 178, 262
162 263

Proverbs
3 .... 80, 247
10 .... 240, 247
15:4 240
20:22 237
25:15 237

Ecclesiastes
3:1 .... 142, 224
3:11 224

Isaiah
1:18 225
2 199
6 .... 106, 150, 225
9:2 .... 152, 167
9:6 .... 163, 249, 260
11:6 172
12:4 221
14:7 262
25:4 229
26:3 226
26:4 .... 226, 227,
244, 247
26:5 247
27:5 244
30:15 .... 106, 154,
222, 226
34:1 118
35........................ 163
40:29 .... 103, 144,
163, 232, 241
40:31 .... 214, 222,
232, 226
41:10 ...... 80, 238, 247
41:13 241
43:2, 3 228
44:21 238
46:4 237
49:14 238
51:3 259
53:5 171
55 .... 86, 128,
143, 225
57 83

58:11 243
60:1 ...... 152, 163, 167
61:1 249
61:10 221
63 .... 103, 245
64:8 254
65:14 245
65:24 237

Jeremiah
10:23 229
15:16 221
18:6 254
29:11 .... 229, 233
29:13 139
32:17 .... 192, 245
33:3 226

Lamentations
3:22 121
3:23 99
3:24 239
3:26 237
3:27 233
3:41 218

Ezekiel
36:37, 38 242
47:9 247

Daniel
12:3 167

Micah
7:18 99

Habakkuk
3:18 89

Zechariah
9:9, 10 163
13, 14 172

Malachi
3:17 239

NEW TESTAMENT
Matthew
4:4 132
4:14 126

5:12 255
6:6 .... 226, 243
6:13 249
7:7 .... 80, 139, 242
8:23 140
9:36 121
11:28 183
12:28 222
12:34,35 240
14:23 243
15:32 121
16:15 116
16:24 255
18:15 235
27:1-2,32 170
28:18,20 118

Mark
6:31-44 .... 125, 222
  243
11:25-26 ...... 235, 237

16:15 225

Luke
1:78 167
2:8-20 .... 165, 260
6:45 240
8:22 140
9:23 233
14:23 116
14:33 251
18:1 242
23:26 .... 170, 172
23:28 172

John
1:1-4 .... 167, 247, 263
1:5 .... 152, 167
1:12 .... 167, 223
1:14 .... 110, 167,
  249, 263
1:36 114
3:16 .... 167, 171, 210
3:19 152
4:14 .... 128, 247
5:16 110
6:33, 35 126
7:38 247
8:12 .... 152, 167

8:32 123
8:36 114
13:1 247
13:23 247
14:1 .... 220, 227
14:6 ...... 110, 114, 116
14:13 .... 81, 84
14:14 .... 81, 226
14:27 220
15:1 228
15:7 .... 226, 243
15:11 255
15:14-16 .... 79, 225
16:23 238
16:26, 29 242
16:33 .... 212, 220, 237
19 170

Acts
2:46 255
4:31 253
7:59 247
17:24-28 142,
  195, 201

Romans
1:16 116
5:1, 3 .... 220, 228
5:20 247
8:17 239
8:35 212
9:20 254
12:2 243
13:12 233
14:19 227

1 Corinthians
3:23 239
5:18, 19 263
6:19 239
8:16 258
12:7 241
12:28 73
13:1 .... 79, 174,
  231, 257
13:2 257
15:57 258

2 Corinthians
1:7 225

1:22 239
2:14 249
4:6 167
4:7 254
4:15 232
4:16 232
5:7 253
5:18 172
6:17 225
8:16 .... 258, 259
9:15 .... 258, 259
10:4 212
10:11 228
12:9 ...... 241, 244, 247

Galatians
2:20 .... 142, 251
4:10 224
5:23 235

Ephesians
1:4 239
1:15,16 259
3:16 .... 222, 244
4:15, 16 123
4:26 235
5:1, 2 .... 234, 253, 262
5:6 123
5:8 152
5:11 224
5:19 234
6:6 .... 129, 146
6:10 .... 212, 241
6:12, 13 212
6:18 242

Philippians
1:9, 11 .... 81, 249
2:1, 2 234
2:9 249
3:7, 8 251
3:13 233
4:4 .... 85, 221
4:6-7 .... 237, 242, 253
4:8 .... 73, 236
4:13 .... 241, 244

Colossians
1:3, 4 259
1:10, 13 152,
  244, 251

3:3 88
3:12 .... 220, 234, 235
3:15 227
3:16, 17 240
4:2 242
4:6 240

1 Thessalonians
1:2 259
1:7, 8 259
2:7, 8 224
3:3 .... 236, 237
3:9 259
5:16 221
5:17 154
5:18 259

1 Timothy
1:12 259
2:8 235
6:12 212

2 Timothy
2:4 212
2:14 259
2:15 263
2:21 254
3:13 123
4:15 259
4:17 244

Hebrews
2:3 192
4:16 ...... 81, 224, 226
11:6 84
12:1 233
12:7 228
12:9 233
12:11, 12 228
13:5, 6 232
13:8 89

James
1:5 242
1:19 240
3:2 240
4:2 242
4:10 218
4:18 228
5:16 .... 154, 195, 226

1 Peter
1:6, 7 238
1:8 85
1:19 167

4:12 228
5:8 212
5:10 238

1 John
1:7 152
2:3 239
3:1 .... 118, 167, 257
3:16 118
4:7-8 .... 210, 234
4:9 .. 89, 118, 121, 234
4:10 .... 89, 118, 210
4:16 .... 80, 210
5:3 234
5:4, 14 .... 81, 242,
            249, 263
5:15 81

Revelation
11:15 163
19................. 163, 263
22:17 247